Constitutional Environments
and Economic Growth

☆

Constitutional Environments and Economic Growth

☆

GERALD W. SCULLY

PRINCETON UNIVERSITY PRESS

PRINCETON, NEW JERSEY

Copyright © 1992 by Princeton University Press
Published by Princeton University Press, 41 William Street,
Princeton, New Jersey 08540
In the United Kingdom: Princeton University Press, Oxford
All Rights Reserved

Library of Congress Cataloging-in-Publication Data

Scully, Gerald W.
Constitutional environments and economic growth /
Gerald W. Scully.
p.   cm.
Includes index.
ISBN 0-691-04261-6
1. Economic development—Political aspects.   2. Civil rights—
Economic aspects.   3. State, The.   I. Title.
HD87.S38   1992
338.9—dc20   91-42650

This book has been composed in Linotron Zapf International

Princeton University Press books are
printed on acid-free paper, and meet the guidelines
for permanence and durability of the Committee
on Production Guidelines for Book Longevity
of the Council on Library Resources

Printed in the United States of America

1   3   5   7   9   10   8   6   4   2

FOR MY DAUGHTER

AUDRA LAINE

✫ *Contents* ✫

List of Figures and Tables   ix

Preface   xiii

Acknowledgments   xv

CHAPTER 1
Overview   3

CHAPTER 2
The Theory of Economic Growth and Economic Policy   13

CHAPTER 3
The Constitutional Setting and the Gains from Exchange   56

CHAPTER 4
A Theory of the Evolution of the Constitutional Setting   80

CHAPTER 5
Measures of Liberty   106

CHAPTER 6
The Choice of Law and the Extent of Liberty   148

CHAPTER 7
The Constitutional Setting and Economic Development   166

CHAPTER 8
The Constitutional Setting and the Distribution of Income   184

CHAPTER 9
The Economic Effect of the Size of the State   200

CHAPTER 10
What Is to Be Done? Reform of the Institutional Framework
and Economic Policy for Progress

                                                                          212

Notes   221

Index   241

☆ *List of Figures and Tables* ☆

FIGURES

2-1. The Solow Growth Model 16
2-2. Frequency Histogram of Growth Rates 17
2-3. Frequency Histogram of RGDP85 21
2-4. Tsiang's Interpretation of the Solow Diagram 25
3-1. Personal Welfare of Two Individuals, One Living in Anarchy, the Other in a Strong Constitutional Setting 59
3-2. Paths of Efficiency and Equity 61
3-3. Growth Paths of Various Economies 61
3-4. Cooperative Agreement 64
4-1. The Time Path of Income per Capita 82
4-2. Neoclassical Growth Equilibrium for Constitutional Setting θ^0 85
4-3. Neoclassical Growth Equilibrium with Efficient Endogenous Constitutional Change 92
4-4. Neoclassical Growth Equilibrium with Endogenous Constitutional Change 95
4-5. The Time Path of Income per Capita with Different Rule Spaces 99
8-1. The Trade-Off between Efficiency and Equality 186
8-2. U-Shaped Income Distribution Function 187

TABLES

2-1. Growth Rates of per Capita Real Gross Domestic Product, 1950–1985 18
2-2. Economic Growth Rates by Geographic Regions 22
2-3. Average National Investment Share and Trend in Investment Share, 1950–1985 29
2-4. Non-Oil-Exporting Less Developed Countries Classified by Development Status Based on Capital Formation, 1950–1985 30
2-5. Real Interest Rates in Less Developed Countries 33
2-6. Education and Literacy by Continent, 1980 35
2-7. Population Growth by Continent, 1950–1985 37
2-8. Non-Oil-Exporting Less Developed Countries Classified by Development Status Based on Population Growth and Human Capital Accumulation 38

2-9. Measures of the Level of Technology by Continent, 1980   42

2-10. Government Expenditure Share and Trend by Continent
1950–1985   44

2-11. Effect of High Inflation Rates on Real per Capita Growth
Rates, 1951–1987   46

App. 2-1. Education and Literacy by Country, 1980   47

App. 2-2. Population Growth by Country, 1950–1985   52

3-1. Prisoner's Dilemma: Observe or Violate Rights Agreement   62

5-1. Mean Ratings of Political and Civil Liberty by Country,
1973–1986   108

5-2. Countries Classified by Political-Economic Systems   113

5-3. Correlations between Gastil and Humana Freedom
Measures   115

5-4. Attributes of Economic Liberty   119

5-5. Summary of the Eight Liberty Indexes and Overall Index   122

5-6. Correlation Coefficients   128

App. 5-2. Various Liberty Indicators by Country   132

App. 5-3. Rank of Various Liberty Indicators by Country   140

6-1. Test of Statistical Significance of Differences in Mean Values
of Political and Civil Liberty by Type of Legal System   157

6-2. Test of Statistical Significance of Differences in Mean Values
of Liberty Measures, Adjusted for Muslim and Rule of Law
Influences   158

6-3. Stepwise Regressions Relating the Degree of Political and
Civil Liberty to the Type of Legal System   159

6-4. Cumulative Frequency Distribution of the Degree of
Political and Civil Liberty by Type of Legal System   159

6-5. OLS and Maximum Likelihood Probit and Logit Probability
Estimates of the Incidence of Freedom and Tyranny under
Common and Civil Law   160

7-1. Regressions Relating the Separate Effects of Institutional
Variables on Economic Growth over the Period 1960–1980   177

7-2. Average Growth Rates of per Capita Real Gross Domestic
Product by Institutional Attribute   177

7-3. Regressions Relating the Effects of All of the Institutional
Variables on Economic Growth, Economic Efficiency, and
the Change in Economic Efficiency   178

7-4. Regressions Relating the Separate Effects of Institutional
Variables on Economic Efficiency, 1980   180

7-5. Regressions Relating the Separate Effects of Institutional

Variables on the Change in Economic Efficiency between
1960 and 1980   181

8-1. Regressions Relating the Separate Effects of Rights Measures on
Quintile Income Share   189

8-2. Income Shares and Income Inequality by Institutional Attribute   191

8-3. Regressions Relating the Separate Effects of Rights on
Atkinson Measures of Income Inequality   192

8-4. Atkinson Measures of Income Inequality by Institutional
Attribute   193

8-5. Regressions Relating Efficiency and Quintile Income Share   195

8-6. The Relationship between Economic Efficiency and Atkinson
Measures of Income Inequality   195

App. 8-1. Atkinson Measures of Income Inequality for Seventy
Nations   197

9-1. Regressions Relating the Effects of Government Expenditures on
Economic Growth, 1968–1980   205

9-2. Predicted Average Growth Rates for Various Levels of GOVT60
and CHGGOVT   207

9-3. Regressions Relating the Effect of Size of the Government
Sector on Economic Efficiency   207

9-4. Regressions Relating the Effects of Gross Investment Share on
Economic Efficiency in 1980 and the Change in Economic
Efficiency, 1960–1980   209

9-5. Regressions Relating the Effects of Size of the Government
Sector and Changes in Size to Changes in Economic
Efficiency, 1960–1980   211

O N occasion, I have consulted for the International Bank for Reconstruction and Development (the World Bank). By the nature of its charter, the bank is a statist organization. Low interest rate loans are provided through the bank to less developed nations for various government-directed development projects. The professional staff of the bank is drawn mainly from the educated elite of these nations.

Most development economists are statists. The paradigm of the state as central to economic development increasingly is recognized as seriously flawed. Little fruit of economic progress has been harvested from decades of their advice of interventionist economic policy and government-directed planning. Despite substantial amounts of foreign aid and loans, precious few cases of successful economic transformation could be cited. Rather, the successful cases of rapid economic growth (for example, the Asian tigers) followed their own path to economic growth through economic freedom, market allocation of resources, and an outward trade orientation.

Partly because of the solicitous economic results of deregulation in the United States and the privatization policy in Great Britain and partly because of the overwhelming evidence of the failure of central economic planning and socialism, some at the bank were prepared to inquire if there was evidence that private arrangements of organized economic activity yielded results (growth, allocative efficiency) superior to those of statist arrangements. I was asked to look into the broader question of the link between individual liberty and national economic progress.

For a classical liberal, the answer is obvious. At the time of the birth of classical liberalism, China and the West more or less were on a par economically and technologically. The Anglo-American paradigm of free men and free markets unleashed human potential to an extent unparalled in history. The process of economic transformation took several centuries. Many in the West viewed the Soviet Union as a paragon of the new wisdom of authoritarian planning. Allegedly, the Soviets transited from feudalism to a modern economy in less than seventy-five years, despite enormous losses from Stalinism and World War II. Now, it is recognized that the story of the Soviet economic transformation largely is a fairy tale. It is a backward economy. Marx and Lenin must be turning over in their graves as the heirs of their doctrine cautiously turn to the idea of free markets and private property as a means of rescuing the Soviet economy from collapse.

To say that a society organized as free men and free markets is the only model that unleashes human potential is not enough. One needs evidence to persuade those who see promise in extensive government intervention in the economy. I have found such evidence, and the evidence is overwhelmingly strong in favor of the paradigm of classical liberalism. The evidence of the link between liberty and economic progress appeared in the *Journal of Political Economy* in 1988. To my knowledge, this was the first empirical confirmation of such a link. This book is a vast extension of my thinking about freedom and economic progress and the empirical evidence of the solicitude of liberty.

☆ *Acknowledgments* ☆

THE research and writing of this book was facilitated by the provision of financial help from a number of sources and by the willing comments of numerous scholars. The Earhart Foundation provided funding for two summers. The Liberty Fund held a conference on a draft of the manuscript in April 1990. The Heritage Foundation provided an appointment as a Bradley Resident Scholar during the 1990–1991 academic year. The University of Texas at Dallas provided a faculty development grant that facilitated residence at Heritage. To all of these foundations and the individuals associated with them, I acknowledge their support and encouragement.

My debt to a number of scholars is large. Julian Simon encouraged me to expand my earlier work on the link between freedom and economic growth into a monograph. Gary Becker and Richard Epstein initially contributed helpful comments on the nature and scope of the project. Judge Danny Boggs, Tom Borcherding, Milton Friedman, Arnold Harberger, Randy Holcombe, Dwight Lee, Richard McKenzie, Douglas North, Phil Porter, Dan Slottje, George Stigler, Robert Tollison, and Gordon Tullock contributed useful comments on various sections of the book. Finally, my editor at Princeton University Press, Jack Repcheck, kept the book focused and the project on schedule. To all, I express my gratitude.

Two chapters are based on joint work, and parts of some of the chapters have appeared as journal articles. Chapter 4 is based on work with Phil Porter; chapter 5 is based on work with Dan Slottje. I am obliged to the editors and publishers of the *Journal of Political Economy* and *Public Choice* for permission to use this material.

Constitutional Environments
and Economic Growth

☆

☆ **CHAPTER 1** ☆

Overview

SOME thirty years ago, Robert Heilbroner wrote that it was settled that collective ownership and government allocation and distribution of resources would bring a standard of living and a degree of social justice to mankind that was not possible under capitalism.[1] Recently, he said that the evidence from the seventy-five-year struggle between socialism and capitalism was that capitalism had won.[2]

Intellectuals have seen in the de-Stalinization of the Soviet Union, in the agrarian economic reforms of the People's Republic of China, and in the political revolutions of Eastern Europe the promise of a sharp move away from government to individual control of the economy. In the USSR and China, these reforms have been mandated by the Communist Party. In Eastern Europe, reform has been a demand of the population. None of the reforms have led, as yet, to a Western system of private property, freedom of contract, free markets, and the rule of law.[3]

The reforms in the socialist bloc have lessened the grip of government, but it is an illusion to believe that the Soviet or Chinese Communist parties are about to proffer freedom as understood in the West.[4] The brutal suppression of the student democracy movement in June 1989 and the reestablishment of state control of the economy point to the reassertion of power by the Chinese Communist Party. The Soviet Central Committee has been unresponsive to the demands for regional and ethnic autonomy. The Communist Party establishment and the bureaucracy resisted Gorbachev's various timid plans for a planned transition to an economy that has some aspects of market allocation. Monopolists of political power naturally resist the surrender of authority. Life in the socialist bloc is so dismal precisely because of the denial of freedom. The Communist leadership has been forced to concede reforms to avoid utter economic collapse and, perhaps, to avoid rebellion.

The uprisings of the people in Poland, Hungary, East Germany, Czechoslovakia, Bulgaria, and violently in Romania, were spontaneous. The reforms of the system are more promising. At the extreme, the two Germanies are reunified as a democratic, capitalist state. The Soviet Union and Europe could do nothing to stop it. Monetary union occurred in July 1990; political reunification, in October. The reticence of the East Germans has been overcome by the vision of prosperity plain to eyes now open and to the willingness of West Germans to buy off any opposition.[5] Yet problems of reunification remain. Unemployment in the east is high, and investment has been hampered by an inability to secure title to property. For the rest of Eastern Europe, at least the monopoly of the Communist Party is broken. The members have re-formed as socialist parties.[6] The ideology of the opposition groups, other than a deep antipathy to past abuses by the Communist Party, is not clear. There seems to be a general interest in incorporating Western economic institutions to one degree or another. Poland and Czechoslovakia have moved most toward the Western model. But there is a reticence, and perhaps resistance, to fostering Western values and ideology. Even as multi–political party states, these regimes at best will be only partly free. The institutions of private property, free markets, and the rule of law and the values and ideology of capitalism that are crucial to the functioning of a free society need to be built from scratch. Certainly, nearly five decades of communist-socialist ideology will color the reforms in Eastern Europe.[7] The model of man and society that ultimately will be adopted is an open question.

Finally, the political revolutions of Eastern Europe have had little discernible effect on the less developed world. Much of the underdeveloped world remains statist, often with a socialist bent. Civilian government and electoral competition now exists in much of Latin America, but the military continues to pose a threat to civilian rule. Some political competition has emerged in Africa, but coups remain the most common form of political change. On the whole, there is no widespread rush to freedom for most of mankind.

PARADIGMS OF HUMAN PROGRESS

The central argument of this monograph is that the material progress of mankind is as affected by the choice of the economic, legal, and political institutions as it is by resource endowment and technological progress.[8] Each economic, legal, and political system embodies a vision of human progress, a model of man and society. This relationship has preoccupied thinkers since ancient times. Hebrew, Indian, Chinese, and Greek prophets and philosophers all struggled with the rights and responsibilities of the individual versus government and the rules and order of a society that were consistent with a particular vision of human progress.

Before the sixteenth century, the feudal institutions of manors and guilds organized production and distribution. The manors and the towns nearby largely were self-sufficient. Little domestic or foreign trade took place. These institutions broke down, first in England, as internal and external trade developed. They were replaced by centralized government control and mercantilist policy. The renaissance of systematic sociopolitical philosophy began in the later half of the seventeenth century. By the eighteenth century, on the foundations of the economic, political, and legal philosophy of the classical liberal thinkers, many of the Western industrial countries and the United States had chosen an institutional framework that permitted a wide latitude for individual initiative, choice, and responsibility, and a very limited role of government. By the nineteenth century, these countries were solidly capitalist, free market, representative democracies, committed to the rule of law.

There are three great themes in the writings of the European and Anglo-Saxon sociopolitical philosophers. The earliest thinkers (Spinoza, Locke, and Smith) celebrated personal freedom and responsibility, the near-absolute right of private property, the virtues of commercialism, and the concept of limited government. The individualist paradigm of human progress is the intellectual legacy of the classical liberals and the revolution of the middle class. The great themes of the classical liberals were indefinite progress, brought about by the incentives and efficiency of private property, private initiative, and free markets, the sanctity of individual liberty, and the harmony of interests—the serving of the public interest (national wealth) by the unfettered pursuit of private interest.

While freedom brings the opportunity to compete for income streams, it does not guarantee that all will prosper. The transition from feudalism and mercantilism to capitalism and laissez-faire that gave rise to the middle class also created a substantial segment of the working class. The poverty of the working class was thought to be a natural result of the competitive process in market capitalism. This led some thinkers and political activists to a vision of individualism, private property, and freedom of contract constrained by government in the public or general interest. Among this group of thinkers, I include David Hume, Jean-Jacques Rousseau, Jeremy Bentham and the Philosophic Radicals, David Ricardo, and John Stuart Mill. The image of a benevolent, activist government leveling the extreme outcomes of a capitalist economy is their legacy. The tension in modern Western representative government between protecting private property, freedom of contract, and individual freedom (negative rights) and subsidizing failure out of general tax revenue (positive rights) is a result of that legacy.

Dictatorship is the oldest form of government. It remains the most common form. Modern authoritarian government has its origins in nationalism and in the paradigm of authoritarian socialism and central planning. The roots of socialism are in the pessimism of the classical economists, the reformist mentality of mainly English nineteenth-century philosophers, and the utopians. The classical theory of labor value and the pessimism of an ultimate state of stagnation in capitalism contributed to Marx's prognosis of the inevitable decline of mature capitalist societies and the assumption that the entire structure of rights, law, and representative government was nothing more than tools used by the propertied interests to exploit the working class.

With the end of World War II, rising nationalism in the colonial world brought independence. These new nations were free to structure the institutional framework by which they could progress. Ghandi, Nehru, Nasser, Nkrumah, and other nationalists became spokesmen for decolonization and for a model of man and society that they thought most suitable for human progress. At the time, the Anglo-American model of individualism and capitalism and the Soviet model of statist socialism competed for hegemony. A few of the newly independent nations chose the path of capitalism. A larger number chose a path of private property and economic liberty, but an authoritarian regime of civil and political rights. Enamored of the Soviet model, most of the newly independent countries chose government control of the economy, economic planning, and some form of socialism as the path to economic development. Concomitantly, those in control of these nations are deeply suspicious of private property, individual initiative, and a market allocation of resources. Much of the economic policy of these nations is neomercantilist. Domestic price regulation, import quotas, high tariffs, foreign exchange controls, and so on are common neomercantilist policies. Individual liberty is not an admired attribute of statecraft in these countries.

ORTHODOX DEVELOPMENT ECONOMICS

Development economics is a very broad field of study. It encompasses the grand issues of income growth, income distribution, and policies; development techniques, such as planning models, cost-benefit analysis, and methods of price and fiscal reform; and the role of institutions, culture, geography, health, and so on in micro-level studies. The objective of this book is limited to the basic questions of the effects of the institutional framework, constitutional setting, or "rules of the game" on the prospects for economic progress. The central question in this debate is the role of government versus that of the individual in transforming a society from backward to developed.

The field of development economics began in the 1940s. The founders were European intellectuals. They were influenced heavily by democratic socialism, Keynesian economics, a disdain for commercialism, and a romantic illusion of the possibility of rapid economic transformation through authoritarian planning. The early and influential writers, such as Paul Rosenstein-Rodan, Ragnar Nurkse, Tibor Scitovsky, and Albert Hirschman, emphasized an extensive role of the fiscal state. All of their work is dominated by the idea of "market failure." All favored substantial government intervention in markets and control of resources, particularly in investment. All saw the effect on citizens of government control as benign. Government or public sector failure, the great theme of the public choice tradition, simply never occurred to them.

In the 1950s, there was a great emphasis on import substitution as a policy of spurring industrialization and growth. An inward-looking development program and protection from foreign competition was advocated influentially by Raul Prebisch and Hans Singer. Citing secularly declining and cyclically unstable terms of trade, economists argued that a policy of unrestricted trade would not produce the massive capital imports necessary for rapid industrialization and growth. Attempts at expanding primary exports through devaluation were thought to be doomed, because foreign elasticities of demand were thought to be low. Without a shred of credible evidence on the terms of trade of the less developed countries (LDCs), trade and exchange rate policies were adopted to shield domestic markets from foreign competition.

Government-directed development was the hallmark of the theory and policy of development economics in the 1950s and 1960s. The important neoclassical resurgence of the view that growth of the factors of production and technical change were the engines of growth contributed nothing to the debate of individual versus government control of the process of growth. The "black box" of neoclassical theory is silent about the institutional framework under which inputs are transformed to output and distribution takes place. Yet writers—who were largely ignored—such as Friedrich von Hayek, Ludwig von Mises, Gottfried Haberler, Peter Bauer and Basil Yamey, and others argued that government control of property and markets and central planning were doomed to failure.

A "greening" of development economics occurred in the 1970s. Partly, disenchantment arose because of the failure of central planning and protectionism to bring sustained economic growth. Instead, these policies brought endemic domestic price distortions (resource misallocation) that has in the extreme precluded economic growth. Partly, this disenchantment was due to the success of the export-oriented Asian economies, which were characterized by a high degree of economic freedom, although political freedom is not a hallmark of these countries. Partly, it was due to a perception that where growth had occurred, it had left the poor behind.

Hope of an increased standard of living through a paternalistic, authoritarian control of man and his resources by the government has turned to despair. Naturally, alternative strategies are being sought. A new paternalism in the form of the "new world order" is the democratic socialist alternative. Myrdal, in his 1975 Nobel Memorial Lecture, states the case for redistributing income from those who have chosen institutions and policies that brought economic success to those who chose institutions and policies that utterly have failed:

> In this situation there are certainly moral and rational reasons for a new world order and, to begin with, for aid on a strikingly much higher level. In particular, people in rich countries should be challenged to bring down their lavish food consumption. It is estimated that if the average American were to reduce his consumption of beef, pork and poultry by 10 percent, 12 million tons or more of grain would be saved. This would mean making so much more food aid possible, saving perhaps five times as many million people as tons released, or even more, from starvation in the poorest countries. This reduction of meat consumption would be in the rational interest of the American people itself and much less is recommended for health reasons by the American Heart Association: one third. To overeating comes the colossal waste by overserving and spoilage. To a varying and usually lesser extent the same hold true in all developed countries.
>
> As has also been amply demonstrated, the cutting down of consumption, and of production for home consumption, of many other items besides food, and in all the developed countries, is rational and in our own interest. This is what the discussion of the "quality of life" is all about. Our economic growth in a true sense could certainly be continued, but it should be directed differently, and in a planned way, to serve our real interest in a better life. At the same time, it would release resources for aiding the underdeveloped countries on a much larger scale and to begin with for solving the acute food crisis.[9]

The paternalistic welfare program of the "new world order" brings new meaning to the word "dependency." An alternative and more optimistic approach is to encourage institutional and policy reforms that have been synonymous with economic growth in the West. The theme of this book is that the institutional framework, constitutional setting, or "rules of the game" are crucial for economic progress.

NEOCLASSICAL GROWTH THEORY AND THE NEW
INSTITUTIONAL ECONOMICS

The neoclassical growth model posits a very simple relationship between the growth rate of per capita national income and the growth rate of the capital-labor ratio, with technology fixed.[10] Two important theoretical extensions of the neoclassical model have been made. Disembodied or embodied technical progress can occur that makes the capital-labor ratio more productive in its production of national output. Exogenous, disembodied technological change is a feature of the Solow model. Arrow showed that technical progress can evolve endogenously through investments in new vintage capital stock.[11] Labor is recognized as reproducible; that is, individuals can accumulate human capital in the form of schooling and job training that augments their productivity. Obviously, such accumulations, like their physical capital counterparts, have positive effects on economic growth. The new neoclassical economics of technical change, pioneered by Paul Romer, Robert King and Sergio Rebelo, and others, endogenizes technological progress through the human capital model and retains exogenous technical change, treating it as an externality or public-type good.

Nothing in the neoclassical theory considers the institutional framework in which capital (physical and human) is accumulated, invention or innovation is made, or inputs are converted to output (the efficiency of the transformation function). The new institutional economics focuses attention on the social, legal, political, and economic framework that sets the range of sanctioned human behavior and choice. The institutional framework affects the allocation of resources within society. The new institutional economics is distinguished from the old in that its proponents are not only not opposed to neoclassical theory but frequently are neoclassical economists. Neoclassical economics and the new institutional economics have been joined most productively in the incorporation of the theory of property rights into the conventional theory of the firm, beginning with the important paper by Armen Alchian and Harold Demsetz.[12] A main purpose of this book is to make a similar contribution at the macroeconomic level; that is, it is possible to incorporate the rule space or the institutional framework into the simple neoclassical growth model. Then, the theoretical effects of the rule space on economic growth can be shown. With suitable measures or proxies for the institutional framework, the effect on economic growth of choices of the rule space can be estimated empirically.

SCOPE AND ORGANIZATION

The range in the human condition is very wide. In 1985, per capita gross domestic product in Zaire was $210, less than a fiftieth of that in the United States, and about what the latter's standard of living was at the end of the Civil War. In Gabon, males can expect to live twenty-five years, about a third of the male life expectancy in the United States. In that country, some 229 babies die for each 1,000 born, a figure about thirty times that of the West. Most of mankind lives under dictatorships, subject to the capricious rule of men, not the rule of law.

Since the time of Adam Smith, economists have had a lot to say about the human condition and how to improve it. What is the conventional wisdom about the sources of economic progress? And what do modern economists say are the key variables that if increased propel man onto a path of pecuniary progress? For the last thirty years the main tool of the analysis of economic growth has been the neoclassical growth paradigm. The insights from neoclassical theory are important. Physical and human capital, technological progress, the savings rate, commercial policy, the size of the state, and population growth do affect material progress. Chapter 2 reviews the neoclassical growth paradigm and the evidence on economic growth, since 1950, for the nations of the world. Also examined is the evidence of the effect of the main neoclassical variables on growth rates.

But the neoclassical growth paradigm is institutionally neutral; that is, the general theory of growth takes the institutional rules of sanctioned behavior as given. Adjusting for the initial level of the capital-labor ratio, raising that ratio in Tanzania or the Soviet Union in theory has the same effect on per capita incomes as in the United States. Clearly, this approach to modeling economic progress is wrong. Adam Smith knew this, more than two hundred years ago. The important part of the story of economic transformation told in *The Wealth of Nations* is about the restructuring of human institutions from government to individual control. Human activity can be organized spontaneously by custom and private (common) law that sanctions legal activity and emphasizes individual rights over state rights. Or human activity can be organized by fiat. Theoretically, what is the effect of the institutional framework on economic growth? And, how might the set of institutional rules be incorporated into the neoclassical growth model in a relatively simple and tractable way? Constitutional settings establish sanctioned behavior and provide for gains from exchange (chapter 3). Features of constitutional settings and changes in the constitutional setting can be classified as Pareto (welfare) efficient and Pareto inefficient. In chapter 4, a theory of the constitutional or institutional setting and its effect on economic growth is derived. The model is an endogenous theory of change in the constitutional setting and the conditions and the timing of rent-seeking (redistributive) activities as substitutes for productive (growth-promoting) activities.

How different are the economic, legal, and political institutions of mankind? What are useful measures of the institutional framework? And, do these measures really tell us anything about the condition of human freedom or lack of it in the world? Political scientists have been seeking to construct a metric of political freedom for about thirty years. The most comprehensive measure now available is from Freedom House, under the direction of Raymond Gastil. He also has constructed a measure of civil liberty that largely captures conformity to the rule of law. Rudimentary work has begun on measuring economic liberty. But there are some serious problems in the construction of these indices, both in the choice of the appropriate attributes of freedom and in the method of weighing them to produce an aggregate index. Political scientists in the main are majoritarians and proponents of human or positive rights. For example, many think that the right of labor to collude and form a union to redistribute income to themselves at others' expense, or the right of special interests to a certain minimum standard of living, or housing, or whatever, at others' expense, so long as it is sanctioned by the sovereign majority, is an enhancement of freedom. Many economists correlate freedom only with negative rights—the absence of governmental interference. In chapter 5, measures of economic liberty are constructed that take some of these problems into account, and the evidence on the status of civil and political freedom is reviewed. Ultimately, freedom is a legal concept. In chapter 6, statistical tests are developed that relate the choice of the legal regime (largely, conformity to the rule of law) to the degree of observed freedom.

With an understanding of the theoretical link between the institutional framework and economic growth and with some measures of the rule space at hand, we can inquire if there is any evidence that the institutional framework has important, observable consequences to economic growth and to the income distribution. In chapter 7, economic growth rates of per capita output and economic efficiency measures for 115 economies over the period 1960–1980 are compared to measures of freedom. It is shown that the rights structure has significant and large effects on efficiency and on the growth rate of economies. Politically open societies, subscribing to the rule of law, private property, and the market allocation of resources, grow at three times the rate and are two and one-half times as efficient economically in transforming inputs into national output as societies in which these rights largely are proscribed.

A recurring theme in the development literature is that economic growth has an adverse effect on income distribution. Income inequality can be traced to two sources: inequality of individual rights (opportunities to compete for income streams) and inequality of outcomes. No work has appeared in the literature that measures the effect of inequality of rights on income distribution. Empirical evidence in chapter 8 verifies that a large fraction of the observed inequality of income across countries is due to inequality in individual rights.

The alternative to economic progress through individual initiative and responsibility and a free market allocation of goods and resources, both internally and externally, is governmental command of resources. It is known that government intervention has efficiency and equity consequences (for example, government regulation, state ownership and licensing, tax and subsidy policy, commercial policy, internal and external public debt, monetary expansion, etc.). In chapter 9, the effect of the size of the state (government expenditures as a share of national output) on economic growth and efficiency is measured. The empirical evidence is that nations with large public sectors grow more slowly.

The Theory of Economic Growth and Economic Policy

AS founded by the Anglo-Saxon classical liberals in the eighteenth and nineteenth centuries, economics was the study of the economy and of the political institutions and policies required to increase material wealth. Such early thinkers as John Locke and Adam Smith lived in an economy made stagnant by the massive intrusion of government into daily economic life. The purpose of government policy (mercantilism) was to develop commerce and industry in the interest not of the material wealth of its citizens but in the interest of national power. To foster the growth of national wealth (that is, the net inflow of precious metals into the vaults of the treasury) labor, capital, and land were regulated in their employments, and internal and external trade was controlled.

Adam Smith viewed national wealth as the sum of invividual wealth and the policies of mercantilism as a corruption of a system of natural liberty that if adopted would bring material benefit to much of society. In particular, he proposed freedom of choice in occupations through the abolition of the guilds and the laws of settlement, free trade in land by the elimination of the restrictions on its use and on title transfer, and free internal and external trade through the elimination of local custom taxes, tariffs, export subsidies, trading monopolies, and other restrictions. The mercantile regulations on commerce and on the factors of production severely inhibited resources from flowing to where returns were highest and, hence, were a drag on economic growth. Thus, part of Adam Smith's theory of economic growth is the increased output from existing resources that is achieved by the substitution of a private, free market mechanism for resource allocation in place of a regulatory mechanism.

Beyond economic growth arising from the superior allocative efficiency of a free market economy, he and the other classical economists viewed growth as being determined by the growth in the supply of factors of production: the accumulation of capital, rising skill (human capital) of the labor force, economies of scale and specialization associated with a widening of the market, and inventiveness. But, there was no role of government in these matters. Necessarily, government contributed to the wealth

13

of the nation, but did so by confining its function to the protection of property and life, the provision of public goods, and defending the nation from foreign aggression. Of the daily economic affairs of mankind, the appropriate policy for increasing material welfare was laissez-faire.

The reforms proposed came to pass, rather quickly. England went through two industrial revolutions in the nineteenth century and became the leader in the policy of free trade. During much of that century government was little more than a "night watchman." And, it was then that the standard of living of the citizens of Great Britain and the United States dramatically surpassed that of the rest of the world.

By the end of the nineteenth century, the politics had been taken out of economics. Matters such as the role of private property, freedom of contract, the rule of law, and public regulation, what is now termed the constitutional setting or institutional framework, and what was much of the substance of the contribution of the classical economists dropped from discussion, perhaps because the issue was considered settled. While inquiry into issues of the economy and growth continued, until John Maynard Keynes, the inquiry mostly was a rehash of the classical economists. Marshallian economics, the theory of the firm and of the allocation of resources, became the preoccupation of the professionals. Becoming more technical, economics became a quasi-science. This technical focus, the need to model and prove interrelationships, necessarily and drastically narrowed the range of questions that economists could ask.

Keynes, in contrast to the supply-side theory of the classical economists, held that the level of national income was determined by the level of aggregate demand.[1] He argued that it was the responsibility of the fiscal state to ensure a level of aggregate demand sufficient to maintain full employment. Absent fiscal stimulation during a cyclical downturn, industry would have excess capacity and little incentive to invest in new capital stock. Unemployment would rise. Moreover, the private, market economy would not automatically adjust to the reduced demand for its output, because product and factor prices were sticky in a downward direction. Roy Harrod and Evsey Domar incorporated the Keynesian theory of aggregate demand into a theory of economic growth.[2]

THE SIMPLE SOLOW MODEL OF ECONOMIC GROWTH

The modern theory of long-term growth is based on the neoclassical model of Robert Solow.[3] He was the first to break with the Keynesian aggregate demand framework and return the focus back to the supply-side,

14

classical theory that the expansion in the supply of factors of production is the engine of real growth of a nation. While it is widely acknowledged that the developed Western nations achieved a high level of material and social progress with institutions that emphasized private property, the rule of law, and market allocation of resources, development economists argued that the rapid economic transformation of the less developed countries could not occur with these same institutions. These economies were seen as so poor and fragile that they were doomed to a "vicious cycle of poverty." Economic transformation was thought possible only through planned industrial development and strategic state control of the economy. Solow and other growth theorists writing then and now do not consider the role of the institutional framework in economic development. Growth is considered as a mechnical process, a sort of alchemy, wholly determined by the growth of certain factors of production and the laws of production.

In the Solow model, national output in a closed economy is produced with only two factors of production, units of homogeneous labor and units of homogeneous capital, with the level of technology fixed through time.[4] Alternatively, the relationship between national output and units of inputs can be expressed in intensive form: per capita national output is determined by capital per worker (the capital-labor ratio).[5]

National output either can be consumed or saved and invested (augmentation of the capital stock). Solow assumes that the fraction of output that is saved is constant and that the basic identity between savings and investment holds at every instant of time.[6] Also, he assumes that population (the labor force, as well, if the labor force participation rate is constant) grows at an exogenous, constant rate.[7]

Within this simple model, Solow shows that there is a rate of capital accumulation that is consistent with the exogenous rate of growth of the labor force and that there is a steady-state growth path for the economy. The solution to the model is the fundamental equation

$$(2\text{-}1) \qquad \dot{k} = sf(k) - nk,$$

where $\dot{k}$ is the rate of change in the capital-labor ratio, s is the constant savings rate, $f(k)$ is national output per capita, n is the constant rate of population growth, and k is the capital-labor ratio.

The interpretation of the result is shown in figure 2-1. In the figure, nk is linear, because n, the population growth rate, is a constant. The function $sf(k)$ is convex to reflex the diminishing marginal productivity of capital. For any capital-labor ratio, k, this difference equation converges monotonically to a unique stationary value, k^*, satisfying $k^* = sf(k^*) - nk^*$. At the point of intersection $\dot{k} = 0$; the equilibrium and stable value

15

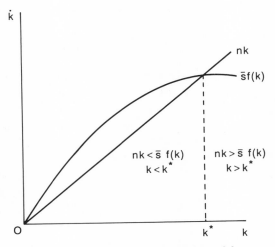

Figure 2-1. The Solow Growth Model

of the capital-labor ratio is k^*. At k^*, under constant returns to scale, the real standard of living grows at the constant rate n. If $k < k^*[nk < sf(k)]$, the capital-labor ratio will rise toward k^*. Conversely, if $k > k^*[nk > sf(k)]$, the capital-labor ratio will fall toward k^*.

An important implication of this growth model is that growth rates will converge across countries through time. The high per capita income, or capital-intensive, economies will have lower rates of return (marginal products) on capital, so capital accumulation and economic growth will be low. The low per capita income, or labor-intensive, economies will have high rates of return on capital, so capital accumulation and economic growth will be high. Additionally, given an open world economy, capital will flow from the rich to the poor nations in search of higher rates of return. In the long run, per capita income of the poor and the rich nations will tend to equalize. How well does this simple model of growth correspond to the observed facts on economic growth?

ECONOMIC GROWTH AMONG NATIONS, 1950–1985

Robert Summers and Alan Heston have produced comparable gross domestic product data for 121 market and 9 centrally planned economies, covering the period 1950 to 1985.[8] The average annual growth rates of per capita real gross domestic product and their standard deviations are pre-

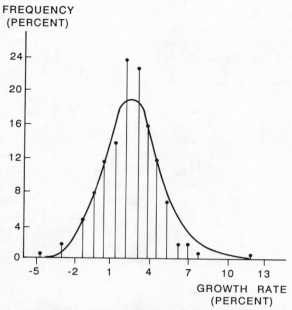

Figure 2-2. Frequency Histogram of Growth Rates

sented in table 2-1. The countries have been ranked by the average annual growth rate.[9] A frequency histogram of the growth rates is given in figure 2-2. The summary statistics on national economic growth rates are as follows. The unweighted world annual average growth rate is 2.34 percent, with a median of 2.3 percent, a mode of 2.03 percent, and a geometric mean of 0 percent. The standard deviation of growth rates is 2.21 percent, with a range of 16.47 percent, a lower quartile of 0.93 percent, and an upper quartile of 3.64 percent. The standardized skewness coefficient is 2.15, which is close to normal. The standardized kurtosis coefficient is 6.47, indicating an excess of observations near the mean and out in the tails. The overall picture is of an enormous range in the economic progress of nations in modern times.

Also shown in table 2-1 are the level of per capita real gross domestic product (RGDP) for 1960 and 1985 and the country's RGDP in 1985 (RGDP85) relative to that of the United States. A frequency histogram of RGDP85 is shown in figure 2-3. The summary statistics of the country data on 1985 per capita RGDP are as follows. The simple average RGDP is $3,725, with a median of $2,265, a mode of $526, and a geometric mean of $2,099. The standard deviation of RGDP85 is $3,638, with a range of $14,658, a lower quartile of $647, and an upper quartile of $5,765. The

17

TABLE 2-1

Growth Rates of per Capita Real Gross Domestic Product, 1950–1985

# Country	Average Growth	St. Dev.	Time	RGDP 1960	RGDP 1985	RGDP85/ US RGDP85
59 Omar	12.15	42.05	1967–85	2,041[a]	7,792	62.2
63 Singapore	7.88	5.86	1960–85	1,528	9,834	78.5
66 Taiwan	6.96	9.50	1950–85	866	3,581	28.6
48 Hong Kong	6.94	4.65	1960–85	1,737	9,093	72.6
53 Japan	6.32	3.58	1950–85	2,239	9,447	75.4
13 Gabon	6.07	1.66	1960–85	804	3,103	24.8
04 Botswana	5.48	3.58	1960–85	493	1,762	14.1
82 Malta	5.38	5.14	1954–85	1,282	5,319	42.4
123 China (P.R.)	5.37	7.44	1950–85	716	2,444	19.5
55 Korea	5.25	4.61	1953–85	690	3,056	24.4
19 Lesotho	5.06	2.27	1960–85	245	771	6.2
69 Yemen	5.00	5.00	1969–85	456[a]	978	7.8
107 Brazil	4.92	7.66	1955–85	991	3,282	26.2
72 Cyprus	4.75	10.68	1950–85	1,692	5,310	42.4
50 Iran	4.67	10.43	1955–85	1,839	3,922	31.3
91 Barbados	4.59	5.04	1960–85	1,747	5,212	41.6
77 Greece	4.50	4.48	1950–85	1,474	4,464	35.6
130 Yugoslavia	4.34	3.77	1960–85	1,778	5,063	40.4
36 Swaziland	4.29	3.28	1960–85	441	1,187	9.5
57 Malaysia	4.27	4.93	1955–85	1,103	3,415	27.3
119 Indonesia	4.21	3.95	1962–85	494[a]	1,255	10.0
85 Portugal	4.10	4.03	1950–85	1,429	3,729	29.8
122 Bulgaria	4.09	4.95	1950–85	2,339	5,113	40.8
86 Spain	4.08	4.63	1950–85	2,425	6,437	51.4
76 West Germany	4.04	2.99	1950–85	5,217	10,708	85.4
80 Italy	3.96	2.73	1950–85	3,233	7,425	59.2
70 Austria	3.95	2.10	1950–85	3,908	8,929	71.2
65 Syria	3.93	10.10	1960–85	1,234	2,900	23.1
10 Congo	3.85	2.76	1960–85	563	1,338	10.7
128 Romania	3.80	3.68	1960–85	1,705	4,273	34.1
52 Israel	3.73	5.56	1950–85	2,838	6,270	58.0
54 Jordan	3.71	9.28	1954–85	1,124	2,113	16.9
39 Tunisia	3.64	2.14	1960–85	852	2,050	16.4
74 Finland	3.56	3.29	1950–85	4,073	8,232	73.7
84 Norway	3.51	2.33	1950–85	5,001	12,623	100.8
114 Suriname	3.49	6.21	1960–85	1,558	3,522	28.1
89 Turkey	3.42	5.80	1950–85	1,255	2,533	20.2
129 USSR	3.39	2.28	1950–85	2,951	6,266	50.0
75 France	3.37	1.87	1950–85	4,473	9,918	79.1

TABLE 2-1, *cont.*

# Country	Average Growth	St. Dev.	Time	RGDP 1960	RGDP 1985	RGDP85/ US RGDP85
67 Thailand	3.28	4.73	1950–85	688	1,900	15.2
07 Cameroon	3.22	2.63	1960–85	507	1,095	8.7
11 Egypt	3.03	2.48	1950–85	496	1,188	9.5
71 Belgium	3.01	2.11	1950–85	4,379	9,717	77.5
102 Panama	3.00	3.84	1950–85	1,255	2,912	23.2
103 Trinidad and Tobago	2.99	8.07	1950–85	4,904	6,884	54.9
47 Burma	2.95	5.67	1950–85	306	557	4.4
125 East Germany	2.93	1.25	1960–85	4,258	8,740	69.7
83 Netherlands	2.88	2.80	1950–85	4,690	9,092	72.6
110 Ecuador	2.88	4.70	1950–85	1,143	2,387	19.0
126 Hungary	2.82	3.04	1950–85	3,218	5,765	46.0
78 Iceland	2.78	4.73	1950–85	4,644	9,037	72.1
73 Denmark	2.76	2.65	1950–85	5,490	10,884	86.8
79 Ireland	2.72	2.07	1950–85	2,545	5,205	41.5
87 Sweden	2.65	1.81	1950–85	5,149	9,704	79.0
94 Dominican Republic	2.64	5.83	1950–85	956	1,753	14.0
100 Mexico	2.60	3.38	1950–85	2,157	3,985	31.8
26 Morocco	2.58	2.58	1950–85	542	1,221	9.7
124 Czechoslovakia	2.53	2.27	1950–85	4,516	7,424	59.2
61 Philippines	2.46	3.18	1950–85	874	1,361	10.9
93 Costa Rica	2.45	4.52	1950–85	1,663	2,650	21.1
62 Saudi Arabia	2.45	9.52	1960–85	3,635	5,971	47.6
92 Canada	2.43	2.92	1950–85	6,069	12,196	97.3
60 Pakistan	2.43	4.07	1950–85	558	1,153	9.2
127 Poland	2.41	3.29	1950–85	2,826	4,913	39.2
109 Colombia	2.30	2.97	1950–85	1,344	2,599	20.7
88 Switzerland	2.29	2.92	1950–85	6,834	10,640	84.9
37 Tanzania	2.28	3.24	1960–85	208	355	2.8
01 Algeria	2.27	2.88	1960–85	1,302	2,142	17.1
51 Iraq	2.27	14.85	1953–85	2,527	2,813	22.4
90 United Kingdom	2.25	1.85	1950–85	4,970	8,665	69.1
43 Zimbabwe	2.15	5.44	1954–85	615	948	7.6
22 Malawi	2.14	2.89	1954–85	237	387	3.1
117 Australia	2.12	3.37	1950–85	5,182	8,850	70.6
118 Fiji	2.08	5.89	1960–85	1,799	2,893	23.1
81 Luxembourg	2.06	3.64	1950–85	6,112	10,540	84.1
64 Sri Lanka	2.06	5.18	1950–85	974	1,539	12.3
99 Jamaica	2.03	5.38	1953–85	1,472	1,725	13.8

TABLE 2-1, *cont.*

# Country	Average Growth	St. Dev.	Time	RGDP 1960	RGDP 1985	RGDP85/ US RGDP85
101 Nicaragua	2.03	9.13	1950–85	1,588	1,989	15.9
32 Sierra Leone	1.99	1.57	1960–85	281	443	3.5
104 United States	1.97	2.68	1950–85	7,380	12,532	100.0
28 Niger	1.95	2.78	1960–85	284	429	3.4
112 Paraguay	1.90	3.98	1950–85	991	1,996	15.9
30 Rwanda	1.89	3.19	1960–85	244	341	2.7
49 India	1.79	4.29	1950–85	533	750	6.0
120 New Zealand	1.69	3.38	1950–85	5,571	8,000	63.8
46 Bangladesh	1.69	6.12	1959–85	444	647	5.2
113 Peru	1.63	4.14	1950–85	1,721	2,114	16.9
34 South Africa	1.57	2.46	1950–85	2,627	3,885	31.0
05 Burkina Faso	1.43	1.87	1965–85	287[a]	377	3.0
25 Mauritius	1.36	2.14	1950–85	1,012	1,869	14.9
24 Mauritania	1.36	2.21	1960–85	414	550	4.4
121 Papua New Guinea	1.33	4.21	1960–85	1,008	1,374	11.0
18 Kenya	1.27	3.37	1950–85	470	598	4.8
14 Gambia	1.21	2.89	1960–85	433	526	4.2
108 Chile	1.21	8.02	1957–85	2,932	3,486	27.8
17 Ivory Coast	.99	4.39	1960–85	743	920	7.3
96 Guatemala	.96	2.54	1950–85	1,268	1,608	12.8
105 Argentina	.93	5.44	1959–85	3,091	3,486	27.8
95 El Salvador	.92	4.28	1950–85	1,062	1,198	9.6
38 Togo	.91	2.82	1960–85	415	489	3.9
29 Nigeria	.90	3.25	1950–85	552	581	4.6
98 Honduras	.74	3.53	1950–85	748	911	7.3
20 Liberia	.69	3.03	1960–85	449	491	3.9
115 Uruguay	.66	4.91	1950–85	3,271	3,462	27.6
40 Uganda	.60	3.04	1950–85	322	347	2.8
12 Ethiopia	.54	2.79	1950–85	285	310	2.5
58 Nepal	.42	2.87	1960–85	478	526	4.2
106 Bolivia	.36	5.04	1950–85	882	1,089	8.7
97 Haiti	.24	3.78	1960–85	605	631	5.0
35 Sudan	.13	2.56	1955–85	667	540	4.3
42 Zambia	.12	8.99	1955–85	740	584	4.7
31 Senegal	.08	2.55	1960–85	756	754	6.0
41 Zaire	.05	6.70	1950–85	314	210	1.7
116 Venezuela	− .08	4.79	1950–85	5,308	3,548	28.3
16 Guinea	− .16	2.61	1959–85	411	452	3.6
111 Guyana	− .23	7.39	1950–85	1,386	1,259	10.0
03 Benin	− .28	2.73	1959–85	595	525	4.2

TABLE 2-1, *cont.*

# Country	*Average Growth*	*St. Dev.*	*Time*	*RGDP 1960*	*RGDP 1985*	*RGDP85/ US RGDP85*
23 Mali	−.30	2.53	1960–85	396	355	2.8
44 Afghanistan	−.31	4.00	1960–85	671	609	4.9
08 Central African Republic	−.39	1.93	1960–85	485	434	3.5
06 Burundi	−.51	1.92	1960–85	412	345	2.8
45 Bahrain	−.79	7.21	1973–85	9,280[a]	8,192	65.4
21 Madagascar	−1.08	2.59	1960–85	659	497	4.0
02 Angola	−1.10	2.35	1960–85	880	609	4.9
15 Ghana	−1.10	3.05	1955–85	534	349	2.8
33 Somalia	−1.12	3.18	1960–85	483	348	2.8
27 Mozambique	−1.45	3.12	1960–85	798	528	4.2
09 Chad	−2.59	1.99	1960–85	515	254	2.0
68 United Arab Emirates	−3.23	14.83	1970–85	23,937[a]	12,404	99.0
56 Kuwait	−4.32	8.21	1960–85	48,987	14,868	118.6

Note: Mean growth rate = 2.3359; standard deviation = 2.2134.

[a] Values of per capita real GDP for these countries are for the following years: Oman—1967; Yemen—1969; Indonesia—1962; Burkina Faso—1965; Bahrain—1973; and United Arab Emirates—1970.

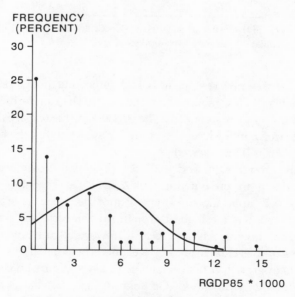

Figure 2-3. Frequency Histogram of RGDP85

TABLE 2-2
Economic Growth Rates by Geographic Regions

Statistic	(1)	(2)	(3)	(4)	(5)	(6)	(7)
Unweighted values							
Growth rate of per							
capita real GDP							
Mean	1.28	3.22	3.43	2.11	1.66	2.29	3.52
Standard							
Deviation	1.92	3.43	.88	1.13	1.54	1.12	.97
Minimum	−2.59	−4.32	2.06	.24	−.23	1.33	2.41
Maximum	6.07	12.15	5.38	4.59	4.92	4.21	5.37
1985 per capita real							
GDP							
Mean	849	4,488	8,110	4,013	2,686	4,474	5,556
Standard							
Deviation	772	4,090	2,749	3,937	913	3,676	1,815
Minimum	210	526	2,533	631	1,089	1,255	2,444
Maximum	3,885	14,868	12,623	12,532	3,548	8,850	8,740
Weighted mean values							
Growth rate of per							
capita real GDP	1.11	2.63	3.46	2.08	3.16	3.93	4.77
Per capita real							
GDP	879	1,964	7,912	9,598	3,075	2,027	3,506

Legend: (1) = Africa; (2) = Asia; (3) = Europe; (4) = Central and North America; (5) = South America; (6) = Oceania; (7) = centrally planned economies.

standardized skewness coefficient is 4.97, indicating an excess of observations of per capita income less than the mean. The standardized kurtosis coefficient is approximately zero. The overall conclusions are that there is a very wide range in the level of economic status and that the income level among nations is badly skewed.

Economic growth rates and 1985 per capita real gross domestic product by continent are presented in table 2-2. The average growth rate and the level of per capita income is lowest in Africa. Among less developed continents, Asia has the highest growth rate and level of per capita income measured by unweighted means. However, South America has the highest rate and level measured by weighted (by population) means. The relatively high growth rate in populous Indonesia (4.21 percent) yields a high weighted growth rate for Oceania. In light of what is now known about the state of the economies of the centrally planned nations, one should treat the estimates of real gross domestic product of these nations with skepticism.

CONVERGENCE OF GROWTH IN THE NEOCLASSICAL MODEL

We have pointed to the implication of the neoclassical model that countries that are capital intensive (high values of k or GDP) will have lower marginal products of capital and thus investment rates and economic growth will be lower in such countries and that countries with little capital per unit of labor (low values of k or GDP) will grow faster.[10] An empirical test of the neoclassical convergence theorem is obtained by regressing the logarithm of the growth rate against the logarithm of RGDP. Convergence is occurring if the regression coefficient is negative. Since Robert Barro and Xavier Martin have tested the convergence theorem with a sample of 114 countries from Summers and Heston, there is no purpose in replicating the result.[11] They correlate the average growth rate of real per capita GDP over 1960–1985 with RGDP in 1960 and find a *positive* correlation of .22. Thus, contrary to the prediction of the model, actual growth rates are diverging across countries.

Robert Lucas has explored the empirical implications of the Solovian model in the context of the question of why capital does not flow from the developed to the less developed countries.[12] Assuming that two countries have Cobb-Douglas-type (constant returns) technology with a common (neutral technology) intercept, $y_i = Ak_i^b$. The marginal product of capital is $r = Abk^{b-1}$, in terms of capital per worker, and thus $r = bA^{1/b}y^{(b-1)/b}$, in terms of output per worker. If the average of the capital share among the countries is $b = 0.4$, Lucas finds that the marginal product of capital in India is $15^{(1.5)} = 58$ times that of the United States! Such an extreme differential in the return to capital is a paradox: Either the neoclassical model is wrong or there must be some other explanation for the lack of a flow of capital in the face of such financial opportunities.

He considers several alternative assumptions. Only the most plausible is treated here. Suppose Indian and U.S. workers are not homogeneous. Using Anne Krueger's estimates to correct for human capital differences in the quality of the labor force, one American worker is worth five Indians, assuming the same physical capital per worker.[13] With this assumption, the ratio of per capita incomes between the two countries becomes one to three rather than one to fifteen. Then, the rate of return ratio becomes $3^{(1.5)} = 5$. While substantially less, the difference in returns after correcting for the human capital differential remains paradoxically large. Obviously, some other factors must be at work that retard international capital flows.

EXTENSIONS OF THE NEOCLASSICAL
MODEL OF ECONOMIC GROWTH

The neoclassical model concludes that all countries are able to grow through capital augmentation and that the rate of economic growth is given by the country's exogenous rate of population growth. But the evidence is that a large portion of the less developed world is stagnant or in economic decline. The simple neoclassical model does not explain why these nations are trapped at such low levels of economic growth. Clearly, the model needs to be extended to allow theoretically for conditions under which increases in the variables that contribute to economic growth do not yield sustained economic growth.

The neoclassical model can be altered to conform to the more realistic pattern of observed growth rates by relaxing some of the critical stated assumptions and incorporating the implicit but unstated assumptions of the model. To incorporate realism and allow for the effect of public policy, but keep the analytics tractable, the assumptions of a variable savings ratio, endogenous population growth (neo-Malthusian), exogenous neutral technological change, the "rule space" or structure of rights, and an open economy need to be incorporated into the model. Additionally, labor now is recognized as reproducible; that is, human capital can augment the quality or skill level of the labor force.

The augmented production function that incorporates some of these more realistic assumptions takes the following intensive form:

(2-2) $$y = f_\theta(k, h)e^{gt}.$$

The structure of rights, θ, is the economic, legal, political, and social rule space in which production takes place.[14] The rules of the game are exogenous at any moment of time to the resources employed in production (and consumption) and to the production function but vary widely across nations. The rate of growth of the labor force is assumed to be a function of the current real per capita income, expressed as

(2-3) $$L_t = L_0 \exp(\int_0^t n[y_t]d\tau),$$

where n is the rate of growth of labor (population), h is human capital per worker, and g is an exogenous, constant rate of neutral technological change.

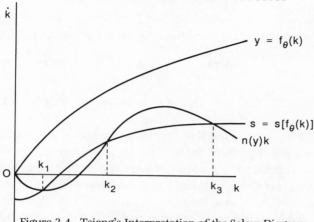

Figure 2-4. Tsiang's Interpretation of the Solow Diagram

We may redraw Solow's diagram, following Tsiang.[15] In figure 2-4, the population growth–capital–labor line is no longer linear, since population growth is endogenous. At low levels of per capita income, below the subsistence level, population growth would be negative and savings would be negative (hence k would fall). Beyond a subsistence level of per capita income, savings would be positive and population would grow to some maximum, and then the rate of growth of population would decline. In Gary Becker and Robert Barro[16] and Becker and Kevin Murphy[17] fertility declines as parents substitute quality for quantity of children. This augmentation of child quality through human capital increases the productivity index of labor.

The savings function is no longer a constant fraction of per capita income. Savings are negative below subsistence per capita incomes. Savings are positive for per capita incomes above the subsistence level.

The savings-investment functions intersect at three points in figure 2-4. At values of the capital-labor ratio between k_1 and k_3, the equilibrium is unstable, while the equilibrium is stable at k_2. For values of the capital labor ratio between k_2 and k_3, economic growth is not sustainable; the capital labor ratio will fall to k_2. For values of the capital labor ratio above k_3, the economy will take off in a self-sustaining process of rising per capita income. The stable equilibrium at k_2 in the figure is stylized as one in which per capita income is near the subsistence level. The economy is trapped in a low-level income equilibrium, with a small savings rate and a low capital-labor ratio. In terms of the model, the problem of economic progress is to raise the capital-labor ratio above k_3, from which the economy will take off on a self-sustained growth path until some higher ($k^* >$

25

k_3) stable equilibrium is reached. There are various policies to raise the parameters of the variables of the neoclassical growth model to values that lead to sustained growth.

PUBLIC POLICY AND THE NEOCLASSICAL GROWTH MODEL

According the model depicted in figure 2-4, the goal of economic development is to raise the capital-labor ratio to a level beyond k_3, that is, to move economies that are in a low-level equilibrium trap (for example, k_1) and those that are developing but are unstable ($k_2 < k < k_3$) on to a path of self-sustaining economic growth.

It is believed that several policies can move developing economies to the takeoff point. One policy is to raise the marginal propensity to save. This would shift the $s[f(k)]$ curve upward. There is skepticism about the sensitivity of savings relative to the interest rate. However, some developing countries increased domestic interest rates and experienced high rates of capital formation and economic growth. Taiwan pursued a policy of relatively high interest rates and domestic price stability. There was a six- to sevenfold increase in its savings rate over a thirty-year period. Korea followed a similar policy beginning in the mid-1960s and also achieved strong growth. Singapore increased its savings rate when it established the Central Provident Fund.

Other developing countries have followed a Keynesian policy of maintaining low nominal rates of interest. Combined with relatively high rates of inflation, this policy led to negative real interest rates. Negative real interest rates induce wasteful employments of capital. Since capital is, in effect, subsidized, a scarce resource is overemployed (production is made more capital intensive) in some industries and flows into otherwise marginal employments. These inefficient employments of capital raise the $n(y)k$ curve in figure 2-4 higher than it would be if the real interest rate reflected the opportunity cost of capital.

If the definition of capital is expanded to include human capital (investments in schooling and on-the-job training), policies that promote human capital formation (wage differentials that make it economically rational to enroll and stay in school) raise the overall level of capital in the economy. Such wage differentials have income distribution consequences.

A second growth-enhancing policy is the liberalization of foreign trade. The liberalization promotes comparative advantage, reduces distortion in the allocation of resources by bringing domestic prices into conformity with world prices, induces capital inflows, and promotes technology transfer. This liberalization injects additional capital and raises the marginal efficiency of investment. However, many developing countries have followed a strategy of promoting the growth of import-substituting industries that are protected by quantitative import controls or high tariffs. Economies of scale were quickly exhausted in small, protected domestic markets. Any growth gains from such policies were quickly offset by scale and allocation inefficiencies arising from the domestic distortions induced by protectionist policies. Moreover, the coincident policy of fixed exchange rates maintained an overvalued currency. This policy discouraged exports, thereby reinforcing stringent trade and exchange controls in the interest of maintaining the balance of payments.

Another method of lowering the $n(y)k$ curve in figure 2-4 is through the adoption of policies that lower the rate of population growth. While the growth rate of the labor force contributes to economic growth, its effect is positive when the rate of capital formation (physical and human) is greater than the rate of growth of the labor force. Such countries as Somalia, Taiwan, Brazil, Colombia, Mauritius, Korea, Sri Lanka, and Singapore have had strongly declining rates of population growth. Such nations as Liberia, Zambia, Gambia, Algeria, Cameroon, Nepal, Burundi, and Gabon have had strongly rising rates of population growth.

In most less developed countries, government plays a large role in the modern sector of the economy, and individual economic, civil, and political rights are limited. The size of the role of the state can be measured crudely by the extent of investment in state enterprises and in the share of government expenditures relative to gross domestic product. Resources in the public sector are allocated on political criteria. There is no guarantee that they are employed in their highest valued economic use. Moreover, political control of the economy leads to rent-seeking behavior. In the extreme, rent-seeking may take the form of endemic corruption. Inefficiency and low growth result. Limits on economic freedom are a form of taxation that lowers the rate of private capital formation, discourages innovation, and interferes with the gains from exchange. Some developing countries have granted wide latitude to economic liberty (Hong Kong, Taiwan, Singapore, Korea, Dominica, Costa Rica, Mauritius, etc.), often with the result of strong economic growth. However, much of the less developed world is deeply mistrustful of individual initiative as the engine of growth.

The discussion, then, suggests that certain policies promote economic growth: high capital formation, positive real interest rates, high human capital formation, low population growth, rapid technological change, liberal commercial policy, economic freedom and market allocation, a small public sector, and a low inflation rate. In the following discussion, each variable is taken up one at a time and the empirical evidence of its effect on economic growth is established. No attempt is made here to construct and estimate an integrated model of growth. These are simple correlations; partial correlations likely would differ, at least in magnitude.

CAPITAL FORMATION AMONG NATIONS, 1950–1985

Capital formation and the level of per capita real GDP and the growth rate in real per capita GDP are correlated. No one seriously questions the role that capital accumulation plays in economic growth; at issue is whether its accumulation and allocation is best left in private or in government hands. The simple correlation between the average share of investment out of GDP over the period and per capita real GDP in 1985 is 0.57. The simple correlation between the average investment share of GDP and the growth rate in per capita real GDP is 0.40.[18]

Table 2-3 presents data on the average fraction of gross domestic capital formation out of gross domestic product and the trend in the investment share by continent over the period 1950–1985. Africa has the lowest rate of capital formation and the highest relative variation in the investment share among the continents. Average investment shares in Africa at one standard deviation are in the range of 6.7 to 21.8 percent of GDP. Economic growth rates in Africa at one standard deviation are in the range of –0.6 to 3.2 percent (see table 2.2). Unweighted mean rates of relative capital formation are comparable in Asia and Central and North America, in the range of about 10 to 24 percent of GDP. Weighting by population yields a lower investment share in Asia. The range (at one standard deviation) in economic growth rates is –0.2 to 6.7 percent in Asia and 1.0 to 3.2 percent in Central and North America. The investment share in Latin America is the highest of the continents of developing nations. At one standard deviation, economic growth is in the interval 0.1 to 3.2 percent per year.

The trend in capital formation is strongly positive in Asia, moderately positive in Africa (weighted mean), weakly positive in Central and North America, and moderately negative in Latin America. Trends in investment shares are moderately related to average rates of growth of per capita real domestic product. The simple correlation between the variables is .23.

TABLE 2-3

Average National Investment Share and Trend in Investment Share, 1950–1985

Statistic	(1)	(2)	(3)	(4)	(5)	(6)
Unweighted values						
Investment as a share of GDP, 1950–85						
Mean	14.23	17.34	25.28	16.49	19.42	21.03
σ	7.49	7.64	4.87	5.88	7.52	6.88
Minimum	4.11	5.86	16.48	7.10	9.92	14.12
Maximum	36.00	32.24	36.24	24.04	31.81	31.87
Trend in investment as share of GDP						
Mean	.082	.507	.058	.090	−.079	.122
σ	.499	.500	.197	.237	.241	.332
Minimum	−1.54	−.57	−.26	−.56	−.43	−.16
Maximum	1.19	1.53	.47	.43	.41	.67
Weighted values						
Investment share	12.43	15.79	22.76	19.86	21.90	15.84
Trend in share	.159	.293	.072	.058	−.194	.573

Legend: (1) = Africa; (2) = Asia; (3) = Europe; (4) = Central and North America; (5) = South America; (6) = Oceania.

The level and pattern of gross domestic capital formation over the period can be used to roughly classify the developing nations into three categories: (1) underdeveloped and stable or stagnant, (2) developing but unstable, and (3) developing and stable. Countries are classified as stable-underdeveloped or stagnant (US) if the average investment share is 12 percent or less, with a cyclically unstable or a falling pattern in the investment share. Countries classified as developing but unstable (DU) have average investment shares in the 12 to 15 percent range, with a cyclically unstable or a falling pattern in the investment share. Countries classified as developing and stable (DS) generally have average investment shares of 15 percent or higher with an upward trend in the investment share or have investment shares above 15 percent but with some instability in the investment share over time.

Table 2-4 presents the data on rates of capital formation for the non-oil-exporting less developed countries and their development status classifications based on these criteria. To a certain extent these classifications are sensitive to the assumptions that have been made regarding the criti-

TABLE 2-4

Non-Oil-Exporting Less Developed Countries Classified by Development Status
Based on Capital Formation, 1950–1985

Country	I/GDP	σ	Trend	g_{RGDP}	Pattern	Status
Zambia	36.00	17.41	−1.52	.12	Cyc. Fall	DU
Singapore	32.24	9.92	.98	7.88	Stead. Rise	DS
Guyana	31.81	7.53	−.16[a]	−.23	Cyc. Const.	DS
Israel	31.35	7.50	−.57	3.73	Cyc. Fall	DS
Chile	29.71	5.36	−.35	1.21	Cyc. Fall	DS
Congo	28.82	10.63	−.38[a]	3.85	Cyc. Const.	DS
Botswana	28.39	4.36	1.19	5.48	Cyc. Rise	DS
Zimbabwe	26.53	13.11	−1.10	2.15	Stead. Fall	DU
Mauritani	25.62	12.02	−.60	1.36	Cyc. Const.	DU
Argentina	25.15	4.09	−.09[a]	.93	Cyc. Const.	DS
Brazil	24.43	4.60	−.31	4.92	Cyc. Fall	DS
Algeria	24.14	8.65	.80	2.27	Cyc. Rise	DS
Panama	24.04	6.07	.27	3.00	Cyc. Rise	DS
Ecuador	23.88	3.24	.12	2.88	Cyc. Rise	DS
Jamaica	22.48	6.28	−.56	2.03	Cyc. Fall	DS
Gabon	22.13	11.40	.41[a]	6.07	Cyc. Const.	DU
Liberia	21.51	14.68	−1.20	.69	Cyc. Fall	DU
Malaysia	21.37	6.92	.73	4.27	Stead. Rise	DS
South Africa	20.91	3.02	.12	1.57	Cyc. Rise	DS
Kenya	20.71	6.33	−.44	1.27	Cyc. Fall	US
Fiji	20.64	2.72	−.11[a]	2.08	Cyc. Const.	DS
Trinidad and Tobago	20.33	7.29	.31	2.99	Cyc. Rise	DS
Hong Kong	19.92	2.99	.11[a]	6.94	Cyc. Const.	DS
Barbados	19.60	2.14	.10	4.59	Stead. Rise	DS
Korea	19.53	9.47	.92	5.25	Stead. Rise	DS
Suriname	19.45	6.00	−.43	3.49	Cyc. Fall	DU
Colombia	18.90	2.12	−.14	2.30	Stead. Fall	DS
Turkey	18.41	3.99	.32	3.42	Stead. Rise	DS
Gambia	18.16	7.20	.65	1.21	Cyc. Rise	DU
Tanzania	18.05	3.43	.22	2.28	Cyc. Rise	DS
Swaziland	17.73	4.81	.18[a]	4.29	Cyc. Const.	DS
Taiwan	17.39	7.13	.59	6.96	Stead. Rise	DS
Dominican Republic	16.29	5.97	.18[a]	1.33	Cyc. Const.	DS
Papua New Guinea	16.29	4.83	.33	2.64	Cyc. Rise	DS
Mauritius	16.17	3.90	.14	1.36	Cyc. Rise	DS
Syria	15.99	3.64	.31	3.93	Cyc. Rise	DS
Jordan	15.86	8.24	.76	3.71	Stead. Rise	DS
Egypt	15.81	2.72	.10	3.03	Cyc. Rise	DS

TABLE 2-4, *cont.*

Country	I/GDP	σ	Trend	g_{RGDP}	Pattern	Status
Thailand	15.75	4.52	.34	3.28	Stead. Rise	DS
Togo	15.54	7.74	.54	.91	Cyc. Rise	DU
India	15.28	3.09	.26	1.79	Stead. Rise	DS
Philippines	14.20	2.74	.12	2.46	Stead. Rise	DS
Costa Rica	14.15	2.87	.10	2.45	Cyc. Rise	DS
Sri Lanki	14.15	3.40	.12	2.06	Cyc. Rise	DU
Tunisia	13.89	2.39	.21	3.64	Cyc. Rise	DS
Somalia	13.81	4.94	.59	−1.12	Stead. Rise	DU
Honduras	13.56	2.45	.05[a]	.74	Cyc. Const.	DU
Nicaragua	13.54	4.45	.02[a]	2.03	Cyc. Const.	DU
Peru	13.16	3.33	− .21	1.63	Cyc. Fall	DU
Cameroon	12.90	3.25	.38	3.22	Stead. Rise	DU
Bolivia	12.75	3.65	.00[a]	.36	Cyc. Const.	DU
Burkina Faso	12.74	3.93	.12[a]	1.43	Cyc. Const.	DU
Lesotho	12.67	6.45	.77	5.06	Stead. Rise	DS
Ivory Coast	12.45	4.16	.18	.99	Cyc. Rise	DU
Malawi	12.29	3.99	.17	2.14	Cyc. Const.	DU
Sudan	12.25	3.22	.26	.13	Cyc. Rise	DU
Uruguay	12.22	4.05	.06[a]	.66	Cyc. Const.	US
Burma	11.70	3.08	.04[a]	2.95	Cyc. Const.	US
Sierra Leone	10.95	2.16	.02[a]	1.99	Cyc. Const.	US
Guinea	10.85	1.42	− .01[a]	− .16	Cyc. Const.	US
Benin	10.84	2.42	− .03	− .28	Cyc. Const.	US
Pakistan	10.80	3.19	.11	2.43	Cyc. Rise	DU
Central African Republic	10.55	1.76	− .04[a]	− .39	Cyc. Fall	US
Niger	10.39	5.83	.47	1.95	Cyc. Rise	US
Paraguay	9.92	4.83	.41	1.90	Stead. Rise	DS
Nigeria	9.91	6.28	.50	.90	Stead. Rise	DS
Senegal	9.61	1.70	− .03[a]	.08	Cyc. Const.	US
Ghana	9.34	2.11	− .13	−1.10	Cyc. Fall	US
Guatemala	8.75	1.91	.03	.96	Cyc. Const.	US
Morocco	8.49	3.16	.07[a]	2.58	Cyc. Const.	US
Rwanda	7.99	2.81	.31	1.89	Stead. Rise	US
El Salvador	7.48	1.73	.07	.92	Cyc. Rise	US
Mali	7.32	2.06	− .03[a]	− .30	Cyc. Const.	US
Madagascar	7.12	1.23	.01[a]	− .08	Cyc. Const.	US
Haiti	7.10	3.57	.43	.24	Stead. Rise	US

TABLE 2-4, *cont.*

Country	I/GDP	σ	Trend	g_{RGDP}	Pattern	Status
Chad	6.99	2.85	.06[a]	-2.59	Cyc. Const.	US
Afghanistan	6.92	1.44	.01	$-.31$	Cyc. Const.	US
Bangladesh	6.76	2.20	$-.09$[a]	1.69	Cyc. Fall	US
Zaire	6.33	3.44	.20	.05	Cyc. Rise	US
Mozambique	6.17	1.12	$-.03$[a]	-1.45	Cyc. Const.	US
Nepal	5.95	2.98	.37	.42	Stead. Rise	US
Angola	5.85	1.20	.02[a]	-1.10	Cyc. Const.	US
Burundi	5.13	2.70	.31	$-.51$	Stead. Rise	US
Ethiopia	4.79	1.73	.10	.54	Cyc. Rise	US
Uganda	4.11	1.12	.01[a]	.60	Cyc. Const.	US

[a] Trend is not statistically significant at a conventional level.

cal investment shares. Misclassifications are inevitable. Nevertheless, the assumptions are reasonable. For moderate changes in the assumptions, the classifications will not change materially. Of the countries classified as underdeveloped-stable, 70 percent are in Africa, 15 percent in Asia, and 15 percent in Central or South America. Of the countries classified as developing but unstable, 65 percent are in Africa, 25 percent in Central or South America, and 10 percent in Asia. Of the countries classified as developing-stable, 37 percent are in Central or South America, and 26 percent each are in Asia or Africa.

Real Interest Rate Policy

Under the fashionable Keynesian monetary policy, most less developed countries have held interest rates at artificially low levels. Combined with high inflation rates, real interest rates frequently are negative. Table 2-5 presents data on the average real interest rate and the percentage of the period that real interest rates were negative. Of the fifty-four countries, only eight had positive real interest rates. This tells us how endemic is the policy of low nominal interest rates combined with inflation. While there is controversy concerning the elasticity of savings with respect to the interest rate, certainly negative real interest rates depress domestic capital formation and distort the allocation of a scarce factor of production.

The average real interest rate is correlated with the average real growth rate, but not with RGDP85. The simple correlation with the growth rate

TABLE 2-5
Real Interest Rates in Less Developed Countries

Country	Time Period	Average Real Interest Rate	% Period Negative	Country	Time Period	Average Real Interest Rate	% Period Negative
Argentina	1977–85	−24.7	66.7	Malaysia	1971–86	−.4	43.8
Benin	1971–82	−2.4	83.3	Malta	1969–86	2.0	22.2
Bolivia	1958–84	−56.4	37.0	Mauritius	1967–87	−1.8	33.3
Botswana	1976–87	−2.2	66.7	Mexico	1978–86	−4.0	66.7
Brazil	1964–86	−22.0	82.6	Morocco	1958–85	−2.0	64.3
Burkina Faso	1973–85	−.4	46.2	Niger	1967–81	−5.6	93.3
Burundi	1974–86	−4.2	76.9	Nigeria	1960–85	−5.9	50.0
Cameroon	1970–83	−5.9	92.9	Pakistan	1960–87	−.8	50.0
Chile	1974–84	−130.2	54.5	Papua New			
Colombia	1958–87	−1.2	56.7	Guinea	1974–84	−.1	54.5
Costa Rica	1961–86	−2.7	38.5	Peru	1961–84	−13.4	70.8
Cyprus	1969–87	−1.9	52.6	Philippines	1958–87	−3.1	66.7
Ecuador	1958–84	−3.9	48.1	Senegal	1969–81	−.6	38.5
Egypt	1960–83	.0	45.8	Sierra Leone	1965–83	−.6	47.4
Fiji	1973–86	−4.8	71.4	Singapore	1972–87	3.0	20.0
Ghana	1960–83	−18.2	75.0	Sri Lanki	1958–84	−1.5	48.1
Guatemala	1958–86	−.5	34.5	Syria	1961–86	1.2	11.5
Guyana	1966–83	.8	33.3	Taiwan	1952–86	6.9	14.3
Honduras	1958–86	4.3	34.5	Tanzania	1971–85	−9.4	100.0
India	1963–86	−.5	45.8	Thailand	1959–87	4.4	13.8
Iran	1960–83	4.1	12.5	Togo	1971–83	−2.2	46.2
Jamaica	1961–86	−5.1	61.5	Trinidad and			
Jordan	1970–86	−2.9	70.6	Tobago	1966–85	−6.1	65.0
Kenya	1968–85	−.7	33.3	Tunisia	1961–83	−1.2	56.5
Korea	1958–87	−1.5	53.3	Turkey	1958–83	−9.0	61.5
Libya	1963–82	−2.5	65.0	Venezuela	1958–86	.5	25.0
Madagascar	1969–82	−5.3	71.4	Zaire	1978–87	−38.3	100.0
Malawi	1963–87	−2.1	56.0	Zambia	1965–86	−5.3	63.6

Source: IMF, International Financial Statistics; Taiwan Statistical Data Bank.

is .31. The correlation with RGDP85 is .18. Of course, one should not expect that interest rate policy and the level of income necessarily are related.

HUMAN CAPITAL AND POPULATION GROWTH

Early neoclassical growth models treated labor inputs as homogeneous and population growth as exogenous. Yet the increase in the quality of the labor force is recognized as a major source of economic growth. Thomas Malthus emphasized the endogenous relationship between population growth and per capita income.

Recently, Gary Becker and Nigel Tomes, Becker and Robert Barro, and Becker and Kevin Murphy have begun to model the connection between education and other investments in knowledge and skills and the Malthusian behavior of fertility within the neoclassical framework.[19] In the simple version of the Becker and Murphy model, three steady states exist. The underdevelopment steady state is characterized by high population growth, little human capital, and subsistence income levels. The development steady state, which is globally unstable, has some human capital accumulation, declining population growth, and rising income. In this development state, the economy either returns to an underdeveloped steady state with low human capital and constant high population growth or transits to a stable developed steady state with a constant low population growth rate, a perpetual growth in per capita income, and a perpetual rise in per capita human capital, depending on the interrelationship among the rate of return on investment, the rate of altruism time preference, and the fertility rate. This model also has equity implications similar in spirit to those described by Simon Kuznets.[20] Transmitters of human capital accumulate more human capital than do workers, and producers of new knowledge accumulate more than do teachers. Efficient specialization requires income differentials among these skill classes, and income inequality rises during development. As the economies reach a perpetual steadily developing state such skill-based income differentials tend to narrow.

The available stylized facts of the relationship among human capital, population growth, and economic progress are consistent with the model. Table 2-6 presents by continent evidence on simple averages and weighted (by population) averages of literacy rates, educational expenditures as a fraction of GNP, enrollment ratios, and the fraction of the population age

TABLE 2-6
Education and Literacy by Continent, 1980

Statistic	(1)	(2)	(3)	(4)	(5)	(6)	(7)
Unweighted values							
Mean literacy 1980	20.8	48.3	92.5	72.4	80.0	70.6	89.3
σ	16.2	29.0	11.3	22.9	9.8	29.0	15.7
Min	2.0	5.0	60.0	24.0	63.0	32.0	50.0
Max	61.0	98.0	100.0	99.0	93.0	100.0	100.0
Mean literacy 1960	17.0	42.2	90.3	66.9	72.4	63.0	88.9
σ	3.1	28.7	15.7	26.1	17.0	33.7	16.5
Min	2.0	5.0	46.0	10.0	32.0	25.0	50.0
Max	60.0	98.0	100.0	99.0	91.0	99.0	99.0
Mean educ. exp./GNP	4.7	3.6	5.2	4.7	3.8	4.6	5.0
σ	1.8	1.8	1.9	2.1	2.3	1.6	1.2
Min	1.8	1.5	2.1	1.5	1.3	2.0	3.2
Max	9.4	8.3	9.1	8.0	9.8	6.0	7.2
Mean primary school enrollment ratio	69.7	90.3	99.0	96.6	107.2	99.6	100.9
σ	29.6	21.1	11.5	17.3	11.6	21.2	8.6
Min	20.0	30.0	64.0	64.0	84.0	62.0	91.0
Max	116.0	116.0	118.0	120.0	128.0	112.0	121.0
Mean secondary school enrollment ratio	18.5	47.3	78.6	48.6	45.6	53.8	71.7
σ	15.3	24.5	14.7	27.5	12.0	32.6	23.5
Min	2.0	10.0	37.0	12.0	26.0	12.0	40.0
Max	76.0	91.0	94.0	95.0	60.0	86.0	105.0
Mean post–secondary schooling as % of pop. aged 25 +	.4	4.4	4.9	6.1	3.63	9.9	5.1
σ	.8	5.1	2.8	10.7	1.39	10.0	1.9
Min	.1	.1	1.0	.3	1.0	1.0	2.0
Max	3.7	20.1	11.0	31.1	6.3	21.5	8.5
Weighted mean values							
Literacy 1980	23.3	43.3	91.3	89.3	73.7	61.8	64.0
Literacy 1960	21.3	37.7	88.9	86.8	67.2	48.4	63.8
Educ. exp./GNP	4.3	3.3	4.5	5.8	3.4	2.5	5.4
Primary school	78.6	80.8	102.8	102.0	103.1	110.8	115.8
Secondary school	24.2	36.6	77.3	75.8	39.7	33.7	58.2
Post–secondary schooling	.7	3.2	5.3	22.1	4.0	5.3	3.3

Legend: (1) = Africa; (2) = Asia; (3) = Europe; (4) = Central and North America; (5) = South America; (6) = Oceania; (7) = centrally planned economies.

twenty-five or older with postsecondary schooling. These variables are available by country, ranked according to the literacy rate in 1980 in Appendix 2-1. Among the less developed continents, Africa has the lowest level of human capital, with a mean 1980 literacy rate of 20.8 percent (weighted mean = 23.3 percent), comparatively low enrollment ratios, especially at the secondary school level, and a very low fraction of the population with more advanced schooling (a mean of 0.4 percent and a weighted mean of 0.7 percent). Asia is next in relatively low levels of human capital, but has a much higher level of accumulation than Africa. Particularly, note that the fraction of the population with postsecondary school training in Asia is comparable to that of Europe, South America, Oceania, and the centrally planned economies, although the overall literacy rate is below the levels of these continents.

Human capital as measured by the literacy rate is significantly related to the average rate of growth in per capita real gross domestic product and the level of real GDP in 1985 across the 130 countries. The simple correlation between the average growth rate and the literacy rate is 0.31. The simple correlation between real GDP in 1985 and the literacy rate is 0.42.

Population growth remains high throughout the less developed world. Table 2-7 presents by continent unweighted and weighted average population growth rates and the trend in population growth rates (in Appendix 2-2 data is available by country). Africa has the highest weighted average population growth rate at 2.8 percent, followed by South America (2.5 percent), Asia (2.3 percent), Oceania (2.2 percent), and Central and North America (1.9 percent). The population growth rates (weighted means) continue to rise in Africa and to a lesser extent in Asia, but are declining on the other continents.

High population growth rates are associated with low rates of growth of per capita real GDP and with low levels of real GDP per capita in 1985. The simple correlation between the growth rate of real per capita income and population growth is −0.37. The simple correlation between the level of real GDP per capita in 1985 and population growth is −0.15, which is not statistically significant at the 5 percent level. The negative relationship between human capital and population growth predicted by the Becker, et.al. models also is confirmed. The simple correlation between the literacy rate and the population growth rate is −0.50.

Using the criteria of population growth, human capital accumulation, economic growth, and the level of per capita income, one can roughly classify the development status of nations. Using arbitrary but reasonable criteria of a population growth rate of 2.75 percent or less, a literacy rate

TABLE 2-7

Population Growth by Continent, 1950–1985

Statistic	(1)	(2)	(3)	(4)	(5)	(6)	(7)
Unweighted values							
Average pop. growth							
Mean	2.70	3.33	.76	2.30	2.27	2.04	.86
σ	.56	2.33	.50	.90	.75	.33	.58
Min	1.57	1.06	.25	.38	.91	1.54	−.08
Max	4.39	13.19	2.54	3.31	3.66	2.30	1.96
Trend in average pop. growth							
Mean	.020	−.072	−.014	−.019	−.031	−.029	−.041
σ	.046	.272	.024	.033	.043	.035	.060
Min	−.136	−1.350	−.051	−.079	−.125	−.064	−.199
Max	.140	.152	.062	.044	.020	.011	−.003
Weighted values							
Average pop. growth	2.84	2.25	.86	1.85	2.53	2.16	1.71
Trend in average pop. growth	.019	.006	−.019	−.027	−.030	−.001	−.028

Legend: (1) = Africa; (2) = Asia; (3) = Europe; (4) = Central and North America; (5) = South America; (6) = Oceania; (7) = centrally planned economies.

of 30 percent or more, an average per capita real economic growth rate of 1.5 percent per annum or better, and a per capita real gross domestic product in 1985 of $1,000 or more, the non-oil-exporting less developed countries were classified by development status. The results appear in Table 2-8. About 35 percent of the countries in the sample were classified as underdeveloped-stable or stagnant, some 70 percent of which were African countries. Only 10 percent were classified as developing-unstable, with the vast majority being African countries. Some 55 percent, three-quarters of which were non-African nations, were classified as developing-stable. Of course, these classifications of development status are sensitive to changes in the assumptions regarding the critical values of population growth, literacy, economic growth, and the level of per capita income associated with a takeoff into self-sustained permanent growth. Also, as partial explanations, they ignore other variables associated with the process of economic transformation. Nevertheless, the general conclusions of a stagnant Africa and a transforming Asia and Latin America (with considerable variance in the pace of development among the countries) will hold for reasonable changes in the parameters of these criteria.

TABLE 2-8

Non-Oil-Exporting Less Developed Countries Classified by Development Status
based on Population Growth and Human Capital Accumulation

Country	Pop. Growth	Trend	Literacy Rate	Economic Growth	RGDP85	Development Status
Ivory Coast	4.39	.016[a]	5	.99	920	US
Botswana	3.58	.081	33	5.48	1,762	DS
Zimbabwe	3.55	−.031	40	2.15	948	DS
Israel	3.54	−.136	88	3.73	7,270	DS
Kenya	3.37	.068	20	1.27	598	US
Syria	3.34	.016	40	3.93	2,900	DS
Honduras	3.31	.006[a]	57	.74	911	US
Swaziland	3.28	.019	30	4.29	1,187	DS
Niger	3.25	.029	2	1.95	429	DU
Tanzania	3.24	.022	29	2.28	355	DU
Rwanda	3.19	.017	17	1.89	341	DU
Somalia	3.18	−.049	2	−1.12	348	US
Costa Rica	3.13	−.053	88	2.45	2,650	DS
Mozambique	3.12	.075	12	−1.45	528	US
Nicaragua	3.06	.044	58	2.03	1,989	DS
Ghana	3.05	−.025[a]	31	−1.10	349	US
Uganda	3.04	−.001[a]	35	.60	347	US
Liberia	3.03	.042	9	.69	491	US
Guatemala	3.01	−.002[a]	46	.96	1,608	DS
Jordan	2.98	−.002[a]	33	3.71	2,113	DS
Zambia	2.92	.042	48	.12	584	DU
Malawi	2.89	.022	23	2.14	387	DU
Gambia	2.89	.079	6	1.21	526	US
Algeria	2.89	.054	28	2.27	2,142	DS
El Salvador	2.83	−.032	50	.92	1,198	DS
Dominican Republic	2.82	−.028	68	2.64	1,753	DS
Togo	2.82	.007[a]	17	.91	489	US
Ecuador	2.81	−.010	74	2.88	2,387	DS
Philippines	2.80	−.010[a]	83	2.46	1,361	DS
Ethiopia	2.79	−.016[a]	6	.54	310	US
Nigeria	2.78	−.031[a]	16	.90	581	DU
Congo	2.76	.043	17	3.85	1,338	DS
Taiwan	2.74	−.078	85	6.96	3,581	DS
Benin	2.73	.024	8	−.28	525	US
Bangladesh	2.71	−.031[a]	21	1.69	647	DU
Paraguay	2.69	.010[a]	81	1.90	1,996	DS
Malaysia	2.68	−.025	54	4.27	3,415	DS

TABLE 2-8, *cont.*

Country	Pop. Growth	Trend	Literacy Rate	Economic Growth	RGDP85	Development Status
Brazil	2.66	− .041	66	4.92	3,282	DS
Pakistan	2.64	.038	15	2.43	1,153	DS
Panama	2.63	− .027	79	3.00	2,912	DS
Cameroon	2.63	.073	19	3.22	1,095	DS
Guinea	2.61	− .136[a]	9	− .16	452	US
Colombia	2.60	− .050	81	2.30	2,599	DS
Thailand	2.60	− .016	79	3.28	1,900	DS
Madagascar	2.59	.033	34	1.08	497	US
Morocco	2.58	− .005	22	2.58	1,221	DS
Sudan	2.56	.050	15	.13	540	US
Senegal	2.55	.028	6	.08	754	US
Mali	2.53	.001[a]	3	− .30	355	US
Zaire	2.49	.032	32	.05	210	US
Egypt	2.48	.010[a]	43	3.03	1,188	DS
Peru	2.46	.007[a]	73	1.63	2,114	DS
South Africa	2.46	− .005[a]	57	1.57	3,885	DS
Bolivia	2.42	.020	63	.36	1,089	DU
Afghanistan	2.40	.025	12	− .31	609	US
Angola	2.35	.025	3	− 1.10	609	US
Hong Kong	2.32	− .050[a]	77	6.94	9,093	DS
Fiji	2.30	− .064	64	2.08	2,893	DS
Papua New Guinea	2.28	.011[a]	32	1.33	1,374	DS
Nepal	2.28	.036	19	.42	526	US
Lesotho	2.27	.032	56	5.06	771	DS
Mauritania	2.21	− .009	4	1.36	550	US
Tunisia	2.14	.030	38	3.64	2,050	DS
Mauritius	2.14	− .069	61	1.36	1,869	DS
Korea	2.12	− .045	88	5.25	3,056	DS
India	2.11	.019	33	1.79	750	DS
Sri Lanka	2.09	− .041	77	2.06	1,539	DS
Burma	2.01	.007[a]	60	2.95	557	DS
Chad	1.99	.028	7	− 2.59	254	US
Chile	1.93	− .031	88	1.21	3,486	DS
Central African Republic	1.93	.048	8	− .39	434	US
Burundi	1.92	.068	14	− .51	345	US
Burkina Faso	1.87	− .024	3	1.43	377	US

TABLE 2-8, cont.

Country	Pop. Growth	Trend	Literacy Rate	Economic Growth	RGDP85	Development Status
Singapore	1.78	−.078	69	7.88	9,834	DS
Trinidad and Tobago	1.76	−.079	92	2.99	6,884	DS
Haiti	1.67	.012	24	.24	631	US
Gabon	1.66	.140	14	6.07	3,103	DS
Argentina	1.59	.002[a]	93	.93	3,486	DS
Sierra Leone	1.57	.035	12	1.99	443	US
Jamaica	1.45	.006[a]	82	2.03	1,725	DS
Suriname	1.24	−.089[a]	84	3.49	3,522	DS
Uruguay	0.91	−.035	93	.66	3,462	DS
Barbados	.38	.001[a]	98	4.59	5,212	DS

[a] Trend coefficient not statistically significant.

TECHNOLOGICAL CHANGE

Output per worker has risen manyfold throughout the industrial history of Western nations. These increases in labor productivity are a multiple of the increases in the capital-labor ratio. Since Robert Solow, these increases in labor productivity have been attributed to technical progress.[21] In the Solow-type model of economic growth, technical change is disembodied knowledge that evolves exogenously. Disembodied technological progress is an intuitively appealing concept in that it describes an important aspect of technological change. The assembly line was a revolutionary change in industrial design that rapidly spread beyond the automotive industry. Hence, disembodied technical change has the feature of being an externality. Consequently, the innovator is unable to capture much or any (if the innovation cannot be patented) of the gains from disembodied technical change, since the innovation can be replicated costlessly. The unappealing aspect of exogenous technical change in the Solow model is that while output depends on technological change, the production function is homogeneous of degree one, and by Euler's theorem, factor payments to capital and labor exactly exhaust national income. As a result, conceptually, technology is produced as a free good without resources.

Since Kenneth Arrow, the alternative view of technological progress is that it is embodied in the factors of production.[22] In the Arrow model, technical change evolves endogenously and is embedded in the capital stock. The increased efficiency of capital is captured as returns to the firm. Following Hirofumi Uzawa, Paul Romer, Robert King and Sergio Rebelo and Gary Becker and Kevin Murphy have specified models of economic growth in which knowledge is accumulated endogenously and is embodied as human capital.[23]

Much of technological progress is embodied in the human capital skills of individuals. In the extreme, such embodied skills disappear with the individual: Pablo Casals, Auguste Rodin, etc. Such individuals capture all the gains from their human capital investment or talent. However, many forms of technological change that involve the interaction of specialized human capital (for example, genetic engineering) exist independently of those involved in its production. Current research on endogenous technical change attempts to blend these two themes. The modeling is of a process that involves embodied knowledge through human capital appreciation as a separate factor of production and disembodied technical change that has fixed costs and externalities from knowledge spillovers.[24]

Changes in technology are extremely difficult to measure. A crude measure of the level of technology embodied in the labor force of a country may be the fraction of the labor force that comprises technical workers. A rough measure of the level of disembodied technology of a country may be the number of patents in force. Such measures are more likely to be impressionistic than definitive. Limited data is available on these variables and is presented by continent in table 2-9. Africa has the lowest level of technology by either measure. Asia, Central and North America, and South America have a comparable fraction of technical workers (measured as an unweighted average), but Asia (Japan) and Central and North America (United States) have more patents in force.

Technological change is dynamic. Neither variable captures the dynamic aspect of technology. Nevertheless, these variables are positively correlated with per capita real domestic product and the growth rate in per capita real domestic product over the period 1950–1985. The simple correlation between per capita GDP and the fraction of technical workers in the labor force is .73. The correlation between the logarithm of per capita GDP and the logarithm of the number of patents in force is .62. The simple correlation between the fraction of technical workers and the average growth rate is .11, which is not statistically significant. The correlation between the growth rate and the logarithm of the number of patents is .36.

41

TABLE 2-9

Measures of the Level of Technology by Continent, 1980

Statistic	(1)	(2)	(3)	(4)	(5)	(6)	(7)
Unweighted values							
Technical workers							
as % of labor force							
Mean	3.3	6.5	11.0	6.6	6.4	9.1	13.1
σ	2.1	4.9	5.4	4.2	1.5	5.7	5.2
Min	1.1	.5	3.7	1.0	4.2	1.9	7.6
Max	9.6	21.5	25.1	14.7	9.5	14.1	20.8
Patents in force							
Mean (000's)	4.0	30.3	70.9	130.3	14.4	27.8	107.4
σ (000's)	9.6	94.3	91.5	331.3	29.2	39.0	225.9
Min	52	9	102	166	7	187	11,195
Max (000's)	39.4	370.3	346.5	1,113.9	80.0	55.3	619.0
Weighted values							
Technical workers	2.2	3.3	10.3	11.7	6.5	3.1	3.5
Patents (000's)	3.3	44.8	137.8	725.8	11.1	4.7	123.9

Legend: (1) = Africa; (2) = Asia; (3) = Europe; (4) = Central and North America; (5) = South America; (6) = Oceania; (7) = centrally planned economies.

COMMERCIAL POLICY AND ECONOMIC GROWTH

In a formal sense, the Solow differential equation can be extended to an open economy by incorporating the trade sector. Economists widely believe that trade openness is growth promoting. There is some empirical evidence that more open economies have higher growth rates than more closed economies. The classical arguments for free trade rest on the static gains in efficiency arising from resource reallocation due to comparative advantage and expansion of market size and the dynamic gains through the spread of technology and the inflow of foreign capital associated with a high volume of trade.[25] Arguments against a policy of free trade are based on the notions of infant industries, factor market distortions (for example, interindustry wage differentials), and unfavorable terms of trade (that is, secularly declining and cyclically unstable).[26] Gottfried Haberler showed that allocative efficiencies arise from trade-induced changes in consumption.[27] Thus, while factor market distortions in less developed countries might neutralize the efficiency gains from trade on the production side, consumption gains are still realized.[28] The terms of trade argument for protectionism has survived without much evidence of support.

Several Asian countries (for example, Taiwan, Korea, and the entrepôt economies of Hong Kong and Singapore) have adopted an export-based development strategy, with rational foreign exchange policies, low domestic inflation, and a more open attitude toward foreign investment. The success of this strategy, which has been associated with extraordinarily high rates of economic growth, has weakened the intellectual arguments of the strategists of import substitution policies.

The measurement of the dynamic effect of commercial policy on economic growth is hampered by a lack of appropriate measures of trade openness. An ideal measure of trade liberalization would be an aggregate weighted index of the divergence between world and domestic prices. An alternative but problematic measure would be an index of weighted average tariff and implicit tariff (quantitative restrictions) rates.[29] Neither measure has been constructed. A measure such as overall imports plus exports divided by GDP is useful, but may be distorted by the effects of customs unions (for example, the European Common Market) and the size of the domestic economy (for example, the large U.S. economy, or the very small economies). Nevertheless, such a measure of trade openness is correlated with economic growth. The simple correlation of imports plus exports divided by GDP in 1980 and the growth rate in real per capita GDP from 1960 to 1980 is .36. The correlation of the growth rate and the change in openness of the economy between 1960 and 1980 is .21. The correlation between trade openness in 1980 and the 1980 RGDP (RGDP80) is .13, which is not significant. The correlation between the change in openness and RGDP80 is .10.

GOVERNMENT EXPENDITURES, 1950–1985

On the whole, over the period 1950–1985, government expenditures (public consumption) were 15 to 20 percent of gross domestic product. The share of resources allocated by the public sector rose during the period. Table 2-10 presents data by continent on the average and weighted average government share and the trend in the share. Africa has the largest public sector (measured by weighted averages, Asia and Africa are about equal in the relative size of the state sector). Moreover, the growth of rel-

TABLE 2-10

Government Expenditure Share and Trend by Continent, 1950–1985

Statistic	(1)	(2)	(3)	(4)	(5)	(6)
Unweighted values						
Government expenditure						
as share of GDP, 1950–85						
Mean	20.47	15.92	15.51	14.45	15.81	19.54
σ	5.67	7.84	4.57	5.08	5.58	9.28
Min	8.94	4.34	7.40	6.74	9.19	11.56
Max	32.18	32.89	24.97	24.96	27.91	34.46
Trend in government						
share of GDP						
Mean	.263	.281	.023	.160	.076	−.008
σ	.321	.585	.166	.257	.407	.313
Min	−.484	−.631	−.287	−.244	−.649	−.509
Max	.975	2.172	.314	.732	.912	.323
Weighted values						
Government share	17.24	17.36	16.02	14.60	13.97	12.31
Trend in share	.314	.079	−.026	−.065	−.196	.110

Legend: (1) = Africa; (2) = Asia; (3) = Europe; (4) = Central and North America; (5) = South America; (6) = Oceania.

ative government expenditure (weighted average) is the highest among the less developed continents. Central and North and South America have the smallest public sectors (weighted average) and the growth rate in relative government expenditures is declining.

Do the level of government expenditures out of GDP and the growth of public expenditures contribute to or retard economic growth? Barro has developed a model that theorizes that the level of government expenditures up to a large level (for example, 25 percent of GDP) contributes positively to economic growth and there is an optimal size of the public sector.[30] But most of the empirical evidence shows a negative effect of size of the public sector on economic growth. The simple correlation between the average real growth rate over 1960–1980 and government expenditures as a fraction of GDP in 1980 was −.34. The simple correlation with RGDP80 was −.53. Roger Kormendi and Philip Meguire, Grier and Gordon Tullock, and D. Landau also have found a negative relationship between relative government spending and economic growth.[31]

INFLATION AND GROWTH

Monetary policy can have effects on real economic growth. Inflation introduces relative price distortions into the economy that shift resources from directly productive activities into rent-seeking activities. This reduces the value (information content) of prices as an accurate guide for resource allocation. Hence, the efficiency of the market economy declines and economic growth is reduced.

For regimes with low inflation, there is no observable empirical relationship between the rate of inflation and real economic growth. At some rate of inflation, relative prices become distorted to a sufficient degree that resource allocation based on the information content of prices no longer is efficient. At this inflation rate, there is a negative relationship between the rate of price change and the real growth rate. The critical rate of inflation necessary to distort relative prices sufficiently to induce a decline in real growth largely is an empirical question. A 30 percent annual change in prices is chosen as the critical rate, an arbitrary but reasonable choice.

There are not many economies in the world that have had periods of inflation at 30 percent or higher per annum. The sample over the 1951–1987 period contains eleven countries: three from Africa, seven from Latin America, and Israel. During these countries' bouts with high inflation, the mean annual rate of inflation ranged from 58.6 percent (Ghana) to 902.4 percent (Bolivia). The mean inflation rate during the high inflation periods for these eleven countries appears in table 2-11.

The effect of high rates of inflation on real economic growth is obtained by comparing the mean real rate of growth in per capita GDP during the high inflationary periods with the mean rate during the low inflationary periods. The mean difference in real growth rates is shown in the table. In all cases the real growth rate is lower during periods of high inflation. The reduction in annual real growth is as low as –1.6 percent (Uruguay) and as high as –8.2 percent (Zaire). However, the difference in the mean growth rates for Uruguay (also, Chile) is not significant. Thus the lower bound in the sample is –4.3 percent (Argentina). Therefore, high inflation has an important and large effect on the real standard of living of citizens in regimes that practice monetary excess to acquire public command over resources in the economy.

TABLE 2-11

Effect of High Inflation Rates on Real per Capita Growth Rates, 1951–1987

Country	Period	High Inflation Periods	Mean Inflation	Growth Diff.	t-Value
Ghana	1956–87	1975–85, 1987	58.6	− 5.34	2.82
Sierra Leone	1961–87	1979, 1981–87	87.0	− 6.60	3.22
Zaire	1964–87	1964, 1967–68, 1974–87	52.2	− 8.22	3.93
Argentina	1960–87	1972–73, 1975–87	232.5	− 4.29	2.32
Bolivia	1951–87	1953–59, 1973–74, 1980–86	902.4	− 6.60	5.14
Brazil	1956–87	1962–65, 1976–87	186.0	− 5.72	2.32
Chile	1964–87	1964, 1972–78	175.8	− 3.82	1.08[a]
Mexico	1951–87	1982–87	85.5	− 6.89	5.84
Peru	1951–85	1975–85	78.0	− 4.56	3.36
Uruguay	1951–85	1964–68, 1972–85	65.4	− 1.59	1.01[a]
Israel	1951–87	1952–53, 1974–86	116.5	− 5.72	2.32

Sources: Inflation rates are from *International Financial Statistics* and *World Tables 1989*. The real per capita growth rates are from Robert Summers and Alan Heston, "A New Set of International Comparisons . . . ," *Review of Income and Wealth* 34 (March 1988): 1–25, updated from *World Tables 1989*.

[a] Not significant at the conventional level.

APPENDIX 2-1: EDUCATION AND LITERACY
BY COUNTRY, 1980

Country	(1)	(2)	(3)	(4)	(5)	(6)	(7)
Australia	100	100	98	6.0	110	86	21.5
Finland	100	100	100	5.7	83	90	6.1
Luxembourg	100	100	99	6.7	98	69	NA
Netherlands	100	100	99	8.1	101	94	7.2
USSR	100	100	99	7.2	106	105	7.2
Switzerland	100	100	100	5.0	82	74	2.9
Austria	99	99	98	5.6	98	74	2.6
Czechoslovakia	99	NA	NA	4.9	91	44	4.1
Denmark	99	99	100	6.3	98	87	NA
East Germany	99	NA	99	5.8	96	88	8.5
Iceland	99	NA	100	4.1	99	83	3.7
Japan	99	98	98	5.8	100	91	14.4
New Zealand	99	99	99	5.6	105	81	2.1
Norway	99	99	100	8.1	100	94	8.5
Poland	99	98	98	NA	100	81	5.7
Sweden	99	99	100	9.1	97	86	NA
United Kingdom	99	99	99	5.7	104	82	11.0
United States	99	99	99	6.4	99	95	31.1
West Germany	99	99	99	4.7	96	90	4.3
Barbados	98	98	95	8.0	117	85	1.2
Canada	98	98	99	7.7	100	90	3.9
Hungary	98	98	98	4.0	97	40	5.1
Ireland	98	98	96	6.8	102	93	4.6
Western Samoa	98	98	NA	8.4	NA	NA	NA
Belgium	97	97	99	6.1	101	89	7.2
France	97	97	99	3.5	112	85	NA
Bulgaria	96	91	85	5.3	97	86	5.2
Italy	95	94	92	4.6	102	73	2.6
Trinidad and Tobago	95	92	80	4.2	94	56	1.2
Argentina	94	93	91	3.4	116	56	4.0
Romania	94	89	99	3.2	101	75	4.6
South Korea	94	88	71	3.4	107	85	6.9
Spain	94	90	87	2.1	109	87	3.7
Greece	93	85	82	2.3	103	81	2.5
Israel	93	88	90	8.3	96	71	2.1
Netherlands Antilles	93	93	NA	1.1	NA	NA	4.4

APPENDIX 2-1, *cont.*

Country	(1)	(2)	(3)	(4)	(5)	(6)	(7)
Uruguay	93	93	90	2.1	105	60	6.3
Yugoslavia	92	84	77	5.4	99	83	3.9
Guyana	91	87	86	9.8	115	59	1.0
Bahamas	90	90	90	9.8	NA	NA	NA
Hong Kong	90	77	71	2.9	109	62	3.8
North Korea	90	NA	NA	NA	116	NA	NA
Chile	89	88	84	3.8	117	55	3.8
Puerto Rico	89	88	81	8.2	82	92	12.1
Cyprus	88	76	76	3.4	64	58	1.4
Thailand	87	79	70	3.2	96	29	1.1
Sri Lanka	86	77	75	2.2	100	51	2.3
Macao	85	80	NA	NA	NA	NA	1.4
Paraguay	85	81	68	1.3	102	26	2.0
Philippines	84	83	72	2.0	110	63	11.9
Suriname	84	84	84	5.5	103	49	NA
Malta	83	NA	63	3.2	112	69	2.4
Peru	83	73	61	1.9	112	56	4.5
Singapore	83	69	60	2.9	107	58	2.0
Colombia	82	81	65	1.9	128	46	3.3
Albania	80	72	NA	NA	NA	63	NA
Burma	80	60	60	1.6	84	20	NA
Mongolia	80	NA	NA	NA	105	89	3.1
Venezuela	80	77	80	5.0	104	32	2.6
Jamaica	79	82	85	7.1	99	57	.5
Panama	79	79	73	5.0	113	65	4.2
Ecuador	78	74	67	3.6	107	40	3.2
Lebanon	78	68	NA	2.5	119	58	3.1
Mexico	78	74	65	4.5	120	37	2.6
Portugal	78	72	62	3.8	118	55	1.0
Grenada	77	77	NA	7.0	NA	NA	.5
Turkey	77	60	46	3.6	101	37	1.8
Cuba	76	78	75	7.1	112	71	NA
Bolivia	75	63	32	3.5	84	36	5.0
Brunei	75	63	NA	2.1	NA	NA	3.1
Mauritius	72	61	60	6.0	102	50	1.2
Fiji	71	64	NA	4.9	109	62	3.3
Indonesia	70	58	43	2.0	112	28	3.5
Brazil	69	66	61	3.6	93	32	4.3
Dominican Republic	69	68	65	2.1	106	32	1.9
Kuwait	68	58	47	2.9	96	75	12.5

APPENDIX 2-1, *cont.*

Country	(1)	(2)	(3)	(4)	(5)	(6)	(7)
Comoro Islands	66	59	58	NA	103	25	NA
Kampuchea	62	36	41	NA	78	43	NA
Zambia	61	48	41	4.6	95	17	.6
Réunion	60	63	NA	NA	NA	84	NA
Solomon Islands	60	NA	NA	4.1	NA	NA	1.6
Syria	60	40	35	4.9	100	46	1.3
Honduras	59	57	45	3.5	89	21	1.0
Malaysia	59	54	43	5.8	92	53	NA
Dominica	58	60	NA	NA	NA	NA	.5
Nicaragua	58	58	50	4.3	100	43	NA
Egypt	57	43	30	4.1	76	52	3.4
South Africa	57	57	35	4.3	105	76	3.7
Seychelles	56	58	NA	5.9	NA	NA	2.6
Guatemala	54	46	38	1.9	69	16	1.2
St. Lucia	51	52	NA	6.7	NA	NA	NA
Tunisia	51	38	30	4.9	103	27	1.2
El Salvador	50	NA	49	3.2	74	23	1.9
Jordan	50	33	35	6.2	102	74	.8
Bahraim	49	39	NA	4.3	102	54	3.8
Zaire	49	32	35	6.3	90	23	NA
Iran	48	37	23	5.7	101	44	.9
Southern Yemen	48	28	28	4.3	72	28	NA
Zimbabwe	48	40	20	4.3	115	13	.6
India	47	33	28	3.2	76	28	1.1
Hamibia	45	38	NA	NA	NA	NA	2.1
Lesotho	44	56	35	NA	104	17	.1
Uganda	44	35	25	1.8	50	05	.1
Ghana	43	31	23	2.9	69	36	.4
Tanzania	43	29	18	5.7	104	04	NA
Algeria	42	28	15	8.1	95	33	.3
Madagascar	41	34	35	3.7	NA	38	NA
Papua New Guinea	39	32	NA	4.7	62	12	NA
Equatorial Guinea	38	NA	NA	NA	78	11	NA
Libya	38	21	30	3.9	NA	64	1.0
Iraq	36	25	20	3.2	116	57	.9
Malawi	34	23	08	2.2	59	4	.2
Morocco	34	22	13	6.0	82	24	NA
Bangladesh	33	21	NA	1.5	62	15	.9
Nepal	33	19	08	1.8	91	21	.1
Cameroon	31	19	10	3.1	104	18	.3

APPENDIX 2-1, *cont.*

Country	(1)	(2)	(3)	(4)	(5)	(6)	(7)
Swaziland	31	30	29	7.2	106	40	NA
Botswana	30	33	20	7.7	102	22	.6
Congo	30	17	23	9.4	NA	NA	NA
Kenya	30	20	23	6.1	108	18	NA
Laos	30	29	15	NA	96	17	NA
Haiti	29	24	10	1.5	64	12	.3
Togo	27	17	8	6.3	116	33	.1
United Arab Emirates	27	18	NA	1.5	116	52	4.3
China	25	NA	50	NA	121	43	NA
Nigeria	25	16	33	3.3	98	24	NA
Sudan	25	15	13	4.7	51	16	NA
Pakistan	24	15	NA	2.0	57	15	3.4
Rwanda	24	17	8	2.6	70	2	NA
Gabon	22	14	8	3.7	NA	NA	NA
Burundi	21	14	NA	2.9	28	3	NA
Afghanistan	19	12	8	1.7	30	10	3.2
Mauritania	17	NA	3	5.3	33	10	NA
Mozambique	15	12	2	NA	93	6	NA
Guinea	14	9	10	4.3	33	16	NA
Liberia	14	9	10	5.6	66	20	1.0
Central African Republic	13	8	15	4.3	70	11	NA
Benin	12	8	5	4.7	NA	16	NA
Chad	12	7	5	2.3	35	3	NA
Oman	10	NA	NA	2.3	62	14	NA
Senegal	10	6	8	4.0	44	10	.1
Gambia	9	6	10	6.7	48	13	.2
Ethiopia	8	6	5	2.3	43	11	NA
Ivory Coast	8	5	20	8.6	76	17	NA
Guinea-Bissau	7	5	5	4.5	95	10	NA
Sao Tomé/Principe	6	NA	NA	NA	NA	NA	NA
Djibouti	5	NA	NA	5.2	NA	NA	NA
Qatar	5	NA	NA	4.1	110	59	NA
Yemen Arab Republic	5	3	NA	1.2	47	5	NA
Angola	4	3	NA	4.7	62	9	NA
Mali	4	3	5	4.6	27	9	.2
Somali	3	2	5	1.8	41	6	NA
Niger	2	2	3	4.3	23	6	NA
Upper Volta	2	2	8	3.5	19	3	NA

Legend: (1) = male literacy rate, 1981; (2) = total literacy rate, 1980–81; (3) = total literacy rate, 1960; (4) = education expenditures/GNP, 1980; (5) = enrollment, primary school; (6) = ratios 1979–80, secondary school; (7) = percentage of age 25 + population with post–secondary schooling.

Sources and notes: (1) George T. Kurian, *The New Book of World Rankings* (New York: Facts on File Publishers, 1984), 357–58, table 28. (2) Simple average of male and female literacy rates: ibid., 357–59, tables 280–81. (3) Charles L. Taylor and David A. Jodice, *World Handbook of Political and Social Indicators*, Vol. 1 (New Haven, Conn.: Yale University Press, 1983), 169–71. (4) Kurian, *New Book*, 377–78, table 295. (5) Ibid., 361–62, table 283. Enrollment ratio may exceed 100 percent if the actual age distribution of pupils spills over the official school age, if there is a significant presence of alien school-going children, or if there is abnormal grade repetition. (6) Ibid., 367–68, table 288. (7) Ibid., 368–69, table 289.

CHAPTER 2

APPENDIX 2-2: POPULATION GROWTH

BY COUNTRY, 1950–1985

Country	Average Pop. Growth Rate	Pop. Growth Rate, 1985	Trend in Growth Rate, 1950–1985
Algeria	2.89	3.22	.054
Angola	2.35	2.44	.025
Benin	2.73	3.14	.024
Botswana	3.58	3.47	.081
Burkina Faso	1.87	1.57	− .024
Burundi	1.92	2.71	.068
Cameroon	2.63	3.21	.073
Central African Republic	1.93	2.46	.048
Chad	1.99	2.45	.028
Congo	2.76	3.19	.043
Egypt	2.48	2.78	.010[a]
Ethiopia	2.79	3.01	− .016[a]
Gabon	1.66	4.57	.140
Gambia	2.89	3.53	.079
Ghana	3.05	3.26	− .025[a]
Guinea	2.61	2.46	− .136[a]
Ivory Coast	4.39	3.81	.016[a]
Kenya	3.37	4.13	.068
Lesotho	2.27	2.62	.032
Liberia	3.03	3.42	.042
Madagascar	2.59	3.22	.033
Malawi	2.89	3.11	.022
Mali	2.53	2.32	.001[a]
Mauritania	2.21	2.05	− .009
Mauritius	2.14	.89	− .069
Morocco	2.58	2.50	− .005
Mozambique	3.12	2.86	.075
Nigeria	2.78	3.00	− .031[a]
Niger	3.25	3.30	.029
Rwanda	3.19	3.23	.017
Senegal	2.55	2.85	.028
Sierra Leone	1.57	2.21	.035
Somalia	3.18	2.43	− .049
South Africa	2.46	2.54	− .005[a]

APPENDIX 2-2, *cont.*

Country	Average Pop. Growth Rate	Pop. Growth Rate, 1985	Trend in Growth Rate, 1950–1985
Sudan	2.56	2.75	.050
Swaziland	3.28	3.70	.019
Tanzania	3.24	3.47	.022
Togo	2.82	3.34	.007[a]
Tunisia	2.14	2.33	.030
Uganda	3.04	3.04	− .001[a]
Zaire	2.49	2.99	.032
Zambia	2.92	3.49	.042
Zimbabwe	3.55	3.69	− .031
Afghanistan	2.40	2.65	.025
Bahrain	4.38	3.72	− .112
Bangladesh	2.71	2.64	− .031[a]
Burma	2.01	1.97	.007[a]
Hong Kong	2.32	1.10	− .050[a]
India	2.11	2.17	.019
Iran	3.00	4.05	.048
Iraq	3.29	4.08	.031
Israel	3.54	.93	− .136
Japan	1.06	.61	− .014
Jordan	2.98	3.68	− .002[a]
Korea	2.12	1.18	− .045
Kuwait	7.44	4.55	− .276
Malaysia	2.68	2.50	− .025
Nepal	2.28	2.40	.036
Oman	4.06	4.14	.152
Pakistan	2.64	3.10	.038
Philippines	2.80	2.53	− .010[a]
Saudi Arabia	4.18	4.05	.058
Singapore	1.78	1.15	− .078
Sri Lanka	2.09	1.48	− .041
Syria	3.34	3.70	.016
Taiwan	2.74	1.29	− .078
Thailand	2.60	2.05	− .016
United Arab Republic	13.19	5.97	− 1.351
Yemen	2.83	2.47	− .040
Austria	.25	.04	− .007[a]
Belgium	.38	.04	− .020
Cyprus	.85	1.22	− .023

APPENDIX 2-2, *cont.*

Country	Average Pop. Growth Rate	Pop. Growth Rate, 1985	Trend in Growth Rate, 1950–1985
Denmark	.52	.04	− .024
Finland	.58	.53	− .022
France	.80	.41	− .019
Germany	.57	− .27	− .047
Greece	.78	.39	− .005[a]
Iceland	1.50	.84	− .042
Ireland	.52	.48	.062
Italy	.57	.25	− .014
Luxembourg	.61	.00	− .016
Malta	.43	− .28	.017[a]
Netherlands	1.03	.46	− .028
Norway	.69	.31	− .022
Portugal	.57	.64	.012[a]
Spain	.94	.49	− .003[a]
Sweden	.50	.16	− .019
Switzerland	.92	.25	− .051
Turkey	2.54	2.49	− .018
United Kingdom	.32	.10	− .014
Barbados	.38	.40	.001[a]
Canada	1.77	.91	− .061
Costa Rica	3.13	2.61	− .053
Dominican Republic	2.82	2.41	− .028
El Salvador	2.83	1.06	− .032
Guatemala	3.01	2.89	− .002[a]
Haiti	1.67	1.82	.012
Honduras	3.31	3.57	.006[a]
Jamaica	1.45	1.42	.006[a]
Mexico	3.13	2.58	− .017[a]
Nicaragua	3.06	3.49	.044
Panama	2.63	2.15	− .027
Trinidad and Tobago	1.76	1.65	− .079
United States	1.30	.96	− .029
Argentina	1.59	1.45	.002[a]
Bolivia	2.42	2.77	.020
Brazil	2.66	2.25	− .041
Chile	1.93	1.65	− .031
Colombia	2.60	1.88	− .050
Ecuador	2.81	2.90	− .010

APPENDIX 2-2, *cont.*

Country	Average Pop. Growth Rate	Pop. Growth Rate, 1985	Trend in Growth Rate, 1950–1985
Guyana	2.27	.61	− .125
Paraguay	2.69	3.24	.010[a]
Peru	2.46	2.30	.007[a]
Suriname	1.24	2.61	− .089[a]
Uruguay	.91	.74	− .035
Venezuela	3.66	2.75	− .029
Australia	1.88	1.34	− .036
Fiji	2.30	1.46	− .064
Indonesia	2.20	2.07	.004[a]
New Zealand	1.54	.65	− .059
Papua New Guinea	2.28	2.60	.011[a]
Bulgaria	.63	.46	− .017
China	1.96	.94	− .025[a]
Czechoslovakia	.65	.30	− .199
East Germany	− .08	.04	− .003[a]
Hungary	.37	− .41	− .024
Poland	1.16	.70	− .033
Romania	.84	.29	− .016[a]
USSR	1.26	.96	− .033
Yugoslavia	.92	.42	− .016

[a] Trend is not statistically significant at conventional levels.

The Constitutional Setting
and the Gains from
Exchange

As an alternative to anarchy, mankind lives under politicolegal regimes of rules and order. The scope and inclusiveness of individual rights and behavior sanctioned under these politicolegal regimes, coupled with the laws of production and distribution, determine the level and distribution of personal well-being. In this chapter, I build on the work of James Buchanan and Gordon Tullock[1] and James Buchanan[2] to derive a theory of the range of the constitutional setting or the institutional framework based on the assumption of wealth maximization. The discussion that follows is highly abbreviated and assumes that the reader has some familiarity with these works. In the following chapter, an endogenous theory of the evolution of the constitutional setting and its effect on economic growth is developed.

It is assumed that all humans exclusively are self-interested.[3] They seek to maximize self-advantage within the "rules of the game" of sanctioned behavior and of rights that govern the production of income in the private sector. The scope of sanctioned behavior and of rights is contained in the constitutional setting or the institutional framework of society. The constitutional setting is the economic, legal, and political environment in which production, exchange, and human intercourse occur. The rules of the game, under which citizens live and work, give rise to the production of income in the private sector and determine who gets to compete for income streams and who does not. The public sector's domain of influence over private activity, the public sector constitution, is treated fully in the following chapter and is treated only incidentally here.

Any institutional framework embodies a set of rules and institutions that sanction behavior that may be either efficient or inefficient. Efficient rules or institutions are those that define a set of sanctioned activities that when undertaken enhance private wealth or utility.[4] Pareto-efficient rules have the attribute that all members of society benefit from their existence.[5] Rules or institutions in which the total gains to society exceed the total losses are termed Hicks-Kaldor efficient. Since some gain at others' expense, such rules are redistributive. In principle, absent costs of redistributing income, those gaining from the rule can compensate those losing, converting a Hicks-Kaldor-efficient rule into a Pareto-efficient rule.[6] Finally, there are rules and institutions in which the total gains to society are less than the total losses. These rules are called Hicks-Kaldor-inefficient and sanction behavior that is termed rent-seeking. Rent-seeking is a game (zero-sum at best) about redistributing a fixed economic pie.[7] No scheme of compensation can convert a Hicks-Kaldor-inefficient rule into a Pareto-efficient rule.[8]

In addition to structuring the rules of the game that define the scope of opportunities for individuals to compete for income streams, the constitutional setting establishes a mechanism for the provision of public goods (including national defense) and a mechanism for the redistribution of income.[9] Variously structured, these functions affect economic efficiency (wealth creation and, hence, economic growth) and equity (income distribution). Within a constitutional setting the choice between rules that enhance efficiency and rules that promote rent-seeking (income distribution) hinges on decisions made about the division of rights between the ruled and the ruler and on the choice of the type of legal system. Conventionally, the division of power (rights) between ruler and the ruled rests on the constitutional contract (document) and on the standing of the citizen relative to the government before the law. In general, law that arises from the custom of exchange and human intercourse (common law) fosters private wealth maximization and minimizes rent-seeking (income redistribution). The common law is a set of general rules of order, a "commons," and as such is very costly to privatize for the purpose of special interest, rent-seeking. Civil law (statutes and administrative rules) is crafted in a political market. In a dictatorship, civil law may reflect the interests of the ruling class. In representative government, civil law may reflect the interests of a sovereign majority. Legislators seek or retain office by rewarding the coalitions that elect them. Hence law by legislation likely is more redistributive than private law. Unlike judge-made law, where precedent constrains legal innovation, one legislature cannot bind another. Hence a legal framework resting on statutes is more uncertain. Legal uncertainty places rights and assets at risk, making economic progress more uncertain.

A THEORY OF CONSTITUTIONAL CONTRACT

The Scope and Inclusiveness of Rights:
Implications for Efficiency and Income Distribution

Consider the personal welfare of two persons in polar extremes of social organization: anarchy and a constitution of equal and mutually respected rights for all. In figure 3-1, A is the utility levels of person 1 (U_1) and person 2 (U_2) in the natural distribution—the Hobbesian jungle of every man against every man. There is absolute freedom in the jungle—each man is the judge of his own conduct. What a person can consume is what he can produce and keep for his own and what he can steal from another. The utility possibility frontier of enjoyment of goods, X_i, is constrained by the need to devote resources to predation and defense. These resources are necessary in a regime without mutually agreed-upon and respected property rights. In this state there is no production beyond immediate consumption, since property is not secure. The income distribution in a regime of anarchy strictly is a function of the relative natural distribution of physical strength, stealth, and guile of the conflicting parties.

The cooperative constitutional contract in Buchanan (point F in the figure) is the Pareto-frontier reached through an agreement on equal and mutually respected freedoms. The utility of both parties rises because the resources that were devoted to predation and defense (rent-seeking activities) are withdrawn and are channeled into productive activity. The constitutional contract of equal rights then permits efficiency gains from exchange (specialization, economies of scale, etc.) in the postconstitutional stage of the many-goods model (point G in the figure). The income distribution in this postconstitutional stage of equal rights to compete for income streams is strictly determined by unequal personal endowments (talent, ambition, motivation, skill, luck, etc.) that result in unequal economic outcomes.

Between the regimes of anarchy and equal rights there are many "constitutional contracts" or institutional frameworks in which rights are distributed asymmetrically among the parties. Nevertheless, agreement among unequals (in rights) is welfare superior to the anarchistic equilibrium at A. In the extreme, a master-slave society may be preferred to the anarchy of the natural state. The weaker party may obtain the right to a larger consumption stream in return for his labor under the command of the stronger party. If the size of the economic pie expands so that both parties have higher consumption streams, a master-slave rights regime

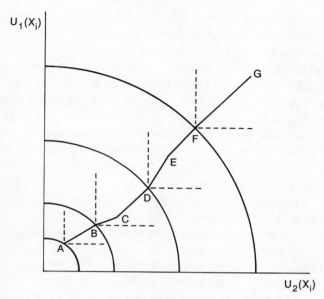

Figure 3-1. Personal Welfare of Two Individuals,
One Living in Anarchy, the Other in a Strong
Constitutional Setting

would be preferred to anarchy. Serfdom is preferred to slavery, if the consumption stream of the serf exceeds that of the slave and that of the feudal lord exceeds that of the slave master. The expanded rights of the serf and the diminished rights of the feudal lord in a feudal society yield efficiency gains compared to a master-slave regime. Free labor and a ruling elite may be preferred to a feudal system for similar reasons. In general, each of the institutional frameworks that we observe in the world can be arrayed hierarchically from the most inequitable distribution of rights or opportunities to compete for income streams to the most equal distribution of rights (that is, B, D, and F in the figure). Each constitutional setting has an income distribution given partially by the rights distribution (opportunities to compete for income streams). Each institutional framework has a level of gains from trade. Each institutional framework has an inherent level of economic efficiency.

A master-slave economy is relatively inefficient, because slaves have an incentive to shirk and masters must devote substantial resources to monitoring slave labor. Serfs shirk less than slaves do, because they have the right to a higher share of the output, but shirking remains and monitoring costs are high in a feudal society. The feudal era in England defined rights and responsibilities linked hierarchically to land tenure. Serfs were confined to the land of their birth and had work requirements meticulously defined and codified.[10] These work laws were designed to prevent a reduction in output due the feudal lord, who in return was obligated to provide protection and other services. In a society of free labor and a ruling elite economic efficiency is higher, because incentives are increased by expanded rights and shirking and monitoring costs are reduced. Economic efficiency is at a maximum in a society of equal rights, since the gains from exchange can be fully exploited only when all have equal opportunities to compete for income streams.

Figure 3-2 describes the paths of economic efficiency and equity or the distribution of rights to compete for income streams of the hierarchy of institutional frameworks. The agreement at B is characterized by wide disparity of rights among the groups. Because rights are unequally distributed, incomes are unequally distributed. Gains from exchange are limited. As a result, economic efficiency under this institutional framework is low. Constitutional settings with less inequality of rights (for example, D) are associated with more equality of opportunity to compete for income streams and wider gains from trade in the postconstitutional stage. Hence, greater income equality and economic efficiency are present in regime D than in regime B. In the constitutional setting of equal liberty for all (F in the figure), inequality of the rights to compete for income streams is zero and economic efficiency is at a maximum (a value of the index equal to one).

As the level of economic efficiency of the institutional frameworks is correlated with the scope and inclusiveness of individual rights, so are the growth paths of per capita income: through the accumulation of capital, physical and human, inventiveness, and economies of specialization and scale associated with a widening of the market and the way that certainties or uncertainties and incentives or disincentives correlated with the rights structure affect these variables. In figure 3-3, the growth paths of economies are arrayed hierarchically according to the scope and degree of inclusiveness of individual rights. For example, the level of per capita income associated with a capital-labor ratio of k_1 is higher in an institutional framework of equal rights for all, $\theta(F)$, than in a setting with limited private rights and/or a very asymmetrical distribution of rights among the members of society, as in $\theta(C)$. The growth rate with respect to an increment in the capital-labor ratio, $\Delta y/\Delta k$, is higher in institutional framework $\theta(F)$ than in institutional frameworks $\theta(B)$ through $\theta(E)$. The

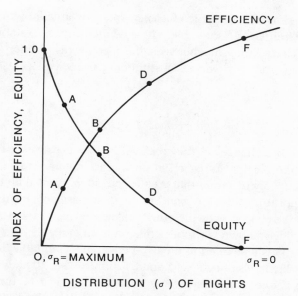

Figure 3-2. Paths of Efficiency and Equity

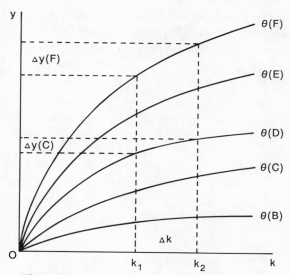

Figure 3-3. Growth Paths of Various Economics

relationship between economic efficiency and economic growth and the institutional framework is testable. These relationships are established in chapter 7. The relationship between the income distribution and the distribution of rights in various institutional frameworks is shown in chapter 8.

Enforcement of Rights

The gains from exchange are fully realized in a cooperative agreement if and only if the parties do not cheat on the agreement. It is a familiar aspect of the theory of games that greater individual gains than the cooperative equilibrium gains (the "core" of the game) are possible if one person violates the contract but the other person adheres to the agreement. This is the widely known "prisoner's dilemma" in game theory. The prisoner's dilemma is illustrated in the two-person model in table 3-1. In the table, the utility levels of persons 1 and 2 arbitrarily are 10 and 5, respectively, when neither party respects the rights of the other. Mutual respect of rights, the cooperative equilibrium, yields utility levels of 20 and 10, respectively. Both parties are better off by moving from a state of noncooperation to a state of cooperation, mutual respect of rights. However, there are gains to unilateral violations of the agreement providing the other party does not retaliate. If person 1 cheats (cell III), but person 2 remains passive, the utility level of person 1 is the highest possible for him

TABLE 3-1
Prisoner's Dilemma: Observe or Violate Rights Agreement

		Person 2	
		Observe Rights	Violate Rights
Person 1	Observe Rights	I $U_1(20)$, $U_2(10)$	II $U_1(7)$, $U_2(12)$
	Violate Rights	III $U_1(25)$, $U_2(3)$	IV $U_1(10)$, $U_2(5)$

and the utility level of person 2 declines to the lowest of all possible states. If person 2 cheats (cell II), but person 1 remains passive, the utility level of person 2 is the greatest he can achieve and is the lowest for person 1. Since either party is better off if one cheats and the other does not, there is a tendency for the game to deteriorate to the anarchistic equilibrium. This tendency is especially true, if the game is transformed from a two-person to a n-person game. The incentives to cheat on the agreement increase, since the actions of a few cheaters are less discernible to the mass of others who abide by the agreement. If cheating is a widespread phenomenon, the n-person game will deteriorate to the anarchistic equilibrium.

The cooperative core of the game can be maintained, if an external enforcing agent is introduced to prevent unilateral violations of the agreement. This is a function that legitimizes the existence of the state. It is in the interest of all individuals who have gained by the cooperative agreement to devote resources to a neutral agent (a referee) that enforces the agreement (protects rights) and punishes violators of others' rights. This role is performed by law backed by the coercive power of government. However, the coercive power is narrowly construed and confined to dispute resolution and enforcement of the agreement.

The Provision of Public Goods

Beyond the mutual gains from private exchange, all parties to the cooperative agreement can be made better off if public goods are produced. This is illustrated as point H in figure 3-4, northeast of point G. Pure public goods have the characteristic of consumption jointness and nonexclusion.[11] In the modern theory of public goods it is demonstrated that, because of their properties, private markets will fail to produce the appropriate amounts.[12] The transaction costs of securing a private agreement on the production of a pure public good are high, because individuals have an incentive not to reveal their preferences and because individuals can consume the collective good without paying their share of the cost (the "free rider" problem). Thus while all parties gain from the provision of public goods, it is more beneficial to each if someone else pays for them. Hence, the solution to the problem is to pay for public goods out of general revenue. Justice in the provision of public goods requires that they serve the general interest. For the interest to be "general," all individuals must receive positive utility (net benefits) from the provision of public goods. This result is ensured only if the public finance of public goods is constrained by a Wicksellian unanimity (approximate) voting rule.

63

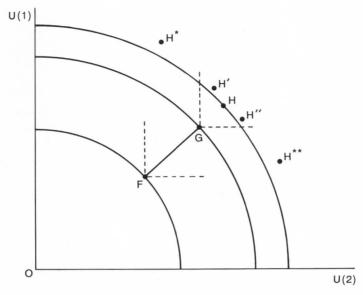

Figure 3-4. Cooperative Agreement

Where H lies relative to G or, for that matter, F in the figure depends upon the decision rule governing the fiscal state and on the type of tax employed to finance the provision of the public good or on an agreement of constitutional constraint on the fiscal enterprise. If decisions on the quanity and cost sharing of the public good are made under a rule of unaminity and if free riders can be excluded,[13] then the Pareto-efficient level of the public good will be provided. Each person will receive and pay for a level of provision of the public good such that for each the marginal benefits arising from its provision will exactly equal the marginal cost (taxes) necessary to provide it. This is point H in figure 3-4. Under a voting rule of less than unaminity (simple majority is ubiquitous in representative democracies) but a constitutional constraint on the fiscal state that requires net benefits to all from the provision of the public good, the utility of person 1 and person 2 will lie somewhere on the line segment $H'H''$ through H in the figure, depending on whose preference for the level of the public good prevails and its method of financing (for example, head tax, proportional taxation, progressive taxation, etc.). Both parties are "better off" through the provision of the public good (the solution remains in the northeast quadrant), but since neither can make a full marginal adjustment with respect to its quantity and tax price, the amount provided is Hicks-Kaldor efficient but not Pareto efficient. Under a voting rule of less than unaminity and absent constitutional constraint on the fiscal state, whoever gets to choose (that is, the dictator, the ruling elite, the winning coalition) the level of provision of the public good and the method of financing it has the opportunity to concentrate the benefits to themselves and impose the costs on others. Under such an arrangement, H may lie outside the northeast boundary; that is, to the northwest, H^*, or the southeast, H^{**}, of G, depending upon who rules. Note that under such an arrangement one of the parties loses some of the gains from trade arising from the constitutional contract that governs private exchange. If redistribution through the provision of the public good is severe enough the losing group may be made worse off than if they had never entered the original constitutional contract (that is, movement in the postconstitutional contract with a mechanism for the provision of a public good northwest or southeast of point F in the figure).

Income Redistribution

It may be rational for individuals at the level of constitutional contract to engage in income distribution during the stage of the constitutional contract and to bind themselves to a mechanism of income distribution at the postconstitutional stage. The scope of the constitutional agreement (point F in figure 3-1 containing all Pareto-efficient agreements on mutually respected rights) may be expanded through income redistribution. Some rights are valued by some but not by others. Side payments by those desiring the right to overcome the disutility of those associated with respecting the right may expand the scope of the constitutional contract beyond point F in the figure and increase the gains from exchange beyond point G. These compensated elements in the constitutional contract properly are termed Hicks-Kaldor-efficient agreements.

Second, the mutual respect of rights to compete for income streams does not ensure equal economic outcomes. Uncertainty of economic outcome in the postconstitutional stage may induce individuals at the constitutional contract stage to agree to a mechanism for the redistribution of income. Buchanan and Tullock conceptualize the mechanism as an "income insurance" scheme.[14] Individuals know where they will lie in the income distribution in the postconstitutional stage in terms of the present discounted stream of lifetime income, but wish to intertemporally smooth out the stochastic elements in the income stream (periods of good and bad fortune). In John Rawls's contractarian analysis, individuals at the constitutional stage dwell behind a "veil of ignorance," with no knowledge of their attributes relative to one another and, hence, incapable of knowing their position in the income distribution in the postconstitutional stage.[15] Whether the conceptualization is "income insurance" or a "veil of ignorance," total lifetime utility can be shown to increase if at the constitutional contract stage, individuals bind themselves to some mechanism of income redistribution. However, while at the level of constitutional contract with a unaminity rule, in theory the individuals could agree on a Pareto-optimal (utility-maximizing) level of redistribution; in the postconstitutional stage, an unrestrained majority could impose taxes on the minority and obtain net subsidies that yield a level of income redistribution beyond the Pareto-optimal amount.[16] The voting rule in the postconstitutional stage turns a Pareto-efficient agreement on income redistribution into a Hicks-Kaldor-inefficient (rent-seeking) result.[17]

CONSTITUTIONAL PROTECTION OF RIGHTS, CHOICE
OF THE LEGAL SYSTEM AND RESTRICTIONS
OF THE FISCAL FUNCTION

Constitutional Protection

Part of the institutional framework is the constitutional document; the other part is sanctioned customs and institutions and the legal and economic systems. Almost all modern states have constitutions that define the scope and inclusiveness of the rights of citizens and the structure and powers of government. Some constitutions rest on democratic foundations; others, on theocratic or socialist principles. Many constitutions are modeled after the U.S. Constitution. In some instances, these constitutions are as sacred a bond between citizen and government as in the United States; in other instances, the constitutional protection of rights is worthless.

The protection of private property, freedom of contract, and other individual rights are features of some constitutions and/or legal frameworks. The free market, private property economic system is not an explicit part of the U.S. Constitution, although freedom of contract is a constitutionally protected right (Article I, Section 10). Defenders of the absolute right to private property have pointed to the natural rights philosophy of the Founders as expressed in their speeches and writings (for example, the *Federalist Papers*), the specific constitutional provision that common law remains in force, the ex post facto law clause of Article I, Section 9, of the

U.S. Constitution, and the due process clause of the Fifth Amendment and Fourteenth Amendment to the U.S. Constitution.[18]

Other absolute individual rights reserved to the people are mandated in the first ten amendments to the U.S. Constitution. The Bill of Rights is a constitutional restriction on the arbitrary exercise of power by the government in the name of the public interest, special interests, or whatever other justification the government wishes to use to abridge personal freedom. The amendments are a guarantee that individuals are free to go about their business without government interference. Freedom of person is a natural corollary of freedom of property and freedom of contract. In the Lockean tradition of classical liberals, individual liberties are inseparable from private property and freedom of contract. For example, freedom of the press has little meaning if the citizen is denied the right to own the printing press. Where individual liberties are corollaries of freedom of property and freedom of contract, their effects on allocative efficiency and economic growth are similar. For example, freedom of ideas and the right to speak and publish them clearly is a right that fosters economic efficiency and growth. Justice Holmes in *Abrams v. United States*, 250 U.S. 616, 630 (1919), wrote that ideas are a useful product produced in a highly competitive market. The "marketplace of ideas" sorts out the "truth" of ideas, with good ones having a characteristic of survivability and bad ones falling into the trashbin of history. The judgment of the validity of an idea is best left to the competition of the marketplace. The market values the wisdom of ideas, and resources flow to the applications of ideas with the highest valued use. Government regulation of ideas is irrational and inefficient.[19]

Powers not expressly reserved to the people and their nongovernmental institutions (for example, the family, the church, the press, etc.) or the several states (federalism) that comprise the nation are reserved by the central government. All governments have three functional divisions: executive, legislative, and judicial. The U.S. Constitution institutionalized Montesquieu's (*L'Esprit des lois*, 1748) separation of powers doctrine by constitutionally mandating division of powers and responsibilities. The theory behind the separation of powers doctrine, as with the theory of federalism, is that it disaggregates the powers of the central government and thereby is consistent with the philosophy of limited government. Countries with a federalist structure (that is, the United States, Canada, Switzerland, and Australia) have lower total government expenditures as a share of GNP, a simple measure of the extensiveness of government, than do countries with similar levels of GNP per capita and with centralized government. Article III, Section 2, of the Constitution provides for independent judicial review of the laws of the United States. Judicial review of the constitutionality of Congressional statutes was settled in *Marbury v. Madison*, 5 U.S. (1 Cranch) 137 (1803).

Under the British system, executive power is with the prime minister, whose party is in control of Parliament. The judiciary is independent (Act of Settlement, 1701) but has no power to review statutes passed by Parliament. Parliament is the supreme power. The legal tradition of continental Europe and most of the non-European world is codified or civil law. Law emerges discretely with the act of codification. Usually, it was stipulated that all law before the new code was nullified (for example, the Code Napoleon, 1804). Thus law in France and in other civil law countries, unlike the common law of England, derives its legitimacy not from custom and prior legal tradition, but from the act of codification by the state. Individual rights and law are more uncertain in a regime of civil law, since the law does not evolve slowly and smoothly but in wrenching, discrete jumps. For example, France had twelve constitutions from the monarchical constitution of 1792 to the republican constitution of 1870–1875. In civil law nations with a tradition of rule of law[20] the effect of this recodification of law on individual liberty may be attenuated, but in nations with no such tradition no law or right is sacrosanct to those changing the social order and the structure of rights through the legal code.

The separation of powers doctrine, of course, exists in civil law countries as well, but the independence of the judiciary is not nearly as meaningful. Civil codes are detailed documents designed to minimize judicial interpretation and discretion. The Prussian Landrecht of 1794 contains some sixteen thousand provisions. Yet such codes, no matter how extensive and detailed, are neither complete nor coherent. Judges continuously seek legislative intent. To prevent independent judicial interpretation, the legislature plays some role in judicial review. In France, constitutional questions are settled by the Constitutional Council, a body composed of the former presidents of France, and members chosen by the president of France, the president of the Chamber of Deputies, and the president of the Senate. Thus the constraints on legislative power are weaker in civil law countries. Rights are at the sufferance of a legislature, which responds to the political will of the majority of citizens that elects its members to office.

Choice of the Legal System

All societies live under some system of law, which may be part sanctioned custom and part legislative code. In England and the United States, institutions of rules and order have emerged spontaneously as creatures of human intercourse and not as creations of government: sanctioned custom and private (common) law. An alternative way of organizing human activity is through fiat. In modern government law mainly is by legislative statutes and by administrative rules authorized by statutes and enforced by bureaucratic agencies of the executive branch.

Custom grew spontaneously out of each tribe's circumstances and evolved by trial and error. "Individuals had learned to observe (and enforce) rules of conduct long before such rules could be expressed in words."[21] Some customs are ubiquitous, such as the taboo on incest or cannibalism. Some norms are very widespread across cultures, such as the rule of first come, first served, reciprocity, retribution, codes of honor, and fairness. Other customs are peculiar to a people, such as the Semitic ban on the eating of pork, which has a health (trichinosis) as well as a religious basis.

The body of custom is transmitted to each generation by parents and by other institutions, which spontaneously evolved as human society became more complex. Initially, custom governed such institutions as marriage, religion, the socialization of children into the life of the community, warfare, and all manner of exchange. Custom still governs much of human intercourse. Custom is a way of life and a moral catalog of rights and wrongs and duties and responsibilities. Often custom determines the way men see the world and their place within it. Custom governs family life and one's relations with one's fellowmen. Custom defines attitudes toward authority. A narrow definition of culture is the sum of a society's customs.

In earlier times, custom characterized the class structure and economic organization of society. Class is not a deterministic feature of some modern societies and is a declining feature of others. Mass education has created a variety of paths of upward social mobility. Custom and culture are features of heterogeneous groups in society. The culture of the Mormons, Quakers, or Amish differs from that of Unitarians. Lawyers, doctors, steelworkers, economists, artists, musicians, country club members, street gangs, and so on each have a culture, codes, and language that separate them from other groups in society. Presumably, the rules of order in these subcultures have been devised less for purposes of exclusion than because they enhance the efficiency of communication between members. Rarely are these group customs sanctioned by law. They are as spontaneous and evolutionary as the customs of society were before being institutionalized in law.

In some instances, strict custom and ritual may be a feature of the exchange process. The customs and ritual not only sanction the exchange but enforce the contract. Where there is a divergence between ex ante terms of exchange and ex post realization (the bride or the mule had a hidden defect), custom may dictate resolution. Or a neutral arbitrator (for example, a wise elder of the community) may be selected to settle the dispute. In religious communities many of the rules of order governing exchange and commercial intercourse are based on theocratic principles. Those schooled in the religion serve as judges of the conformity of the act with its tenets.

One view is that law is institutionalized or sanctioned custom enforced by a controlling authority. In the case of common law, this view has considerable merit.[22] A more modern view is that law is a positive instrument of social control. Law is viewed as a tool of social engineering or ideology that will transform a society from a rude customary order to a more idyllic order.[23] Law is obeyed naturally when it takes mankind as it is and when it conforms to the social norms of society as they have evolved out of the common wisdom of mankind's experience. Law is not obeyed or enforceable when it conflicts sharply with custom. It does not seem true that law or a legal order can be a substitute for custom and a natural moral order that has evolved spontaneously. Much of modern life is regulated by law that is not rooted in custom. Such law is obeyed when the coercive power of government credibly is present. Laws based on custom, since they arise from the community itself, are self-enforcing and require much less credible presence of a controlling authority.[24] According to Iredell Jenkins:

> When it is functioning properly, what this institutional structure collectively does is to provide law with a relatively finished human and social product. Law is then able to deal with men who have already been domesticated: imbued with common habits, attitudes, and models of behavior, and trained to live together peacefully and to work together in cooperation. In short, the legal apparatus has at its disposal the two invaluable ingredients of a body of *citizens* who already constitute a *community*. Given these materials, it is but a short and easy step to those

70

familiar figures of jurisprudence: the *legal person*, with his rights and duties clearly spelled out; and the *state*, with its powers and responsibilities sharply defined. Conversely, to the extent that this institutional foundation is weakened, the legal framework is at once subjected to intolerable stresses and strains. Law then has to work with the raw material of human nature, which eludes its grasp and confronts it with tasks for which it is ill-equipped.[25]

All societies have some private law (custom) that sanctions and governs the terms of exchange. England developed the private law of custom into the grand institution of common law. The common law of England, which was adopted by the United States, and prevails more or less in other former English colonies, developed over a span of seven centuries. Increasingly, its function is preempted by statutory law. The common law has evolved over the centuries from judge-made rulings on a case-by-case basis and subject to the authority of a single, binding, and often ancient precedent. Thus common law does not emerge in a political market that is subject to the sovereign will of the majority. Common laws are general rules that emerge from the judicial resolution of disputes between parties of equal standing before the bench, importantly including the circumstance when one of those parties is the state. There is a laissez-faire quality to the common law. Individuals seek the sanctioning of private arrangements and the resolution of disputes before a neutral referee whose interests in the matter are confined to the issues at hand. The system of private law or common law is a path by which law is to be "discovered more than enacted and that nobody is so powerful in his society as to be in a position to identify his own will with the law of the land."[26] In this tradition, judicial intervention is by request of those concerned, is applicable mainly to the parties affected, and is decided in collaboration with the powerful legal constraint of stare decisis.

The early impetus of English law was to force kinsfolk to take money compensation for a slain or injured relative to prevent endless and distressing rounds of retaliation. Compensation depended on rank and the extent of the injury.[27] Common law of property and property transfer arose as lands were granted to individuals by the king and the process of subinterfeudation arose. As feudalism broke down and market exchange became more extensive, a law of contract developed that by tradition set normal terms of exchange. The third body of law developed in common law was torts. In the beginning, common law torts were criminal harms. Later, civil torts were recognized under the common law. Importantly, neither state-granted monopolies (*Case of Monopolies*, 11 Co. Rep. 84b, 77 Eng. Rep. 1260, K.B. [1602]) nor cartel agreements [*Croft v. McConoughy*, 79 Ill. 346 [1875]) were sanctioned under common law. Nor was competition (new entrants into a line of activity) recognized as a tort (*Keeble v. Hickeringill*, 11 East. 574, 103 Eng. Rep. 1127, K.B. [1706]). The effect of these decisions was to prevent the sanctioning of monopoly under common law. Commercial law developed naturally within the common law in the eighteenth century. Lord Chief Justice Mansfield queried experts on the then newly emerging features of commercial exchange, such as negotiable paper instruments, to discover what was the prevailing practice that might be sanctioned in law.[28] In the American West in the nineteenth century, water was made transferable as private property on the basis of the doctrine of the first occupant, a common law tenet. In the beginning, the radio spectrum was privately owned. Rights to a radio frequency were obtained on a first come, first served basis. When interference on an existing frequency occurred from an adjacent frequency, an injunction was sought. A common law case casuistry was just beginning to emerge when the U.S. Congress in the name of the public interest socialized the electromagnetic spectrum.[29]

The common law is efficient because it provides a general framework that sanctions and makes secure (the characteristic of legal certainty) joint gains from voluntary exchange. The certainty of the legal setting makes rights and assets secure. The security of rights induces productive behavior, fostering capital accumulation and economic growth. Because the legal rules are a "commons," it is extraordinarily costly for individuals or specialized coalitions to change the rules. However, there is nothing in the common law that precludes private parties that find it mutually beneficial from contracting around the rule. Freedom of contract within the common law sanctions any terms of exchange that are mutually beneficial (joint wealth maximization), as long as they met standards of consideration, mutual assent, and absence of fraud, incapacity, or duress.

In economic analysis an allocation of resources is said to be privately efficient if and only if all resources are employed in their highest valued use. Property must be owned by someone, be exclusive, and be transferable for it to have value. The legal protection of property creates the incentives to use resources efficiently. Exclusivity of the right of property, transferability, and freedom of contract permit resources to be shifted to their highest valued use. When a complicated exchange process is carried out over time, a divergence between the ex ante terms of exchange and the ex post realizations of the process may occur. The law of contracts minimizes breakdowns in the exchange process by imposing sanctions for breach of contract. These protections and remedies reduce the risk and the transaction costs associated with such exchanges. Further, by supplying a set of normal terms of contracting, contract law reduces the complexity (transaction costs) and the uncertainty of the exchange process.[30]

Richard Posner[31] believes that the system of common law is efficient in the sense that it stipulates general rules that permit resources to flow to their highest valued use and minimizes the costs of transacting:

> The common law method is to allocate responsibilities between people engaged in interacting activities in such a way as to maximize the joint value, or, what amounts to the same thing, minimize the joint cost of the activities. It may do this by defining a property right, by devising a new rule of liability, or by recognizing a contract right, but nothing fundamental turns on which device is used.
>
> Since growth is fostered by efficient resource use, there is a sense, but a rather uncontroversial one, in which the common law, insofar as it has been shaped by a concern with efficiency, may be said to have fostered growth. . . . If the common law played any role in accelerating economic growth, it must have been by making capital investment more profitable.[32]

The alternative to private law is public or statutory law. Traditionally, statutes were royal prerogatives issued for the benefit of the monarch. In dictatorships, statutes frequently are legal instruments that embellish the interests of the dictator and the ruling class. In socialist countries, law is a political instrument of the Communist Party. In some Muslim countries, law is a religious instrument. In governments where sovereignty lies with the majority of the electorate and is exercised through the legislature, statutes are legal instruments arising in a political market subject to the majority will or the will of special interests and coalitions of special interests (legislative vote trading) to extract special benefits at the expense of other interests or the general interest. Moreover, unlike judge-made, common law, which is bound by precedent, one legislature or political party cannot bind another. Thus statutory law is more uncertain—in the West, subject to change as political coalitions shift and representatives adjust legal positions in an effort to get elected and retain office; elsewhere, as power bases representing secular, religious, or class interests change through time.

In the West, a rough and imperfect (partly because of vote trading) measure of the generality or specificity of the interest being served by the statute is the fraction of legislatures voting for the measure. Except for statutes passed in times of high passion (for example, declarations of war), unanimity or approximate unanimity may be a signal of the general nature of the interest served by the statute.[33] Significant opposition to a statute is a signal that some minority interest is harmed (taxed directly or indirectly through restriction of rights or regulation) for some other interest that has succeeded in collecting a majority of the votes.

If the function of private (common) law is to increase economic efficiency by providing a general set of rules by which individuals in voluntary exchange can maximize joint value, the function of statutory law under a voting rule of less than unanimity (approximate) is to provide a political market for the redistribution of income (wealth) by special interests. A voting rule of unanimity or even a supermajority voting rule prevents (or at least drives up the decisionmaking or transaction costs of) statutes that distribute net benefits (benefits minus taxes) to special interests. Only statutes in the general interest will pass. That individual rights are correlated with the type of legal system is a testable hypothesis: This test is the subject of chapter 6.

Restrictions on the Fiscal State

Until the twentieth century, government was a modest enterprise, at least as measured by government expenditures as a share of gross national product. Prior to 1900, government expenditures seldom constituted more than 10 percent of GNP. Now, the size of government is three to five times that size among the Western nations. What is the cause of this secular rise, and what is the consequence for economic efficiency and growth?

Property qualifications were restrictions on suffrage in England and the United States until well into the nineteenth century. Now, universal adult suffrage is the rule in representative government. Where the income (property) distribution is skewed, a rule of one man, one vote and majority rule bring a tendency to citizens and their representatives to vote for schemes that tax the upper half of the distribution and subsidize the lower half. This fear has long been held, even among social democrats, such as John Stuart Mill. Since the legislature is granted authority, bound only by the will of a sovereign majority, to tax and spend, the opportunity for politicians to redistribute income is widespread in representative, constitutional government.

Generally, economists view such large-scale income redistribution as deleterious to economic efficiency and to economic growth for several reasons. Taxing successful outcomes and subsidizing unsuccessful ones on a large scale has incentive effects. At the margin, income redistribution alters the incentives to save and invest in physical and human capital and engage in inventive activity, the engines of economic growth. Second, resources increasingly are allocated in the political market rather than the economic market. There is no guarantee that a political allocation of resources will be to their highest valued use. Third, since significant sums are available for redistribution, citizens will withdraw resources from the productive sector in search of net benefits in the redistribution or rent-seeking game in the political market.

There are three devices by which citizens can ensure that the public purse is employed for efficiency, but not for income redistribution. These are constitutional restrictions on the tax and expenditure side of public finance (for example, proportional to population), on the scope and size of government (for example, government expenditures as a certain fixed size of gross national product), and on intergenerational transfers (for example, a balanced budget requirement); a Wicksellian voting rule of unanimity; and a principle of taxation equal to benefit received (for example, user fees).

Under the U.S. Constitution (Article I, Section 8), Congress is granted the power to tax and pay for the common defense and general welfare. However, Article I provides that taxes shall be uniform throughout the United States. This constraint was interpreted as a geographical equity requirement of taxation proportional to population. This constitutional requirement defeated schemes (except during the Civil War) for progressive income taxation that arose frequently during the second half of the nineteenth century. Corporation income was taxed beginning in 1909 on the basis of a judicial decision that the tax was an excise tax and as such was constitutionally acceptable. In 1913, the uniformity of taxation provision of the original constitution was abridged. The Sixteenth Amendment to the Constitution gave Congress the power to levy taxes on incomes from whatever source and without apportionment among the separate states. There never was any constitutional constraint of proportionality on the expenditure side. Thus, from the beginning, while taxes were general, Congress could and did distribute expenditures disproportionately. Thus was pork barrel legislation born, along with a political market for confining benefits to special interests, with expenses spread over the taxpayers. Progressive income taxation exacerbated the redistributive character of public finance by concentrating the cost of these special interest benefits on high-income (wealth, property) types.

The constitutional requirement to provide for the general safety, common defense, and general welfare is a constraint on the scope and hence the size of government. However, it is an unbounded constraint. For the first one hundred years of the existence of the United States, these duties of the state required between 1 and 2 percent of GNP.[34] Partly, the rise in the size of federal government to something on the order of 25 percent of GNP (a trend common to Western representative governments)[35] is due to a proclivity to finance all public goods and services out of general tax revenue rather than on the basis of user fees. A large array of public goods and services have the characteristic of exclusivity and as such lend themselves to pricing through user fees (roads, waterways, harbors, irrigation and flood control, recreation facilities, schooling, etc.). More importantly, however, is the fact that the general welfare clause (public interest) and the redistributive bias in the mechanism of public finance permits vote-maximizing politicians to sell redistributive services in a political market. The rise of the political market for redistributive services expanded the scope and size of government. The transfer of resources from the private sector, where resources are allocated to highest valued use, to the public sector, where they are allocated on political criteria, lowers economic efficiency.

Congress also has the power to borrow money on the credit of the United States. There is no constitutional constraint of a balanced budget or a limit to public indebtedness. For the first 150 years of its existence, Congress was fiscally conservative. Taxes were raised or lowered as budget deficits or surpluses were incurred. With the rise in popularity of Keynesian economics (government budget deficit as an engine of aggregate demand), the implicit legislative constraint of fiscal responsibility was abridged. Now, current generations engage in public consumption at future generations' expense. These massive intergenerational transfers reduce current and future savings (investment) and reduce economic growth.

The concern of public finance theorists has been with tax incidence, tax shifting, and the just distribution of the burden of taxation, but not with tax justice and voluntary consent to taxation. The principle of taxation according to ability to pay, resting on the theoretically shaky foundation of declining marginal utility of income, has prevailed over the older precept of taxation according to benefit. Knut Wicksell was the first to point out that if a public expenditure is not useful to the whole of society, then it is a blatant injustice to force someone to contribute to the cost of a public activity that does not further his interests.[36] He proposed that no public expenditure ever be voted without the simultaneous determination of the taxes necessary to cover the cost. Since there are a whole range of types of taxes, if the public expenditure has the characteristic that benefits (utility) exceed or equal taxes for all, the expenditure bill will pass unanimously (all will voluntarily consent). If unanimous (approximate unanimity based on a voting rule between 75 and 90 percent is proposed by Wicksell, presumably to prevent monopolistic exploitation by a tiny minority) consent is not reached, it is proof that the expenditure does not provide the community with benefits corresponding to the necessary sacrifice. Absent a voting rule of approximate unanimity, there is the real danger that the poor "may impose the bulk of all taxes upon the rich and may at the same time be so reckless and extravagant in approving public expenditures to which they themselves contribute little that the nation's mobile capital may soon be squandered fruitlessly. This may well break the lever of progress."[37] Thus Wicksell links the voting rule in matters of public finance to economic growth.

The third device in public finance that has economic efficiency and growth implications is the method of financing public expenditures (that is, general tax revenues or specific taxes equal to benefits, such as user fees). Some public goods have the characteristics that the consumption of one does not diminish the consumption of another and that individuals cannot effectively be excluded from consuming the good (for example, national defense, public safety, monuments, etc.). Such public goods cannot be provided by the private market, because they cannot command a price, and even if they could be priced, it is costly or impossible to prevent "free riders." Legitimately, such goods should be financed out of general tax revenue. Other public goods and services are less "public" in the sense that exclusion is possible and not very costly (for example, roads, waterways, harbors, irrigation, flood control, recreation facilities, schooling, etc.). In some cases there are practical pricing difficulties (that is, divergence between marginal and average cost) of public goods, but these difficulties are not insuperable. In many instances, the benefits to individuals are directly observed, and a user charge is an appropriate and just tax instrument. Financing such public goods out of general revenues and charging the public a zero or near-zero price for the good induces overconsumption of public goods, not to mention the opportunities for redistribution that such a public financing scheme encourages. The fact that the private sector competes with the public sector in the provision of many of these same goods and services indicates that they are less public goods then private goods supplied to the public at general taxpayer expense. When the method of financing these "public" goods induces their overconsumption, fewer resources are available for the private production of goods and services.[38]

Income redistribution is recognized as a legitimate function of government. There exists an income distribution that yields a maximum level of efficiency in society. In neoclassical theory this result occurs with factor prices' being equated with factor value marginal products. It is well known that as an economy grows, the distribution of resources is efficient in an idealized private property, laissez-faire, free trade, perfectly competitive, market exchange economy, but may result in an income distribution that is socially unacceptable. Too much inequality may create incentives for the low-income types to seek another social order. Redistributions that reduce work incentives may be an inexpensive (efficient) means of preserving the social order. Thus the income distribution partly may reflect the opportunity cost of rebellion.

Arguments in a citizen's utility function are his and others' places in the income distribution. In a society of free men, *ceteris paribus*, voters select candidates or sets of policies that reflect their own views. The capture of the state's coercive power by voters to redistribute income toward the middle-class majority in a representative democracy first was clearly articulated in Aaron Director's Law of Public Income Redistribution.[39] Gordon Tullock has extended this concept into a major hypothesis on the determinants of the income distribution.[40] Anthony Downs, James Buchanan and Gordon Tullock, and Mancur Olson extended the theory and the implications of a majority principle of policy in representative government.[41] In a one-issue election with complete voter participation, those who would gain (lose) from income distribution would vote for (against) those candidates or sets of policies that favored (opposed) redistribution. Under universal suffrage and majority rule, income would tend to become more equally distributed. Altruism, less than complete voting, and vote buying (campaign contributions, etc.) ruin the simple correspondence between the income distribution and the distribution of votes. Moreover, in a multi-issue election, nothing can be said about the appropriate set of positions or policies that will win an election. Economic policy affects the income distribution. Low-income groups gain on high-income groups during periods of low unemployment and high inflation. Political parties offer voters choices on economic policy. Voters with different socioeconomic characteristics appear to respond to economic policy differences between political parties and politicians. Finally, income distribution appears to be affected by voter choice on the liberal-conservative continuum.[42]

Economic policy has efficiency effects as well. Regulation, state-licensed monopoly, tariffs, quota restrictions, export subsidies and taxes (marketing boards), foreign exchange controls, government debt, industrial policy, inflation, and so on may shrink the transformation curve, distort resource allocation, and hence reduce economic growth. These policies also redistribute income from one group to another.

A Theory of the Evolution of the

Constitutional Setting

IN their classic work on the constitutional framework, James Buchanan and Gordon Tullock model the costs of collective decision making and the tendency in representative government with a majority voting rule to concentrate public benefits and diffuse costs.[1] Later, Buchanan developed a theory of the static constitutional contract, in which an agreement of equal and mutually respected rights for all leads to the full exploitation of gains from trade.[2] The need to enforce the agreement through a body of law and a coercive agent and to exploit further gains from the provision of public goods justifies a minimal state. Absent constitutional constraints on the fiscal power of government and supermajority voting rules in the legislature, Leviathan emerges.[3] Gary Becker shows that in the political market for redistribution there will be a tendency for political agents to choose wealth-maximizing (efficient) outcomes.[4] Donald Wittman is skeptical of the whole literature on government failure.[5] He argues that like private markets, the market for collective action is organized to promote wealth-maximizing outcomes, that there is competition in political markets, and that political agents are rewarded for efficient behavior.

Here, an endogenous model of the effect of the constitutional setting and changes in the rule space on the path of real full income within a simple neoclassical growth framework is developed. By making the rule space endogenous within the neoclassical growth model, the secular decline in private market return is linked with the return to rule change in the political market. Political agents are the monopoly brokers of the changes in the rule space, and these changes in the constitutional setting affect the path of real full income (positively for efficient rule changes and negatively for Hicks-Kaldor-inefficient changes). A steady-state constitutional setting is defined as one in which all Pareto- and Hicks-Kaldor-efficient rule changes have been incorporated and which is analytically equivalent to the neoclassical steady state. The model yields a theory of revolution based on forces leading to the adoption of Hicks-Kaldor-inefficient changes in the constitutional setting.

Before proceeding, it is important to note that there are some critical assumptions that drive the results in this model of the evolution of the constitutional setting. These assumptions are by no means universally accepted. First, the secular decline in the marginal product of capital in the private sector, a feature of the classical and neoclassical growth models, determines the timing and sequencing of rule change. In the growth models, innovation retards the decline in private rates of return. It is by no means accepted that in fact there has been a decline in the marginal product of capital. Second, the specificity of assets gives rise to net gains or losses to those favoring or opposing rule change. In a world of completely variable (nonspecific) assets, reallocation of the assets eliminates quasi-rents. Third, the classification of rule change arrayed from efficient to inefficient is reasonable, but arbitrary. Fourth, altruism and ideology are not features of political agent behavior, only self-interested gain. Finally, the model applies more to representative than to nonrepresentative government.

The sociopolitical rule space that governs exchange among people configures individual rights, enforces agreement on those rights, provides a body of law that sanctions and limits rights, and provides a public finance mechanism for the provision of public expenditures. The "rules of the game" that define the type of behavior sanctioned by government are set forth in sanctioned custom, in the constitutional document, and in private (common), statutory, and administrative law. Behavior not sanctioned by government is subject to penalty (criminal law, civil law). These sanctions, coupled with the laws of production and distribution, give rise to the costs and benefits that govern individual behavior.

The constitutional setting creates a set of opportunities: protected, legal activities that, when undertaken, increase personal well-being. Discount rates are positive, so the opportunities from sanctioned activities that yield the greatest benefits are exploited first. The time path of the returns to legal activities for a fixed constitutional setting, with fixed technology and resource endowment, is shown in figure 4-1. The vertical axis measures the sum of private, real full income generated from legally sanctioned activities; y^* is the steady state maximum income per capita for a fixed rule space with a fixed technology and the stock of available resources constant. The slope of the profile of per capita income is concave to reflect declining marginal returns from legally sanctioned activity, as the more remunerative activities are exhausted.

Invention, innovation, and the discovery of new resources give rise to new opportunities and the common law of squatter's rights or the system

81

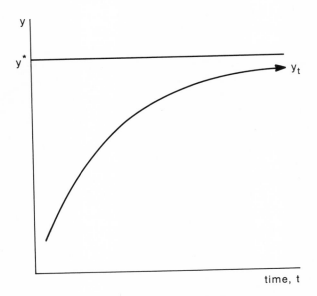

Figure 4-1. The Time Path of Income per Capita

of government-sanctioned patents creates the opportunities to legally exploit new economic opportunities. The effect of technological change or new resources within a fixed constitutional setting simply is to shift upward the per capita income steady-state maximum, y^*.

CHANGE IN THE CONSTITUTIONAL SETTING

The rule space is not time invariant. By an act of Congress and the ratification of three-quarters of the individual state legislatures, amendments to the U.S. Constitution are made. Legislators have been very active in proposing amendments to the constitution (some 5,392 proposals between 1789 and 1963), although the supermajority voting rule has prevented almost all of them from being adopted. Of the thirty-one amendments passing Congress, twenty-six have been adopted. In the post-Lockner era (economic due process, ex post facto, and obligation of contracts), the Supreme Court has been active in changing the constitutional order. William Landes and Richard Posner calculate the depreciation rate of constitutional precedents in Supreme Court decisions for 1949–1973, an era of judicial activism. The average length of life of a constitutional precedent is twenty years.[6]

A second mechanism for making effective changes in the constitutional setting is through changes in the body of law that sanctions activities. The common law does change, but its evolution is slower and the legal decisions are more narrowly construed. Yet new precedents emerge. Landes and Posner calculate a modern length of life of forty years for a common law precedent in the Supreme Court.[7] The doctrine of stare decisis makes the common law more durable and hence more certain. Because the common law is a system of general rules of legal behavior, it is costly to privatize a rule for the benefit of a special interest.

Absent amendments to the constitution or the framing of a new constitution (for example, French constitutions endured an average of less than a decade between 1789 and 1875), legislation is the main route to changing the constitutional setting. Statutes are particular bills introduced by particular legislatures, often for the benefit of the special interests that elected them. The political market for special interest legislation, which can be privatized, is a more powerful force for change in law than the common law, which as a commons has no defenders. Where the two systems of law conflict, statutes prevail. This suggests that over time the domain of private (common) law is gradually eroded and replaced by special interest statutory law.[8]

The vast majority of statutes passed by Congress make relatively marginal changes in the constitutional setting by redistributing net benefits from one group to another. However, in the aggregate these statutes represent very fundamental revisions in the rule space. Some of the statutes are of a major sort that have large effects on the institutional framework. In this category belong fiat money, bankruptcy laws, the Civil Service Act, the Social Security Act, and the Full Employment Act. Forgiveness of debt and paper money are devices for redistributing income from creditors to debtors. A great Populist movement arose in the United States over the issue of debt. Fiat money permits the state to finance the sale of its political services and public consumption through an inflation tax. The Civil Service Act led to the formation of a professional bureaucratic class largely free, within the broad confines of the statutes, to modify what the state considers legally sanctioned behavior. The Social Security Act redistributes income from one generation to another. The Full Employment Act authorized the use of the federal budget (deficit) as an instrument of stimulating aggregate demand. Where deficits are associated with unanticipated inflation, it is a tax on money holders (an increase in the transaction cost of using money in exchange) and creditors.[9] Inflation transfers wealth from net private monetary creditors to net monetary debtors.[10]

83

When the deficit is fully backed by future taxes, it is an intergenerational transfer of income. The implicit legislative rule of fiscal responsibility was replaced by a policy of increasing current public consumption at the expense of private consumption and saving in the future.

THE MARKET FOR CHANGE IN THE CONSTITUTIONAL SETTING

Legal sanctions dictate the ways that productive inputs can be combined, the output that they can produce, and the exchange processes that allocate resources. In short, the rule space determines the output that can be derived from a given set of inputs. In keeping with neoclassical growth theory assume that output is produced with capital, K, and labor, L, and with a constant returns-to-scale production function. To assess the differential impact of a rule change, assume that the aggregate production function can be decomposed into N private production functions that produce output valued as real full income, Y.[11]

Accordingly,

(4-1) $$y = f(k, \theta) = \Sigma_i f^i(k^i, \theta), i = 1, N,$$

where $y = Y/L$ is real full income (output) per unit of labor, $k = K/L$ is capital input per unit of labor, and θ is rule space that delineates the "rules of the game" that govern the production of real full income in the private sector.[12]

When the rule space is fixed, capital accumulation per worker depends on the constant, average propensity to save and the exogenous, constant rate of growth of population, according to the Solow differential equation.[13] While there may be both specific and variable or nonspecific capital in each sector,[14] it is assumed that there is sufficient new and variable capital at any time so that, even in the face of rule changes, aggregate output can be maximized.[15] The rule space defines the marginal product of capital in each sector according to equation (4-1). Private market entrepreneurs continually adjust their inputs so as to receive the maximum return. The traditional neoclassical growth equilibrium is presented in figure 4-2 for constitutional setting θ^0, where $y^*(\theta^0)$ and $k^*(\theta^0)$ solve the Solow differential equation, given the average propensity to save, the population growth rate, and the rule space.

The rule space itself is the product of a production process. Rules are created and changed, sanctions imposed and altered, and enforcement activities undertaken in the public sector. Public sector inputs of capital, K^L, and labor, L^L, produce and maintain the constitutional setting accord-

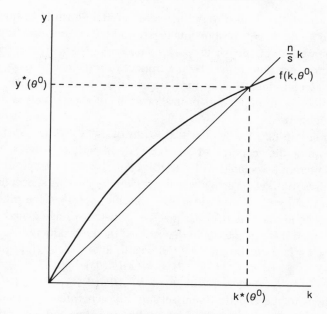

Figure 4-2. Neoclassical Growth Equilibrium for
Constitutional Setting θ^0

ing to a production function that is assumed to be constant returns to
scale. Write the per capita output of rules, θ/L^L as

(4-2) $$\theta/L^L = g(k^L, \Psi),$$

where Ψ represents the public sector rules (partly contained in the constitutional document, Supreme Court decisions on the permissible set of
government activities, legislative innovation, bureaucratic expansion,
etc.) that govern the means of legally altering the rules of the game in the
private sector. As such, Ψ defines both the means of changing the private
rule space (for example, constitutional amendment, legislative or administrative statute, common law) and also which dimensions of the private
constitutional setting are subject to change (for example, which private
rights and properties are inalienable and which are subject to government, public interest reinterpretation, which goods are publicly provided
and which goods are privately acquired, what can be owned, what can be
transferred, what can be taxed or subsidized, etc.). The domain of the
public sector is considered in a later section.

Units of capital allocated to the public sector have an opportunity cost
equal to the returns to assets in the private sector and therefore must be

compensated. The return to public sector capital depends on the willingness and ability of rule proponents to pay and the forgone cost of payment offered by rule opponents. Proponents and opponents among the N private sectors are determined by the impact of a change in rules on their personal well-being. This, in turn, depends on the rule's impact on each production function, f^i, and past allocations of capital between specific and variable uses.

Variable capital may be allocated to any of the $N + 1$ private and public sectors of the economy at any time. By its nature of being variable, there is no rent associated with variable capital. Variable capital earns the competitive market return, given the private sector rule space, and competition dissipates any quasi-rents. A specific input, on the other hand, may realize a quasi-rent (either positive or negative) associated with the use to which it is allocated and determined by the production function in equation (4-1). Accordingly, real full wealth in any sector, i, is given by

$$(4\text{-}3) \qquad w^i = \int_0^\infty [f^i(k^{Fi}, \theta) + k^{Vi} MPk(\theta)]e^{-rt}dt$$
$$= (1/r)[f^i(k^{Fi}, \theta) + k^{Vi} MPk(\theta)].$$

Changes in the constitutional setting, $d\theta$, generate support when the impact of the change on individual wealth is positive and opposition if the change reduces individual wealth. Rule changes influence wealth according to

$$(4\text{-}4) \qquad dw^i/d\theta = (1/r)(f_\theta^i + MPk_\theta k^{Vi}),$$

where, as throughout, subscripts denote partial derivatives. The term f_θ^i is the change in the quasi-rent realized by specific inputs in sector i and MPk_θ is the change in the per-unit return to variable inputs in all sectors when the rule space changes. The distinction between specific and variable assets is central to any conflict that arises over a proposed rule change. If all assets are variable, equation (4-4), with no quasi-rents and $f_\theta^i = 0$, suggests that all sectors will unanimously favor (oppose) the proposed rule change if MPk_θ is positive (negative). In this model, the ability to realize quasi-rents from a rule change underlies the attempt of a subset of the population to secure a rule change that in the aggregate is inefficient, that is, $f_\theta^i > 0$ and $MPk_\theta < 0$. We will return to this point subsequently. Thus, for any rule change, there will be a group of proponents, whose wealth rises as a result of the change, and a group of opponents, whose wealth declines.[16]

For their gains, or to avoid their losses, proponent and opponent groups make political payments.[17] Political payments take many forms. Votes, campaign contributions, ward-heeling activities, etc., provide access to political office and rulemaking power. Political office provides salaries and job perquisites, and political power gives access to direct and indirect payments of cash and goods in kind. If group organization and political payment were free of transaction costs, only wealth-increasing rule changes[18] would be forthcoming, since the opponent group could bid up to the value of its wealth loss under the new rule to prevent change. Of course, organization and political payment are not free of transaction costs. Political groups must coalesce with the associated organizational costs (for example, overcoming inertia, etc.) and free rider problems. Outright payments are not likely to be permitted under the public sector rule space and the access to legal means of payment may differ across groups. Finally, there is no clear permanent property right in rules. It is political influence, not rules, that is bought and sold in political markets. This increases uncertainty and magnifies principal-agent problems.

The willingness and ability of proponent and opponent groups to pay for rule changes depends on their respective monetary and voting resources.[19] The political payments function converts these heterogeneous sources of political pressure into real full income according to the public sector's valuation of votes and cash. Differences in partial influence reflect differing abilities across groups to convert monetary resources into cash payments. For example, if only direct cash payments are permitted, the political influence at the margin of proponents and opponents is equal. When direct payments are not permitted, a producer group—as an example, the proponent of an import restriction—that can offer future employment opportunities to a rulemaker will possess an ability to convert monetary resources into an offer to pay that is greater than that of the consumer group (the opponent group) that cannot make a similar offer.[20] In this instance, proponent political payments at the margin exceed those of opponents.

Monetary resources must be raised by member contributions. They are a function of the members' anticipated gains (losses) under the rule change, reflecting their willingness to pay for the change (or to avoid change), and the size of the group. Presumably, as the size of the group increases, greater internal expenditures to avoid free riding—peer pressure, policing members, structuring member benefits to conform to individual contributions, etc.—become necessary. This reduces the group's monetary resources that can be devoted to obtaining favorable rules. Therefore, the member contribution functions for each group will depend positively on the group's change in wealth under the rule change, negatively on the size of the group, and on other influences on the group's ability to raise money,[21] including the parameters of the distribution of the individual effects, the education and political savvy of the members, and whether the group has other benefits, such as trade association membership, that can be denied recalcitrant members.[22]

Political Market Income

Per capita public sector income, from the production and maintenance of rule changes, y^L, is the per capita payment of proponents net of the political cost per capita of the pressure of opponent groups, $y^L = (P^p - P^o)/L^L$. Relief from opponent pressure can be "purchased" by trading votes[23] so that opponent political payment, P^o, is an explicit cost of rulemaking. Alternatively, opponent pressure can be borne with no compensation given. Since political market competition limits the amount of pressure that can be borne, failing to compensate opponents has an opportunity cost equal to their political payment, P^o. The return to capital and labor dedicated to the public sector, MPk^L, therefore, is

$$(4\text{-}5) \qquad MPk^L = dy^L/dk^L = P_\theta\, g_k,$$

where $P^\theta = \partial P^p/\partial\theta - \partial P^o/\partial\theta$ is the political market's return for a rule change. As in the private sector, it is assumed that there is enough variable k in the political sector at any time to permit assets to efficiently reallocate in response to new alternatives. The existence of specific assets in the political sector gives rise to quasi-rents. Such rents generate rent-seeking behavior by politicians who wish to change the rules that govern the political arena, Ψ. The implication of specific political assets and public sector rent-seeking are considered below. With income-earning opportunities in the public sector, the allocation of capital among the $N + 1$ private and public sectors will result in equal marginal productivity of capital in each sector; that is, the cumulative "supply of rules" is determined by the political market's return for a rule change, P_θ, the opportunity cost of resources, MPk, which is determined in the private sector, and the productivity of resources in producing rules, g_k.

$$(4\text{-}6) \qquad S(\theta) = S(P_\theta, MPk, g_k).$$

Equation (4-6) is a static supply curve with quantity positively related to market value and resource productivity, and inversely related to input cost. The pace of constitutional change is slowed by technological advances in the private sector and hastened by technological advances in the public sector. New technology in the private sector increases the productivity of assets in production and draws resources away from rulemaking. Technological change in the public sector increase the marginal product of resources employed in the production of rules, g_k, and diverts resources from private sector employments. New public sector technology would include, among other things, the centralization of rulemaking authority, the growth of administrative rulemaking agencies, the growth of the seniority system for committee appointments, income taxation, the direct election of senators, and the acceptance and increased use of the institution of logrolling.

When technological change in the two sectors is offsetting, the evolution of the constitutional setting is determined by the secular decline in the marginal productivity of capital in the private sector as capital accumulates through time. In the early stages of the constitutional setting, when capital per unit of labor is small, the high marginal productivity of capital in the private sector precludes all but the most remunerative rule changes. Less remunerative rule changes may evolve later, when the opportunity cost of capital has fallen. In this fashion, rule changes theoretically will be introduced into the constitutional setting over time in order of descending values of the political market's return for rule change, P_θ.

EFFICIENT AND INEFFICIENT CHANGES IN THE CONSTITUTIONAL SETTING

The positive, but secularly decreasing, marginal productivity of capital implies that additional private sector resources increase wealth and that the private market efficiently allocates its resources to their highest valued uses at all times. This need not be true of the public sector. While the marginal return to resources devoted to the public sector declines as returns to capital in the private declines over time, the impact of the rule changes produced with public sector resources may lead to increases or decreases in private wealth and the private impact of rule changes need not flow in an ordered manner. However, some general patterns emerge from the model of the previous section. To facilitate the discussion of the evolution of the constitutional setting consider the following definitions of allocative efficiency in a constitutional setting.

Definition 1: A Pareto-efficient rule change is one in which someone's wealth rises and no one's falls.

Definition 2: A Hicks-Kaldor-efficient rule change is one in which total wealth gains from the change are greater than total losses.

Definition 3: A Hicks-Kaldor-inefficient rule change is one in which total wealth gains from the change are less than total losses.

Political conflict (the posturing of proponent and opponent groups) in the context here depends on the existence of specific capital. Return to equation (4-4) and the following paragraph where proponents and opponents of rule change are defined.[24] If all capital is variable, the increment in wealth $(dw^i/d\theta)$ from the rule change is positive (negative) for all employments of capital as long as MPk_θ is positive (negative). Further, the effect on wealth per unit of resources of a rule change, $d(w^i/k^i)/d\theta$, is the same (MPk_θ) in each sector. When all capital can be costlessly varied among the N private sectors, a rule change that makes resources more productive in the aggregate will be Pareto-efficient, even if it reduces the marginal product of capital in some sectors. This is because inputs rendered less productive in particular employments by the rule change flow to a more productive sector. Thus, if all capital is variable, the benefits (costs) of any change will be shared in the private market on the basis of ownership of resources. Everyone will take the same position on each issue, as either proponents or opponents, and only Pareto-efficient changes will occur.

Efficient changes of the Pareto and Hicks-Kaldor type increase per capita production from the given stock of resources. It may be that this increase is realized in a proper subset of the N private sectors, but the movement of resources from other sectors will ensure that the marginal product of capital increases in all sectors. Similarly, Hicks-Kaldor-inefficient change, by reducing aggregate production, reduces the marginal product of capital. Thus, for efficient rule change, $MPk_\theta > 0$, and for inefficient change, $MPk_\theta < 0$. This implies that, in general, all the N sectors of the economy have an interest in rule changes that change aggregate production possibilities. Even if the sector is one in which its specific capital is unaffected, the value of its variable capital changes if $MPk_\theta \neq 0$.[25]

Rewrite equation (4-5) as

$$(4\text{-}7) \quad MPk^L = [P_1^p M_1^p(dw^p/d\theta) = P_1^o M_1^o(dw^o/d\theta)]g_k$$
$$+ [(P_2^p M_2^p + P_2^p)(dn^p/d\theta) = (P_2^o M_2^o + P_2^o)(dn^o/d\theta)]g_k,$$

where the subscripts, 1 and 2, indicate partial derivatives with respect to the argument in that position in the function. The first bracketed term on the right-hand side of equation (4-7) incorporates the direct effect on public sector income of the wealth changes embodied in rule change $d\theta$. The second bracketed term reflects the distributional nature of the rule change and its effect on the ability of the groups to organize for pressure.

Because the sequence of changes in the rule space proceed in descending order of their political return, depending on the rate of return to capital in the political market, right-hand side values that increase this return shorten the time before the rule change is introduced. Values that decrease the return slow (and possibly halt) a rule change. A sufficient condition for a rule change is that the returns to capital in the political market exceed (or equal) the steady-state marginal product of capital in the private sector.[26] In other words, the rule change will (eventually) be introduced, and become part of the steady-state constitutional setting if its marginal political return is at least as great as the steady-state marginal return to capital in the private sector.

Equation (4-7) reveals a general principle of change in the constitutional setting. When all of the parameters of the groups' political payment and contribution functions are equal and the groups are of equal size, equation (4-7) reduces to

(4-8) $$MPk^L = (dw^p/d\theta - dw^o/d\theta)\, P_1 M_k g_k,$$

where $P_1 M_1 = P_1^p M_1^p = P_1^o M_1^o$. Equation (4-8), in contrast to equation (4-7), states that if proponent and opponent groups have (a) equal voting assets and other influences (equal n and X), (b) equal marginal abilities to convert individual wealth effects into group monetary assets (equal M_1 and M_2), and (c) equal abilities to convert voting and money assets into political currency (equal P_1 and P_2), then MPk^L is a direct function of net benefits, $dw^p/d\theta - dw^o/d\theta$, positive for efficient changes in the constitutional setting and negative for inefficient changes. When one considers rule change in the abstract, without reference to a specific change that identifies the proponent and opponent groups and calls attention to the differences in their political payment and contribution functions, a general pattern of evolution of the constitutional setting emerges. Equation (4-8) identifies the pattern of change: The predominant tendency is for change in the constitutional setting to be efficient in the Hicks-Kaldor sense, with the sequence of change reflecting diminishing net benefits.[27]

Figure 4-3 demonstrates an efficient sequence of the change of rules in a neoclassical growth framework. The vertical axis measures real income (output) from the N private sectors, y^N. The horizontal axis measures total capital, where k^N is capital utilized in the N private sectors. Public sector capital is $k^L = k - k^N$. The initial constitutional setting, θ^0, yields the production function $f(k^N, \theta^0)$. When k_1 capital has accumulated some portion, sufficient to produce Δy^N in the private sector, k^L is used to change the rule space from θ^0 to θ^1. The steady-state return to investment Δy^N is $y^*(\theta^1) - y^*(\theta^0)$. The envelope function, $f(k)$, is the neoclassical production function for this sequence of rule changes. The slope of $f(k)$ at point A defines the minimum, steady-state marginal product of capital. All rule changes, $d\theta$ for which the returns to capital in the political market

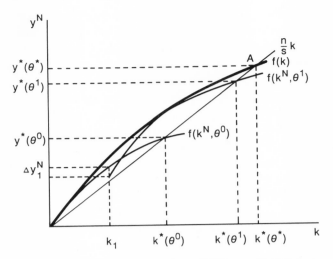

Figure 4-3. Neoclassical Growth Equilibrium with Efficient
Endogenous Constitutional Change

exceed or are equal to those in the private sector are made at point A, and
$\theta^0 + \int d\theta$ defines the steady-state constitutional setting, θ^*.

With regard to specific rule changes, likely differences in the groups'
political payment and contribution functions and in their size can be
identified. Then, the sequence of change will not necessarily follow in descending order of net benefits and may include Hicks-Kaldor-inefficient
change. Refer to equation (4-7). The wealth changes embodied in a rule
change do not translate dollar for dollar into political payments. In contrast to private markets, the rule being traded is a public good (bad) being
given to (taken from) a group, rather than a private exchange between
individuals. The groups must organize and translate their private assets
into political currency, and to the extent that groups differ in their ability
to do so, the resulting exchange may not mirror private exchange in a
Coaseian world of zero transaction costs.

First, P_1 reflects the group's ability to translate its monetary assets into
real full income payments to political brokers of rules. When direct cash
payments are not permitted, $P_1 < 1$, because payments must be made indirectly. Legal forms of indirect payment may include campaign contributions, honoraria, gifts, employment opportunities, etc. The delivery of illegal payments at a future date may be so difficult to detect and prohibit
that the promise to deliver also is a credible and effective means of converting monetary assets into political currency. Second, M_1 (< 1) is the
fraction of the group's benefits (costs) that can be brought to the political

market as monetary assets. When individual rights are not private (individually purchased and enjoyed) free-riding behavior results. If the rule change can be tailored to the behavior of the individual contributor (being more or less favorable depending on the individual's contribution) or if membership in the group conveys private benefits that can be tailored to individual behavior, M_1 will be larger.[28] To the extent these values differ across groups the political market misreads (distorts) the private market effects of a rule change.

Finally, the political market values numbers (votes), and the distribution of proponent and opponent numbers for a rule change typically will not mirror the distribution of wealth effects.[29] The parameter P_2 is the political value of a vote, and there is no reason to expect that this value will differ across groups. Only when the benefit/cost ratio and the proponent/opponent number ratio is equal[30] will the voting effect not distort the political reading of private effects. When votes are associated with individuals and not their wealth, this is not likely.

There is a second, potentially more serious, number effect. Because free riding increases with the size of the group, greater numbers have a negative effect on the group's ability to raise contributions. $P_1M_1 + P_2$ is the total effect of numbers on the political currency of the group. For a given level of benefits, there is an optimal group size, n^{p^*} and n^{o^*}, determined by $P_1M_2 + P_2 = 0$, that maximizes political influence.[31] A rule change that concentrates its benefits among n^{p^*} proponents will generate greater political payments than will a rule change with similar benefits that are more or less concentrated. The same is true of the concentration of costs among the opponents of a rule change. Depending on the relative value of cash and votes in the political market and the degree of free riding, the optimal size of the group may be quite small. If so, rule changes that concentrate their benefits and widely disperse their costs could generate large political returns in spite of causing net wealth reductions in the private sector. Similarly, some Hicks-Kaldor-efficient rule changes with dispersed benefits and concentrated costs might not generate enough political support to be accepted.

Thus, when differences in proponent and opponent characteristics are included, the path to the steady-state growth equilibrium is not likely to be the smooth envelope presented in figure 4-3. Inefficient rule changes become possible, and the sequence does not always progress in lockstep from the most valuable change to the least. To what extent group characteristics alter the political interpretation of the wealth effects of a rule change is an empirical issue. The array that ranks the total wealth effects of rule change, $dW^p = dW^o$, from highest (positive) to lowest (negative) will not correspond perfectly to the array that ranks the political returns from rule change, $dP^p = dP^o$, but because wealth effects are an important part of political returns, the correspondence is expected to be positive and significant. Thus, the early stages of constitutional evolution, when the high opportunity cost of resources demands a high political return, would tend to be characterized by efficient rule changes. The later stages of the development of the rule space, when the opportunity cost of resources is lower, increasingly are more likely to be characterized by Hicks-Kaldor-inefficient rule change. With inefficient rule change, the growth path of per capita income may become negative as the steady state is approached. To appreciate this observation, envision an efficient initial constitutional setting. Because of group characteristic effects, there are likely to be some Hicks-Kaldor-inefficient changes that will, nonetheless, generate positive political returns. In the progress to the steady-state equilibrium, the private market's per capita income is always at least as high as it would be in any other constitutional setting (this most efficient constitutional setting is the envelope of all envelopes generated from any initial rule space). When MPk falls sufficiently to permit change in the rule space, the income per capita growth path will become negative. Under any other constitutional setting, where MPk is lower, this change would have been forthcoming at an earlier time.

Figure 4-4 presents a sequence of changes in the constitutional setting in a neoclassical growth framework. The original constitutional setting is θ^0, and through rule space θ^2 the changes presented are efficient. θ^E is the efficient constitutional setting, that is, where all efficient changes are included, and $f(k^N, \theta^E)$ is the efficiency envelope. When k_3 resources have accumulated, an inefficient change in the constitutional setting is made (from θ^2 to θ^3) that diverts resources from the private markets (shifts the private sector production functions down) and lowers the marginal product of capital (the slope of the private sector production function). The growth equilibrium is achieved at point A. The emboldened path $f(k^N)$ is the neoclassical production function with endogenous change in the constitutional setting, and includes Hicks-Kaldor-inefficient change.

EVOLUTION OF THE STEADY-STATE CONSTITUTIONAL SETTING

By expanding the role of the monopoly agents of government to include the brokering of changes in the structure of rights, a pattern of the evolution of the institutional framework to something akin to a steady-state

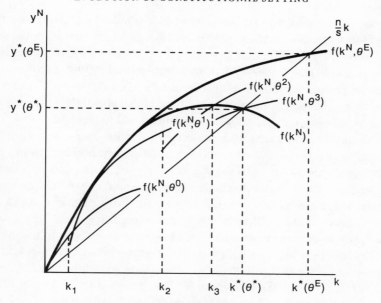

Figure 4-4. Neoclassical Growth Equilibrium with Endogenous
Constitutional Change

constitutional setting emerges. As long as the returns from legally sanctioned activities within a fixed constitutional setting exceed the returns from changing the sociolegal framework, no revision of the rule space will be initiated. Recall figure 4-2. The slope of the per capita income function, $f(k, \theta^0)$, represents the return to constitutionally protected activities. The return, then, represents the opportunity cost of resources and effort expended to secure private gains through changes in the rule space. In the early stages of a constitutional setting, the returns from legally sanctioned activity are high. As capital and labor accumulate, marginal returns fall. At some point in time, the returns from change in the rule space become competitive with the returns from legally sanctioned activities. This is when the process of rule space change sets in and rent-seeking begins. Given the assumption that the opportunity cost of resources declines over time, those changes in the constitutional setting that yield the greatest net benefit to political entrepreneurs will be undertaken first. Given the definitions of efficient change in the rule space above, the sequence of change will tend to be from efficient change of the Pareto or Hicks-Kaldor variety to Hicks-Kaldor-inefficient change, in descending order of the greatest net benefit. The process of change in the constitutional setting will continue as long as the return to resources used in the public sector exceeds the steady-state private return to resources. Change in the constitutional setting ends when the returns to capital in the private and the public sectors are equalized. This is the steady-state constitutional setting. In the steady state, all private pockets of wealth from legally sanctioned activities and gains from changes in the rule space have been exploited so that the returns to all resources and effort is determined and unchanging.

First consider Pareto institutions and their relation to the constitutional setting. In private contracting sanctioned under common law and in the voluntary formation of clubs for sharing the benefits and costs of production and consumption of goods that have a degree of publicness over a membership, absent any external effects, the institution is Pareto efficient.[32] Since some constituency favors and no constituency is credibly opposed, Pareto-efficient institutions are likely to be sanctioned in the initial constitutional setting. When they are not, perhaps because of oversight or because unanticipated technological changes subsequently create Pareto-efficient institutions, the brokerage fee for implementing change is high, since there is no political cost of (i.e., no opposition to) change.

Rules that arise from Pareto-efficient change, because their political return is high, will be common to most constitutional settings. Some examples of Pareto-efficient changes in various constitutional settings are the allocation of resources and commodities in a market of free exchange, free trade in foreign commercial relations, the adoption of a commodity-backed money (but not fiat money) as an efficient replacement for barter exchange, the substitution of a system of command in production organized as a firm for production based on contracting and market exchange,[33] the development of financial instruments of exchange (for example, bills of exchange, letters of credit, etc.), the rise of an insurance market to diversify risk, the separation of ownership (risk) and control (the corporate form of the firm), the development of commodity, credit, and stock markets, changes in common law, etc. These innovations are likely to emerge quickly under a constitutional setting, with the pace of innovation governed solely by the costs of organizing the proponents for change relative to the benefits to be accrued from the change.

Some constitutional changes are Pareto-efficient for all but the ruler. The only persons who are harmed are those who lose command and control over the actions of others. For example, the rights to engage in free exchange, to develop commodity, credit, and stock markets, and so on benefit all but the central planner. If the original constitutional setting gives disproportionate political power to the few, however, these changes may be slow to evolve. For example, under Muslim law, which now is incorporated in the constitutions of most Islamic states, usury is forbidden and commercial law is more narrowly construed and religiously flavored than in Western practice.[34] While Muslim bankers have gotten around the ban to a degree by charging fees on loans and distributing profit on savings, the arrangement is uncertain, and efficient credit and financial markets have been retarded by the constitutional ban on usury. Recall that during the medieval period usury was also forbidden (except to Jews) and a principle of just price was enforced. Without the constitutional ban on usury this institution was soon replaced. Usury ceilings, common in the past, have all but disappeared in the United States.

As constitutional settings evolve over time, change frequently is more typified by Hicks-Kaldor-efficient changes. These might include constitutionally legal activities with relatively low external (localized) costs (smokestack industry, water pollution, deforestation, etc.), coercive taxation for the provision of pure public goods, the introduction of fiat money, bankruptcy laws, the regulation of market exchange in cases where the information cost of consumers exceeds that of producers and/or their bargaining strengths differ, warranty legislation, regulation of monopoly, a change from *caveat emptor* to *caveat venditor*, etc. Statutory laws that prevent significant negative externalities or promote significant positive externalities might fall into this category. This might include the public provision through coercive taxation of some private goods with significant positive externalities that cannot be captured by the private provider (for example, schooling, roads, waterways, irrigation, harbors, etc.). However, to the extent that the private market is a more efficient provider (for example, health care delivery systems), public provision through taxation is Hicks-Kaldor-inefficient.

The pressure for Hicks-Kaldor-efficient change by proponents is positive as is the pressure to prevent change by opponents, so long as organization costs are relatively low. Pressure takes the form of payment for favorable rulings or legislation. The courts and the legislature will act first where the surplus is greatest. As aggregate net benefits are positive, *ceteris paribus*, Hicks-Kaldor-efficient changes are the most likely legislative/judicial changes to provide sufficient surplus to move the monopoly suppliers of statutes and legal rulings to make changes.

A maturing constitutional setting increasingly is characterized by Hicks-Kaldor-inefficient changes. As is the case with Hicks-Kaldor-efficient changes there is a group of opponents and a group of proponents that, if organizational costs are sufficiently low, will exert pressure on the monopoly brokers of rules. For Hicks-Kaldor-inefficient changes to occur, however, the organization advantages of the proponents vis-à-vis those of the opponents must be sufficient to overcome the benefit/cost difference that militates against such change. Accordingly, the surplus, P_θ, that can be extracted by the monopolist broker of rules likely is lower than for Hicks-Kaldor-inefficient changes. One expects these changes to be the last set of rules brokered. Hicks-Kaldor-inefficient changes might include progressive income taxation, government ownership of emerging property rights or existing private rights (for example, the electromagnetic spectrum, outer space, genetic engineering, Western water rights, declining industry, the "commanding heights," etc.), plant closing laws, corporate reform (workers, environmentalists on the board), the licensing of business and occupations, the recognition of trade unions, price supports, and other subsidies, protective tariffs and quotas, deficit financing of current public consumption, etc.

There are several other features of this final stage of change in the rule space through special interest statutes. Since the common law is far less capable of being privatized for special interest—that is, benefits cannot be concentrated and costs cannot be dispersed to increase P_θ—statutory law begins to dominate common law. By corollary, the legislative (political) market begins to dominate the judicial market, since legal rulings under common law are more alterations of the parameters of general rules of legally sanctioned behavior. Moreover, stare decisis and precedent bind future judges but legislators cannot bind future legislators (*lex posterior derogat priori*).[35] This fact means that, unlike legal rulings, statutes cannot grant exclusive and permanent rights in the future. What one legislature grants, another can take away or modify. Statutory transfers of the Hicks-Kaldor-inefficient sort are transfers of short-term rents rather than the transfer of a permanent right.[36] This view of the dynamics of Hicks-Kaldor-inefficient changes in the constitution is also at variance with Whittman's view of the efficiency of the legislative process and statutory law.[37]

ON THE ENDURANCE OF CONSTITUTIONAL SETTINGS

The durability of a constitutional setting depends upon the returns to legally sanctioned behavior and the breadth of the provisions in the original document for initiating Pareto-efficient changes in the institutional framework. Consider two constitutional settings with different potentials

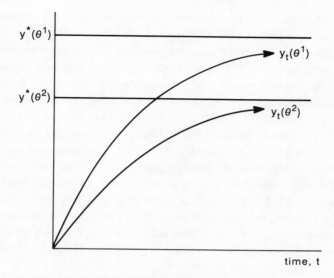

Figure 4-5. The Time Path of Income per Capita with
Different Rule Spaces

for private wealth. In figure 4-5, under the rule space with the lesser potential, the marginal return from legally sanctioned behavior in private markets declines more quickly. Pressure to change the original constitutional setting will emerge more quickly. If the changes are not Pareto-efficient, opposition to changes grows. The movement to Hicks-Kaldor-inefficient changes will occur much earlier with this type of constitutional setting.

This likely explains the contrast in the evolution of human behavior in China and the Soviet Union under communist rule and the Western representative democracies. While the communist constitutional settings are much younger than the U.S. framework, their prohibitions on private property, on the ownership and control of capital, and on market allocation of resources prevent many Pareto-efficient changes. Access to wealth through control of the political market becomes attractive more quickly. There have been some fairly radical institutional changes in China, and to a lesser degree in the Soviet Union, in the last few years that are Pareto-efficient. First, China allowed the farmers to sell a substantial portion of their crops in a legally sanctioned private market. This led to a doubling of crop output in a short interval with relatively little change in resource endowment. Private incentives are a powerful force for productivity. Next, farmers and others in rural areas were allowed to engage in small-scale manufacturing. While private firms represent a very small fraction of industrial enterprise in China, they represent a substantial fraction of industrial output. While farmers still are prohibited from owning land, a system of long-term leases that are in principle exchangeable has been put into place. This reform creates the incentives to conserve the land as a resource and offers some opportunity for an allocation of land to highest valued use. Secondly, China opened up its borders in a limited fashion to foreign investment. Much of this activity is confined to economic zones and conditions of technology transfer, foreign exchange and repatriation restrictions, and domestic content requirements that have slowed the pace of foreign investment. China's main partner in foreign joint ventures has been Hong Kong. Thirdly, China has attempted to put state enterprise onto a for-profit basis and appears to be prepared to let inefficient state firms go bankrupt. But, while there is a cautious interest in permitting the allocation of some goods by market price, a fear of inflation and "profiteering" ("profit" remains a four-letter word in China) has limited its application. Moreover, capital is allocated by the government, the labor force is immobile (workers belong to work units; while work units are free to trade labor, workers cannot initiate moves without the loss of a very substantial array of subsidies and access to social services), and government enterprise remains jointly administered by a manager, who is instructed to seek profit, and a Communist Party official, who imposes the political ideology of the Communist Party.

Similar changes are occurring in the Eastern bloc countries, where the idea of free market allocation of resources is gaining momentum, opposition political parties and free trade unions are being permitted, and emigration restrictions are being loosened. The Soviet Union's hold over the empire has been relaxed.

As the analysis suggests, not all radical reforms of constitutions are Pareto-efficient. Constitutional change can be harmful to some and may serve to lower aggregate wealth. In the early 1970s Iran was on a path of economic development more or less along Western lines. But many aspects of Western culture are deeply offensive to the sensibilities of Muslims. The ideology of the fundamentalist mullahs prevailed, and the rule space of Iran changed from that of a monarchy with some autonomous secular legislative (Majilis) power to that of a fundamentalist Islamic state under the rule of mullahs. Islam has not settled the debate of whether the ideal Muslim economy is private enterprise or socialist. The Pareto-inefficient changes in the rule space in Iran have returned the country to the fifteenth century.

The steady-state constitutional stage is postponed to the degree that technological progress and resource growth occur. But the rate of technological change and resource growth are not exogenous with respect to the institutional framework except in settings that initially sanction Pareto efficient behavior and provide for Pareto-efficient changes in the framework. In constitutional settings that initially limit the scope of Pareto-efficient behavior and block Pareto-efficient changes in the rule space, the rate of technological progress and resource growth is likely to be low.

The extent of Hicks-Kaldor-inefficient change in the constitutional setting is controlled by the voting rule in the legislature and the legislative rule that permits vote trading (logrolling). If the voting rule is Wicksellian unanimity (approximate) and income redistribution is costless, only Pareto-efficient and Hicks-Kaldor-efficient changes in the rule space will occur. What would otherwise be Hicks-Kaldor-efficient change will occur, because under costless income redistribution there exists a redistributional structure that will make Hicks-Kaldor-efficient change Pareto efficient. Where the voting rule is simple majority, Hicks-Kaldor-inefficient change in the constitutional setting is the final stage toward the steady-state rule space. This is so because the sovereign majority can impose a legal tyranny over the minority. The legislature has an incentive to provide redistributional services, since it earns a brokerage fee on the surplus P_{θ}. With vote trading, minority special interests can obtain a majority on statutory legislation and redistribute income from the actual majority.

RENT-SEEKING AND CONSTITUTIONAL REVOLUTION

Constitutional revolution is a discrete change of large magnitude in the constitutional setting. It arises typically because a galvanizing event makes obvious an inefficiency in the existing constitutional setting. In this theory of the evolution of the constitutional setting, changes in the rules that govern the private production of personal well-being have been discussed. It has been argued that an overriding document, Ψ, defines the public sector's domain of influence and the mechanisms by which this influence is administered. Because of the existence of specific resources in the private sector, incentives exist to seek changes in the rules of the game. Proposed rule changes that are not Pareto-optimal create private sector proponent and opponent groups. If the proponent group can raise enough political currency, it will prevail even if the social consequences are negative. Thus one source of inefficiency in political allocations is the expected

101

value of Hicks-Kaldor-inefficient change in the rule space, E(HKIC). In private sector exchange, where the opponent group must be fully compensated, E(HKIC) = 0.

A second source of inefficiency involves the public sector's domain of influence over private activity, as defined by the public sector constitution, Ψ. That public sector allocations tend to be efficient in the *sequence* of changes they promote does not imply that they tend to be efficient in the *method* of change they utilize. Consider the private market alternative to political allocation. In the absence of constitutional constraint, the private sector would reallocate rights by exchange. In this instance the proponents (as buyers) and the opponents (who must be compensated as sellers) of a rule change would bear the cost of the transaction by

(4-9) $$\theta/L = h(k, \Psi),$$

where h defines the private sector resource cost of producing and maintaining θ. With private sector exchange the proponent and opponent groups[38] share the net benefits of the change less the resource cost, $dw^P/d\theta - dw^o/d\theta - (h_k L)MPk$.

In the political market, the proponent group's benefit is its value of the change less the political payment, $dw^P/d\theta - P^P$. The opponent group's loss is the value it loses with the change less the amount it can extract in political payments (for example, logrolling) as compensation, $dw^o/d\theta - P^o$. The political rights brokers collect the difference in political payments less their resource costs, $P^o - P^P - (g_k L^L)MPk$. With public sector change, the aggregate effect is $dw^P/d\theta - dw^o/d\theta - (g_k L^L)MPk$. Inefficiency associated with the method of changing rules arises when the domain of public sector rulemaking includes rules that are more costly to change in the public sector than in the private sector, $h_k L < g_k L^L$. With the two sources of inefficiency an ideal constitutional setting includes in the public sector's domain only those rule changes whose private sector costs exceed their public sector costs, as in

(4-10) $$(h_k L - g_k L^L)MPk - E(HKIC) > 0.$$

Now consider the public sector constitution, Ψ. Unlike the private rule space, there can be no individual or group entrusted to administer the public sector rule space. At some point, the rules that govern the governors must be subjected to an open arena where pressures (potentially physical force as well as financial pressure) from all sources are weighed and balanced. In this arena the will of the public sector is an important influence in the determination of the public sector rule space. If there are fixed assets in the public sector (legal capital of judges and political capital of legislators that rises with length of tenure) that can earn quasi-rents, changes in the public sector rule space that increase the return to those assets will be favored by their owners.

Write the per capita wealth of individuals in the public sector with specific and variable resources, k^{FL} and k^{VL}, as

(4-11) $\qquad w^i = (1/r) \, [k^{FL} \, MPk^L \, (\Psi) + k^{VL} \, MPk],$

where $MPk^L(\Psi)$ is the quasi-rent returned to specific political assets. Changes in the public sector rule space that increase the scope of public sector influence, that is, that increase the number of allocative decisions that government makes, will produce quasi-rents in the political market when (1) there are specific political resources and (2) the political market's payment for rule change, P_θ, in its expanded dimension is greater than in its existing dimensions. In other words, government, as a special interest, favors expanding its control when the new dimensions of its control offer greater remuneration than do existing dimensions. This is properly termed regulatory imperialism. As in private markets the existence of quasi-rents in the public sector depends on specific resources. If all public sector resources are variable, inefficient changes in the scope of public sector influence will lower MPk, the competitive return to resources, and hence w^L in equation (4-11). Politicians then would uniformly oppose such changes. The decline of P_θ over time, then, will drive the evolution of Ψ. The passage of time increases the incentive for regulatory imperialism by government.

A sufficient condition for extension of the political domain is that the proponent group be able to make a payment to the public sector that is greater than the political cost of opposition and resources.[39] Proponents will be willing to pay in the political market for a rule change, if the political price is less than the private market cost.[40] These two conditions imply that the scope of political allocations will increase if the sufficient condition is met, and

(4-12) $\qquad dw^o/d\theta - dP^o/d\theta > -(h_k L - g_k L^L)MPk.$

The left-hand side of equation (4-12) is the difference between the private and political cost of a rule change. The right-hand side relates directly to the domain of the ideal constitutional setting expressed in equation (4-10). When the opposition group finds it difficult to translate its losses under the rule change into political currency,[41] the domain of the public sector will tend to expand to include dimensions that are not appropriate to an ideal constitutional setting. The opposition group's difficulties in this translation arise when it is too large to efficiently organize ($n^o > n^{o^*}$) and when it cannot easily convert its members' contributions into political currency ($P_1^o < 0$). From the sufficient condition it is seen that

103

the proponent group must be more efficient in translating its gains into political currency than the opponent group. Its group size must be closer to its optimum (n^{p^*}) and/or it must be more efficient in converting cash into political currency $(P_1^p > P_1^o)$.

Thus, over time, the scope of government influence will tend to grow, if there are specific political resources. The new dimensions increasingly will be those not found in an ideal constitutional setting and increasingly embrace Hicks-Kaldor inefficient change. It will do so by concentrating the gains of a rule change and dispersing the costs as this is necessary to overcome the advantages of private market exchange, which does not permit Hicks-Kaldor-inefficiency. The public sector, with the passage of time, will increase its support for private monopolies (increased licensing) that concentrate benefits and disperse costs; it will support redistribution to narrowly defined interest groups through widespread taxation; and it will tend to favor business and trade groups that can promise future payments and that can more effectively police their members.

With the kind of evolution of the constitutional setting described here, the size and losses (but not the political influence) of the group opposed, for one reason or another, to the constitutional setting grows. Numbers and losses grow as more groups are forced to accept Hicks-Kaldor-inefficient changes. Political influence will not grow so long as the individuals identify only with their group. However, any event that discretely alters the parameters of the political payment and group contribution functions will cause a discrete change in political influence and in the constitutional setting. For example, it is not uncommon to find the seeds of a constitutional revolution among membership of an otherwise nonpolitical group (members of trade unions in the United States in the nineteenth century and in the 1980s in Poland, members of black churches in the 1960s, students in China and Eastern Europe, etc.). The opposition group, organized for another purpose, but sharing a common opposition to the existing constitutional setting, suddenly finds its organizational effectiveness enhanced by increased policing power and more effective peer pressure (M_1 and $P_1 M_2 + P_2$ increase). As the real world shows us, this can lead to a peaceful revolution (for example, the Glorious Revolution of 1688, the civil rights movement in the United States) or a violent one (for example, the American and French revolutions). In a violent revolution, the shift from peaceful change in the constitutional setting to forcible change alters the value of the number of members and the money resources of the group in securing constitutional change. In one case P_2 converts membership size into potential votes and P_1 converts money resources into advertising dollars and campaign contributions; in the other case P_2 converts size into potential troops and P_1 converts money into arms! The ratios P_2^p/P_2^o and P_1^p/P_1^o likely are not the same in peaceful and violent revolutions, and the opposition group can be expected to choose the more favorable form. In a dictatorship, where numbers (as votes) have little value, or a political regime that controls media access, opposition is more likely to lead to violent revolution. In a democracy, with free speech, change is more likely to be peaceful.

Following a constitutional revolution, the process begins once again. The demise of any rule space has its roots in the presence of specific political capital and differences in the abilities of interest groups to translate member desires into political currency. The Achilles' heel of democratic capitalism appears to be the voting rule that allows a redistributional tyranny of the majority of the active pressure groups over the remainder of the citizens and the reelection advantage (specific political capital) of incumbents.

Measures of Liberty

Measuring the amount of political and civil liberty available to citizens of countries throughout the world has been in the domain of political scientists. Early efforts were made by A. Banks and R. Textor, Robert Dahl, and R. P. Claude.[1] These early studies suffered from limitations on source material and in the comprehensiveness of the freedom measures and of the attributes that made up the indexes.

The most comprehensive measures available today are those constructed by Raymond Gastil. He has constructed indexes annually, since 1973, of political and civil rights for virtually all nations.[2] Political rights are ranked from 1 (highest degree of liberty) to 7 (the lowest), based on rankings of several subjective criteria. The criteria are the meaningfulness of elections for the executive and legislature as an expression of the will of the polity, election laws and campaigning opportunities, voting power of the electorate (electoral vote weighing), political competition (multiple political parties), evidence of political power shifting through elections, significant opposition voting, freedom from external and military control of domestic politics, minority self-determination or pluralism, decentralization of political power, and the attempt of political agents to reach a consensus on major national issues.[3] The measure of civil liberty, ranked on a similar scale, is based on rankings of such criteria as freedom of the press from political censorship, freedom of speech, freedom of assembly and peaceful demonstration, freedom to organize for political purposes, equal protection under the law, freedom from arbitrary search and seizure of property, an independent judiciary, freedom from arbitrary imprisonment, freedom from government terror and abuse, free trade unions and worker associations, free business and professional associations, freedom of religion, protected social rights (including freedom of property, internal and external travel, choice of residence, marriage, and family), socioeconomic rights (including freedom from dependency on landlords, bosses, union leaders, or bureaucrats), freedom from gross socioeconomic inequality, and freedom from gross government indifference or corruption.[4]

Charles Humana has developed ratings of human rights for nations based on conformity to the United Nations Universal Declaration of Human Rights, the International Covenant on Economic, Social and Cultural Rights, and the International Covenant on Civil and Political Rights.[5] His attributes of human rights include many of those considered by Gastil, but also include freedom from compulsory work permits or conscription of labor; freedom from capital punishment and corporal punishment; freedom from mail censorship or telephone tapping; political, legal, social, and economic equality for women and ethnic minorities; the right to free legal counsel; and freedom of personal rights (interracial marriage, equality of the sexes, use of contraception, homosexuality).

MEASURES OF POLITICAL AND CIVIL LIBERTY

Table 5-1 presents the average values and standard deviations of Gastil's measures of political and civil rights by country from 1973 to 1986. Broadly speaking, about 30 percent of the nations in the world have free political and legal institutions. About 35 percent of the nations in the world have no freedoms. The remainder of the nations in the world are partly free.

In table 5-2, countries are classified by type of economic system (capitalist or socialist) and type of government (multiparty political system or dictatorship). Capitalist systems range from those having a high percentage of private property, free enterprise, and free market systems to systems with a considerable government presence and control of the economy and to systems with some elements of socialism present in the basic capitalist structure. The range in the type of capitalist system is arrayed vertically in the table. The purest form of capitalism is at the top and the least pure at the bottom. Socialist systems similarly are arrayed from mixed (with some elements of capitalism) to pure forms.

Dictatorship is the most common form of government in the world. About three-quarters of the countries in the world are dictatorships. Dominant-party states, such as Malaysia, Taiwan, Mexico, etc., are classified as implicit dictatorships. All socialist countries are dictatorships. Government ownership of property and the allocation of resources by command and individual political choice are not compatible. The monopoly of power of the Communist Party (now weakened by the political reforms in part of the socialist bloc) and state ownership of property remain

TABLE 5-1

Mean Ratings of Political and Civil Liberty by Country, 1973–1986

Country	Political Liberty		Civil Liberty	
	Mean	St. Dev.	Mean	St. Dev.
Afghanistan	6.8	.8	6.5	.7
Albania	7.0	.0	7.0	.0
Algeria	6.1	.3	6.0	.0
Angola	6.8	.4	6.0	.0
Antigua and Barbuda	2.0	.0	2.6	.5
Argentina	4.2	2.0	4.6	2.4
Australia	1.0	.0	1.0	.0
Austria	1.0	.0	1.0	.0
Bahamas	1.4	.5	2.0	.0
Bahrain	5.4	.7	4.5	5
Bangladesh	4.6	1.7	4.2	.7
Barbados	1.0	.0	1.2	.4
Belgium	1.0	.0	1.0	.0
Belize	1.2	.4	1.8	.4
Benin	7.0	.0	6.5	.7
Bhutan	4.5	.5	4.5	.5
Bolivia	4.5	2.0	3.8	.9
Botswana	2.1	.3	3.1	.3
Brazil	3.7	.8	4.2	2.5
Brunei	6.0	.0	5.0	.0
Burkina Faso	5.2	1.8	4.5	1.0
Burma	6.8	.4	5.7	1.4
Burundi	6.8	.6	6.2	.4
Cambodia	6.8	.4	6.8	.6
Cameroon	6.1	.3	5.5	1.1
Canada	1.0	.0	1.0	.0
Cape Verde	5.8	.4	6.0	.6
Central African Republic	7.0	.0	6.3	.8
Chad	6.7	.5	6.4	.5
Chile	5.9	1.6	4.8	.8
China (P.R.)	6.3	.5	6.2	.6
China (R.)	5.2	.4	4.9	.5
Colombia	2.0	.0	2.8	.4
Comoro Islands	4.5	1.1	4.1	1.3
Congo	6.5	.9	6.2	.4
Costa Rica	1.0	.0	1.0	.0
Cuba	6.4	.5	6.2	.4

TABLE 5-1, *cont.*

Country	Political Liberty		Civil Liberty	
	Mean	*St. Dev.*	*Mean*	*St. Dev.*
Cyprus (G)	2.3	1.2	3.1	1.0
Cyprus (T)	3.4	.9	3.0	.0
Czechoslavakia	7.0	.0	6.2	.4
Denmark	1.0	.0	1.0	.0
Djibouti	3.2	1.3	4.2	1.4
Dominica	2.0	.0	2.4	0.5
Dominican Republic	2.4	1.3	2.5	.5
Ecuador	4.0	2.3	3.2	1.3
Egypt	5.1	.6	4.6	.8
El Salvador	3.4	1.3	3.8	.8
Equatorial Guinea	6.7	.5	6.5	.5
Ethiopia	6.8	.6	6.6	.7
Fiji	2.0	.0	2.0	.0
Finland	2.0	.0	2.0	.0
France	1.0	.0	1.8	.4
Gabon	6.0	.0	6.0	.0
Gambia	2.4	.5	2.8	1.0
Germany, East	7.0	.0	6.7	.5
Germany, West	1.0	.0	1.6	.5
Ghana	5.7	1.8	4.8	1.1
Greece	2.1	1.3	2.3	1.1
Grenada	3.3	1.8	3.8	1.1
Guatemala	4.1	1.2	4.3	1.3
Guinea	7.0	.0	6.5	.9
Guinea-Bissau	6.2	.4	6.1	.3
Guyana	4.1	1.0	3.8	1.0
Haiti	6.5	.7	5.8	.6
Honduras	4.5	1.9	3.0	.0
Hungary	5.8	.4	5.3	.5
Iceland	1.0	.0	1.0	.0
India	2.0	.0	3.4	1.2
Indonesia	5.0	.0	5.2	.4
Iran	5.5	.5	5.8	.4
Iraq	6.8	.4	6.9	.3
Ireland	1.0	.0	1.2	.4
Israel	2.0	.0	2.4	.5
Italy	1.3	.5	1.6	.5

TABLE 5-1, *cont.*

Country	Political Liberty		Civil Liberty	
	Mean	*St. Dev.*	*Mean*	*St. Dev.*
Ivory Coast	5.8	.4	5.2	.4
Jamaica	1.7	.5	2.8	.4
Japan	1.5	.5	1.0	.0
Jordan	5.8	.4	5.8	.4
Kenya	5.2	.4	4.6	.5
Kiribati	1.7	.5	2.0	.0
Korea, North	7.0	.0	7.0	.0
Korea, South	4.8	.4	5.5	.5
Kuwait	4.9	1.0	3.9	.6
Laos	6.6	.8	6.6	.8
Lebanon	4.0	1.0	3.7	.8
Lesotho	5.2	.6	4.5	.5
Liberia	5.8	.4	4.8	.9
Libya	6.4	.5	6.2	.4
Luxembourg	1.3	.5	1.0	.0
Madagascar	5.3	.5	5.2	.9
Malawi	6.4	.5	6.5	.5
Malaysia	2.9	.3	4.1	.6
Maldives	4.5	.8	4.4	1.2
Mali	7.0	.0	6.3	0.5
Malta	1.7	.5	2.6	1.1
Mauritania	6.4	.7	6.0	.0
Mauritius	2.2	.4	2.5	.9
Mexico	3.7	.6	3.7	.5
Mongolia	7.0	.0	7.0	.0
Morocco	4.2	.7	4.5	.7
Mozambique	6.6	.5	6.8	.4
Nauru	2.0	.0	2.0	.0
Nepal	4.5	1.5	4.5	.5
Netherlands	1.0	.0	1.0	.0
New Zealand	1.0	.0	1.0	.0
Nicaragua	5.1	.5	4.8	.7
Niger	6.9	.3	6.0	.0
Nigeria	4.8	2.1	3.9	.9
Norway	1.0	.0	1.0	.0
Oman	6.2	.4	6.0	.0
Pakistan	5.3	1.5	5.0	.4
Panama	5.6	1.2	5.0	.4
Papua New Guinea	2.3	.6	2.0	.0

TABLE 5-1, *cont.*

Country	Political Liberty		Civil Liberty	
	Mean	St. Dev.	Mean	St. Dev.
Paraguay	4.9	.3	5.2	.4
Peru	4.1	2.1	3.8	.9
Philippines	4.7	.5	4.6	1.0
Poland	5.9	.3	5.2	.7
Portugal	5.2	.4	5.0	.0
Qatar	5.0	.0	5.0	.0
Romania	7.0	.0	6.2	.4
Rwanda	6.4	.5	5.6	.5
St. Kitts-Nevis	1.8	.4	2.5	.9
St. Lucia	1.8	.4	2.6	.5
St. Vincent	2.0	.0	2.0	.0
São Tomé and Principe	6.0	.8	5.9	.9
Saudi Arabia	6.0	.0	6.3	.5
Senegal	4.5	1.2	4.0	.8
Seychelles	4.8	2.0	4.3	1.8
Sierra Leone	5.2	.7	5.0	.0
Singapore	4.6	.5	5.0	.0
Solomons	2.4	.8	2.2	.4
Somalia	7.0	.0	6.8	.4
South Africa	4.8	.5	5.8	.5
Spain	2.6	1.7	3.1	1.4
Sri Lanka	2.3	.5	3.3	.6
Sudan	5.5	.7	5.5	.5
Suriname	4.2	2.4	3.7	1.9
Swaziland	5.3	.6	4.7	1.1
Sweden	1.0	.0	1.0	1.0
Switzerland	1.0	.0	.0	.0
Syria	5.7	.6	6.5	.5
Tanzania	6.0	.0	6.0	.0
Thailand	4.2	1.6	4.0	.9
Togo	6.8	.4	5.9	.3
Tonga	4.9	.3	2.9	.3
Transkei	5.2	.4	5.7	.5
Trinidade and Tobago	1.7	.5	2.1	.3
Tunisia	5.7	.5	5.0	.0
Turkey	2.9	1.1	3.9	1.0
Tuvala	1.7	.5	1.9	.3
Uganda	5.8	1.2	5.8	1.2
USSR	6.5	.5	6.5	.5

TABLE 5-1, *cont.*

Country	Political Liberty		Civil Liberty	
	Mean	St. Dev.	Mean	St. Dev.
United Arab Republic	5.3	.6	5.0	.0
United Kingdom	1.0	.0	1.0	.0
United States	1.0	.0	1.0	.0
Uruguay	4.7	1.4	4.6	1.4
Vanuatu	2.8	.8	3.3	.5
Venezuela	1.2	.4	2.0	.0
Vietnam	7.0	.0	6.8	.4
Western Samoa	4.0	.0	2.5	.5
Yemen Arab Republic	5.5	.7	4.8	.4
Yemen, South	6.5	.5	7.0	.0
Yugoslavia	6.0	.0	5.3	.5
Zaire	6.6	.5	6.2	.4
Zambia	5.0	.0	5.2	.6
Zimbabwe	4.7	1.2	5.1	.5

Source: Calculated from data in Raymond D. Gastil, *Freedom in the World* (Westport, Conn.: Greenwood Press, 1987), 54–65.

in the Soviet Union and the People's Republic of China. The reform movement in Eastern Europe beginning in 1989 (earlier in Poland), which has overthrown the monopoly of the Communist Party, promises a movement away from complete government ownership of property and command allocation of resources. Where the reforms will lead in the restructuring of the constitutional setting is unpredictable. It is doubtful that the popular pressure for a veer to the right on the institutional spectrum will move these systems much beyond some form of democratic socialism. While the prospects of private property, market allocation of resources, and the rule of law in these former socialist states promise an expansion of the opportunity set for the citizens, government subsidies in housing, health care, transportation, food staples, and other cradle-to-grave welfare policies are hard to give up. Multiparty political systems in which there is credible political competition are found mainly in capitalist systems. Predominantly these nations are characterized by private property, free enterprise, and free markets. About 40 percent of the capitalist countries have multiparty political systems. The remaining capitalist countries, dominated by a significant presence of the government in the economy, are dictatorships.

TABLE 5-2
Countries Classified by Political-Economic Systems

Capitalist Economic System						
Multiparty Political System			Dictatorship			
Antigua and Barbuda	Iceland	Australia	Malaysia	Dijibouti	Chile	Jordan
Bahamas	Ireland	Belgium			Suriname	Western Samoa
Barbados	Japan	Canada				
Belize	South Korea	West Germany				
Colombia	Luxembourg	Lebanon				
Costa Rica	Mauritius	Switzerland				
Cyprus (G)	New Zealand	United States				
Cyprus (T)	St. Kitts-Nevis					
Dominica	St. Lucia					
Dominican Republic	St. Vincent					
El Salvador		Spain				
Ecuador	Thailand	Botswana	Liberia	Cameroon	Chad	Bhutan
Fiji		Papua New Guinea	Transkei	Comoro Islands	Haiti	Maldive
Gambia		Solomons		Gabon	Lesotho	Nepal
Guatemala				Ivory Coast	Niger	Swaziland
Honduras				Kenya	Yemen Arab Republic	Tonga
				Malawi		Tuvalu
Argentina	Sri Lanka	Brazil	China (R.)	Sierra Leone	Ghana	Bahrain
Grenada	Turkey	Trinidad and Tobago	Mexico		Nigeria	Brunei
Italy	Venezuela					Kuwait
Jamaica	Panama					Nauru
South Africa						Qatar
						Saudi Arabia
Bolivia		India	Bangladesh	Zaire	Central African Republic	United Arab Republic
Morocco		Vanuatu	Indonesia		Equatorial Guinea	Kiribat
Pakistan			Iran		Mauritania	Oman
Peru			Paraguay		Uganda	
			Philippines			
Austria	Netherlands		Egypt	Burundi	Guinea	
Denmark	Norway		Nicaragua			

TABLE 5-2, *cont.*

Capitalist Economic System			
Multiparty Political System		*Dictatorship*	
Finland	Portugal	Senegal	
France	Sudan	Singapore	
Greece	Sweden	Tunisia	
Israel	United King-	Zimbabwe	
	dom		
Malta	Uruguay		

Socialist Economic System				
Guyana	Libya	China (P.R.)		
Syria	Seychelles	Poland		
		Yugoslavia		
Madagascar	Burma		Mali	Burkina Faso
	Cape Verde		Rwanda	
	Congo		Togo	
	Somalia			
	Zambia			
	Algeria	Albania	Hungary	
	São Tomé	Bulgaria	North Korea	
		Cuba	Mongolia	
	Angola	Czechoslo-	Romania	
		vakia		
Benin	East Germany		USSR	
	Guinea-Bissau		Vietnam	
	Iraq	Afghanistan		
	Mozambique	Cambodia		
	Tanzania	Ethiopia		
	Southern	Laos		
	Yemen			

Source: Raymond D. Gastil, *Freedom in the World* (Westport, Conn.: Greenwood Press, 1987), pp. 74–75.

Comparisons between Gastil and Humana Freedom Measures

How descriptive of the actual levels of personal freedom among countries is the Gastil ranking of political (civil) rights? What freedoms do these rankings measure? The reliability of the Gastil rankings can be verified by a comparison with rankings of various human rights originated and compiled by Humana. Apparently, Humana's main concern is in measuring signatory compliance with the United Nations Declaration of the Rights of Man. Humana codes adherence to thirty more or less separate rights on a

TABLE 5-3

Correlations between Gastil and Humana Freedom Measures

Freedom or Right	(1)	(2)	(3)	(4)
1. Of internal migration	−.4946	−4.44	−.5771	−5.52
2. Of emigration	−.6010	−5.87	−.6868	−7.38
3. From nationality removal	−.3487	−2.91	−.4306	−3.73
4. To seek/teach ideas	−.6752	−7.15	−.7557	−9.01
5. From forced labor	−.5566	−5.23	−.5829	−5.60
6. Of political opposition	−.7727	−9.51	−.8615	−13.25
7. Of assembly	−.7141	−7.97	−.8170	−11.07
8. Of sex equality	−.4915	−4.41	−.5405	−5.02
9. From state-directed work	−.3617	−3.03	−.3382	−2.81
10. Of choice in marriage	−.0930	−.73	−.1525	−1.21
11. Of religion	−.4256	−3.67	−.4800	−4.27
12. From ideology in school	−.3576	−2.99	−.4227	−3.64
13. From press censorship	−.7351	−8.47	−.8438	−12.28
14. From arrest without charge	−.6207	−6.18	−.7533	−8.95
15. From search without warrant	−.5071	−4.60	−.6579	−6.82
16. From torture/coercion	−.5973	−5.82	−.7207	−8.12
17. Of innocence at trial	−.5452	−5.08	−.6742	−7.13
18. Of speedy trial	−.6801	−7.25	−.7325	−8.40
19. Of independent judiciary	−.6446	−6.58	−.7207	−8.12
20. From secret trials	−.6035	−5.91	−.7133	−7.95
21. For free trade unions	−.7367	−8.51	−.8455	−12.37
22. From mail censorship	−.6117	−6.04	−.7190	−8.08
23. Of ethnic publication	−.3241	−2.68	−.3578	−2.99
24. Of artistic expression	−.4850	−4.33	−.5145	−4.69
25. From military conscription	−.0435	−.34	−.0979	−.77
26. To consume alcohol	−.2468	−1.99	−.2657	−2.15
27. For adult homosexuality	−.4891	−4.38	−.5041	−4.56
28. To use contraception	−.0268	−.21	−.0123	−.10
29. Of early abortion	−.3930	−3.34	−.4429	−3.86
30. Of divorce (sex equality)	−.2196	−1.76	−.2597	−2.10

Legend: (1) = correlation POLLIB; (2) = Student-*t* POLLIB; (3) = correlation CIVLIB; (4) = Student-*t* CIVLIB.

scale from zero (the lowest level of freedom) to 3 (the highest). These freedoms or rights are listed in table 5-3, along with the simple correlation coefficients and Student-*t* values obtained by regressing them on Gastil's ranking of political liberty (POLLIB) and his ranking of civil liberty (CIVLIB). The Humana data are available for sixty-three countries. Some twenty-five of Humana's separate rankings of human rights are statistically associated with Gastil's ranking of political liberty at the 95 percent level of significance, while twenty-seven out of thirty are statistically associated with the ranking of civil liberty. These statistical results may be interpreted as rather firm support for the accuracy of Gastil's description of the actual levels of political and civil freedoms found in nations throughout the world. No matter how one ranks these thirty freedoms, assuming one is predisposed to ranking preferences for freedoms, and weights the freedoms to construct an overall measure of freedom, the rankings will be related to Gastil's political liberty and civil liberty rankings. These results are reassuring, since it means that Gastil broadly has measured what many would agree is freedom.

While the Gastil freedom measures have gained widespread acceptance among scholars, they are subject to criticism because they do not distinguish between natural (negative) and human (positive) rights. Negative rights are those that freely constituted societies reserve for themselves exclusively, denying the government any, or giving it little, power to interfere. These are the individual rights articulated in the Constitution of the United States and in the Bill of Rights. Human rights are those rights granted by the government to all or some individuals at the expense of other individuals. Being redistributive in character, positive rights interfere with and diminish negative rights. The government cannot simultaneously protect individual freedom and inject its coercive power to redistribute income from one group to another deemed more worthy. The justification for positive rights and the concomitant circumspection of negative rights is that sovereignty rests with the political majority. Many political scientists believe in the notion of majoritarianism, as an ethical principal of sovereignty. Under majority rule individual rights are determined in a political market, where vote-maximizing politicians aggregate coalitions (special interests) to get elected and remain in office. Liberty as understood by classical liberals loses its meaning when individual rights are allocated in a political market, subject to the will of the majority.

MEASURING ECONOMIC LIBERTY

Particular skepticism has been expressed about Gastil's measures of economic liberty.[6] The measure is the average of four subindices of economic freedom: (1) the right to private property; (2) the right to freedom of association; (3) the right to freedom of internal and external travel; and,

(4) the right to information. The four subindices of economic freedom are based on certain characteristics that purport to measure an aspect of the subindices of freedom. The index of the right to private property is based on information about the extent of nationalized and state industries, self-management of enterprise, the incidence of state farms, land reform, ownership and control of capital, taxes, social services, and income distribution. Freedom of association includes not only the right of assembly, but the right to form trade unions and business associations or cartels. Freedom of association, so measured, is freedom to collude to redistribute income, hardly a classic, negative right. The right to freedom of travel includes not only the freedom of internal travel (freedom from forced resettlement, job relocation, forced labor, work permits) and external travel (freedom from exit visa fees, etc.), but also the degree of discrimination and socioeconomic mobility in society. The right to information mainly measures freedom of the media, but includes such attributes as regulation of the economy through price controls, subsidies, and minimum wage.

Alvin Rabushka has argued that a quantitative measure of economic liberty needs to be much more comprehensive in scope and more precise in definition of the attributes that aggregate to an overall measure than is found in the Gastil measure.[7] He would include the right to private property, including freedom of contract, the rule of law (equal protection under the law, an independent judiciary, etc.), the size of the government or its command of resources, public spending, economic regulation of business and labor, the monetary framework and monetary policy, and commercial policy (free versus restricted trade).

In addition to the problem of definition and scope, there is the problem of weighing the attributes to construct an overall measure of economic liberty. Past measures of economic liberty have either adopted the egalitarian standard of equal weighing (a social welfare function that treats each right as of equal utility or preference) of the attributes or involved the researcher's imposing his own standard of relative importance of the attributes.[8]

The purpose here is to construct some aggregate indices of economic liberty and to demonstrate how relative rankings of liberty across countries will vary, contingent on how relative information about liberty, from individual liberty indicators, is aggregated and weighted. This approach is essentially a sensitivity analysis demonstrating how world rankings of liberty vary as the information from several liberty indicators is summarized into one index.

ATTRIBUTES OF ECONOMIC LIBERTY

The objective is to measure economic liberty as comprehensively as possible with available data for as many countries as possible. These objectives force the exclusion of a number of attributes of economic liberty that are important but not widely available. A total of fifteen attributes of economic liberty met the criteria of being credible (that is, essentially natural rights) and being available for a large number of countries. These attributes are listed in table 5-4. The data for these attributes appears in appendix 5-2.

Attribute L1 is the Foreign Exchange Regime (available from *Pick's Currency Yearbook*, which has been renamed as *World Currency Yearbook*). The foreign currency regime is coded as follows: 1 = free; 2 = liberal; 3 = strict; and 4 = dictatorial. These ratings characterize the degree of government control of international financial transfers and the relationship between official exchange rates and market, shadow exchange rates. Since foreign exchange policy is correlated with commercial policy, the measure crudely captures the degree to which the citizens of the home country are permitted to face world prices for commodities. Attribute L2 is Military Draft Freedom, coded 1 to 5.[9] Conscription is a tax on liberty and the probablistic taking of life. Attributes L3, L4, and L5 are Gastil's measures of freedom of property, freedom of movement, and freedom of information. Attribute L6 is the Civil Right index, a measure of the rule of law, coded 1 to 7. Attribute L7 is the Gastil classification of type of economic system, ranging from capitalist inclusive = 1 to socialist nonexclusive = 9. It measures the degree of individual versus government control of property and reliance on the market for the allocation of resources. Attributes L8 and L9 are the freedom of the print and broadcast media, respectively, are coded 1 to 3, and represent the degree of competition in the marketplace for ideas.[10] Attributes L10 to L15 are from Humana, are coded 1 to 4, and are, respectively, freedom to travel domestically, freedom to travel abroad, the right to peaceful assembly, permit not required for work, freedom from public search without a warrant, and freedom from the arbitrary seizure of property.[11] For all of the attributes 1 is free and the highest value represents the least amount of freedom.

There are a sufficient number of attributes employed here over the range of possible states of economic liberty to expect countries to be correctly classified as economically free, partly free, or not free, no matter what weighing technique is employed to aggregate the attributes into a

TABLE 5-4

Attributes of Economic Liberty

Symbol	Description
L1	Freedom of the foreign currency regime, coded 1 to 4
L2	Freedom from military draft, coded 1 to 5
L3	Freedom of property, coded 1 to 5
L4	Freedom of movement, coded 1 to 5
L5	Freedom of information, coded 1 to 5
L6	Gastil's civil rights index, coded 1 to 7
L7	Gastil-Wright classification of type of economic system, coded 1 to 9
L8	Freedom of the print media, coded 1 to 3
L9	Freedom of the broadcast media, coded 1 to 3
L10	Freedom of internal travel, coded 1 to 4
L11	Freedom of external or foreign travel, coded 1 to 4
L12	Freedom of peaceful assembly, coded 1 to 4
L13	Freedom from work permits, coded 1 to 4
L14	Freedom from search without a warrant, coded 1 to 4
L15	Freedom from arbitrary seizure of property, coded 1 to 4

Note: For all attributes 1 is free, and the highest value represents the last amount of freedom.

Sources: See text.

single index. Examination of appendix 5-2 verifies this statement (for example, the United States has an average value of the fifteen attributes of 1.0 (the developed Western nations generally are in the interval of 1.0 to 2.0, for the average), while the Soviet Union has an average of 4.33 (Eastern bloc countries generally have average values of 4.0 or higher). But the set of attributes is not rich enough to make very fine distinctions within these crude categories of economic freedom. For example, the average for Hong Kong is 1.27, compared to 1.0 for the United States. Many observers would rank economic liberty in Hong Kong as higher than in the U.S. The average for Taiwan is 2.53, compared to 2.0 for Mexico. Many would rank economic liberty in Mexico as considerably lower than in Taiwan. Similar anomalies arise from a perusal of the data in the table. As a result of the crudity of the data on the attributes of economic liberty, it should come as no surprise that anomalies of rankings of economic liberty are going to arise. The more that we demand fine distinctions between countries on the degree of economic liberty, the greater will be our disappointment. If we are satisfied with a coarser degree of intercountry comparison, which is proper, given the crudity of the data on the attributes, we will be less disappointed. The measures of economic liberty presented here are the best available in the literature, given the crudeness of the data used to construct them.

WEIGHING THE ATTRIBUTES OF ECONOMIC LIBERTY INDICES

In the construction of indices of liberty, the current practice is to weight each attribute equally. By this egalitarian standard, freedom of property, freedom to form trade unions and other collusive associations, due process of law, the military draft, capital punishment, and so on, are rights of equal preference in a citizen's utility function. Rights are logically separable and may or may not be lexicographically ranked by individuals. If it were possible to rank rights lexicographically in a social welfare function, weights based on the relative rankings of the attributes of liberty could be employed to construct an overall measure of liberty. Of course, this approach is not possible. An alternative is for the researcher to impose his own ranking on the relative importance of rights, but this is ad hoc. There are two objective methods of weighing the attributes of liberty in constructing an overall index of liberty. One method is to weight the attributes by the variance in the attributes. This is the method of principal components analysis. This technique has the feature that the normality assumptions in statistical theory are invoked. A second method is to use an instrumental variable or hedonic approach and weight by the regression coefficients. This technique has the feature that the regression coefficient of the liberty attribute on the instrumental variable (say, per capita income) measures the implicit value assigned to the attribute. These are the techniques employed here in the construction of overall indices of economic liberty.

In the last section the individual economic freedom measures that others have used to examine economic liberty were described. In this section a multidimensional representation of economic liberty is presented, by combining the information from several different individual measures into a class of aggregate liberty indices. As with the construction of any aggregate index, the critical step in combining various attributes into a single summary measure is the choice of appropriate weights. Since the index is a representation of a multidimensional view of a given country's level of economic liberty, several indices that all represent different unidimensional capsulizations are utilized. There are many ways to aggregate information into one broad index. One strategy is suggested by the social choice and income inequality literature. This body of research can be extended to this work by examining the relative ranking of economic liberty between countries. Absolute notions of liberty become meaningless when the absolute metric is based upon an index derived from a vector of characteristics that all purport to measure a different aspect of the same problem. Maasoumi and Nickelsburg and others have used principal components analysis to compare the quality of life between countries.[12] This is a statistical technique, which relies solely on the variation and covariation of the data matrix to construct the weights in the indices.

Griliches has suggested that if there is one attribute which we desire to analyze, but cannot observe directly, such as the level of economic liberty in a country, we can use a hedonic model to see how other factors affect this variable.[13] This generally implies that some variable is used as an instrument for the latent variable and then one can see how other characteristics affect this instrumental variable. Frank is the leader of a new school of economists, who argue that it is the relative levels that matter in the utility economic agents derive from consuming goods.[14] This argument is extended to economic liberty by suggesting that it is relative rankings between countries, given a set of liberty indicators, that have the richest information content in comparing liberty between countries.

Here all of these approaches are used in constructing the economic liberty measures and in comparing the level of economic freedom between countries. Several different measures are constructed where the weights are alternatively determined by ranks of attributes, principal components of the attributes, and a hedonic representation of the attributes. The relative rankings are presented for each index to serve as a sensitivity analysis of the different weighing specifications. Finally, the average rank is taken for each country over all the different indices as the final index of economic freedom. In appendix 5-3 each country is ranked from the lowest level (more liberty) to the highest level of economic freedom for each attribute. These ranks can be used directly as indices. In table 5-5 the average rank is taken across all fifteen attributes for each country given in appendix 5-3, and then these averages are ranked. This is the first liberty index and is called RINDEX1. Also, information about the ranks can be used as the weighing factors, as is discussed below.

TABLE 5-5
Summary of the Eight Liberty Indexes and Overall Index

Obs.	Country	RINDEX1	RINDEX2	RINDEX3	RINDEX4	RINDEX5	RINDEX6	RINDEX7	RINDEX8	INDEX
1	Afghanistan	134	136	111	101	92	113	122	101	116
2	Albania	141	141	140	139	137	124	140	137	142
3	Algeria	114	112	125	95	94	131	118	114	114
4	Angola	139	140	139	137	135	136	139	135	143
5	Argentina	59	51	53	47	38	14	43	40	42
6	Australia	9	13	25	15	17	21	10	13	14
7	Austria	24	10	9	10	6	34	8	5	12
8	Bahamas	13	18	8	13	13	28	12	15	13
9	Bahrain	74	83	20	18	20	12	54	38	39
10	Bangladesh	76	73	97	92	102	97	75	97	86
11	Barbados	19	17	11	14	12	4	12	12	10
12	Belgium	14	5	10	5	3	3	1	4	5
13	Beldize	16	24	60	36	42	42	32	27	32
14	Benin	117	117	85	102	95	143	81	107	110
15	Bolivia	64	55	21	19	15	9	37	20	24
16	Botswana	32	36	71	56	57	57	48	56	52
17	Brazil	46	44	47	41	36	30	35	37	37
18	Bulgaria	141	141	140	139	137	124	140	137	140
19	Burkina Faso	94	87	98	87	91	123	108	90	98
20	Burma	127	130	122	118	121	139	130	124	130
21	Burundi	84	96	107	99	100	112	90	110	100
22	Cameroon	102	102	80	126	118	134	119	127	115
23	Canada	6	7	5	3	7	19	1	6	6
24	Cape Verde	93	89	101	119	123	138	101	128	112
25	Central African Republic	88	77	57	78	75	103	67	82	77
26	Chad	110	122	72	130	128	141	111	133	124
27	Chile	82	79	59	64	60	77	56	64	67
28	China	126	126	91	83	80	83	112	87	99
29	Colombia	54	50	44	80	74	58	73	70	62
30	Congo	105	108	73	106	103	121	86	103	101
31	Costa Rica	8	11	27	21	23	24	17	18	15
32	Cuba	131	129	137	76	77	69	102	84	102
33	Cyprus	47	45	70	84	89	82	72	65	70
34	Czechoslovakia	135	134	138	107	106	85	126	102	120
35	Denmark	29	23	36	24	21	37	22	17	19
36	Dominican Republic	12	16	30	31	34	33	26	32	20
37	Dominica	31	37	34	40	45	36	31	46	34
38	Ecuador	52	46	52	32	28	10	24	34	31
39	Egypt	79	76	77	68	59	32	63	57	64
40	El Salvador	77	75	114	93	86	40	85	81	81
41	Ethiopia	136	135	127	123	119	119	133	121	131

TABLE 5-5, *cont.*

Obs.	Country	RINDEX1	RINDEX2	RINDEX3	RINDEX4	RINDEX5	RINDEX6	RINDEX7	RINDEX8	INDEX
42	Fiji	21	19	29	29	33	45	20	23	21
43	Finland	22	29	33	25	30	56	25	23	25
44	France	41	40	48	26	22	27	21	21	26
45	Gabon	51	61	42	73	72	95	65	86	68
46	Gambia	44	43	35	48	51	72	45	50	50
47	West Germany	5	6	6	16	14	29	12	15	11
48	East Germany	133	131	135	105	105	96	126	106	123
49	Great Britain	27	26	64	34	39	63	30	26	35
50	Greece	38	35	51	35	29	11	29	22	28
51	Grenada	100	85	92	69	69	70	84	62	78
52	Guatemala	60	57	19	86	79	81	74	74	65
53	Guinea	122	123	130	111	116	101	125	108	122
54	Guyana	106	99	115	134	134	128	120	126	126
55	Haiti	96	95	61	109	107	104	93	111	96
56	Hong Kong	20	20	7	1	1	2	11	3	8
57	Honduras	45	41	39	72	68	65	66	61	59
58	Hungary	121	119	124	70	66	80	82	69	92
59	Iceland	11	8	55	37	43	43	32	27	30
60	India	58	59	89	60	65	79	59	66	66
61	Indonesia	90	81	67	112	109	106	103	109	97
62	Iran	120	109	117	90	90	84	114	89	104
63	Iraq	132	128	129	127	124	107	135	123	129
64	Ireland	3	1	1	5	8	15	1	6	1
65	Israel	53	47	58	51	40	6	44	30	40
66	Italy	37	33	75	44	48	38	46	31	44
67	Ivory Coast	65	62	46	82	84	92	71	79	73
68	Jamaica	40	48	79	59	62	64	58	59	61
69	Japan	8	11	27	21	23	24	17	18	16
70	Jordan	75	82	49	46	50	20	76	54	57
71	Kenya	61	63	82	94	101	91	89	96	83
72	South Korea	66	72	88	103	108	90	94	100	89
73	North Korea	143	139	144	138	136	109	140	136	139
74	Kuwait	69	66	18	2	5	13	16	14	18
75	Laos	128	132	131	133	141	127	136	142	138
76	Lebanon	49	56	14	61	58	67	57	63	55
77	Liberia	78	80	24	88	81	87	77	83	76
78	Libya	119	114	116	115	117	114	124	116	121
79	Liechtenstein	3	1	1	5	8	15	1	6	3
80	Luxembourg	3	1	1	5	8	15	1	6	2
81	Madagascar	109	116	109	125	127	120	107	119	118
82	Malawi	99	103	103	100	104	135	80	113	108
83	Malasia	56	65	45	42	47	71	38	58	54
84	Mali	101	101	69	117	112	122	100	115	107

TABLE 5-5, *cont.*

Obs.	Country	RINDEX1	RINDEX2	RINDEX3	RINDEX4	RINDEX5	RINDEX6	RINDEX7	RINDEX8	INDEX
85	Mauritania	108	106	112	143	143	132	129	140	132
86	Mauritius	15	22	31	28	32	35	26	32	22
87	Mexico	48	53	17	50	46	60	42	52	48
88	Mongolia	141	141	140	139	137	124	140	137	141
89	Morocco	83	78	94	67	73	78	92	80	79
90	Mozambique	125	125	132	129	132	142	137	141	136
91	Nepal	68	69	87	65	70	59	62	71	69
92	Netherlands	28	15	15	10	4	5	8	2	9
93	New Zealand	11	8	55	37	43	43	32	27	29
94	Niger	89	92	54	97	97	110	83	98	88
95	Nigeria	50	54	83	74	82	94	68	85	75
96	Norway	30	21	43	20	18	8	15	11	17
97	Oman	95	97	26	27	27	66	64	53	58
98	Pakistan	82	90	99	114	114	99	110	113	106
99	Panama	39	42	13	23	26	39	19	36	23
100	Papua New Guinea	25	30	65	55	56	52	51	48	49
101	Paraguay	72	71	76	57	52	68	52	60	63
102	Peru	62	52	95	85	85	53	78	72	74
103	Philippines	71	70	90	110	111	86	99	93	90
104	Poland	123	121	133	75	76	62	98	73	95
105	Portugal	42	38	86	62	63	41	61	51	56
106	Qatar	85	94	23	17	19	23	54	38	45
107	Romania	137	137	136	120	120	111	131	122	133
108	Rwanda	116	113	104	91	96	118	113	91	109
109	Saudi Arabia	103	105	32	49	49	88	79	76	72
110	Senegal	43	49	41	63	64	73	60	67	60
111	Seychelles	130	133	123	122	126	133	132	132	135
112	Sierra Leone	58	64	50	104	99	93	95	95	82
113	Singapore	71	68	37	52	37	54	47	45	51
114	Somalia	130	133	123	122	126	133	132	132	135
115	South Africa	129	127	126	89	88	50	115	94	105
116	USSR	144	144	134	142	142	140	144	143	144
117	Spain	35	32	81	53	53	22	49	43	47
118	Sri Lanka	55	60	84	77	83	74	70	77	71
119	St. Lucia	18	28	62	45	54	46	39	44	41
120	St. Vincent	17	31	63	54	55	47	49	48	46
121	Sudan	87	91	110	131	131	129	123	131	119
122	Suriname	115	110	121	135	130	98	121	125	125
123	Swaziland	91	98	96	128	129	100	116	130	111
124	Sweden	26	25	40	43	41	55	40	47	38
125	Switzerland	23	14	16	3	2	1	1	1	7
126	Syria	112	115	78	124	122	137	106	129	117
127	Taiwan	67	67	68	30	25	26	23	41	43

TABLE 5-5, *cont.*

Obs.	Country	RINDEX1	RINDEX2	RINDEX3	RINDEX4	RINDEX5	RINDEX6	RINDEX7	RINDEX8	INDEX
128	Tanzania	124	124	120	121	125	130	128	118	128
129	Thailand	63	58	93	113	110	51	109	92	85
130	Togo	93	100	66	98	98	117	86	103	94
131	Trinidad	33	34	74	58	61	49	53	55	53
132	Tunisia	73	74	106	79	78	89	69	78	80
133	Turkey	97	86	118	96	93	61	91	88	91
134	Uganda	118	118	128	132	140	116	117	117	127
135	United Arab Emirates	80	84	22	12	16	7	41	35	33
136	United States	3	1	1	5	8	15	1	6	4
137	Vanuatu	36	39	12	39	35	75	36	42	36
138	Venezuela	34	27	38	33	31	31	28	25	27
139	Vietnam	138	138	143	136	133	108	138	134	137
140	Yemen Arab Republic	111	120	102	66	71	48	96	75	84
141	Yugoslavia	113	107	119	71	67	76	88	68	87
142	Zaire	107	104	108	144	144	144	134	144	134
143	Zambia	87	93	105	108	113	105	97	105	103
144	Zimbabwe	98	88	100	81	87	102	104	99	93

Principal components analysis can be used in several different ways in constructing the indices of economic liberty.[15] Since each principal component is a linear combination of the original attributes, the components themselves can be used as indices. The first component is a linear combination of the attribute values with maximum variance, so it can be calculated. The same thing can be done for all of the components, and when this was done, it was found that the first five components contained 90 percent of the variation. In table 5-5, the ranks for each country based upon their respective first principal component are presented. This is RINDEX2. Only one component is reported, because this component contains 60 percent of the total variation in the attribute data, and the other principal components do not have a strong economic interpretation. While this is a statistical procedure, and perhaps not an economically intuitive one, it still is instructive. It suggests that if the fifteen variables are reasonable indicators of liberty, they can be combined in such a way that different combinations of them create fifteen new variables, which contain as much information as the original fifteen, but without any multicollinearity problems. If one were to rely on any one of them (say the first one), then the coefficients represent the weights that give maximum variance. One is constructed for each country, and then ranked. Thus a country, such as the United States or Luxembourg, that has relatively low attribute values and low variances across all attributes consequently will have a small first principal component, which will rank that country first. A country with a large amount of variation across attributes and large attribute values (low levels of economic freedom) will have larger component values. As one moves to higher-order principal components, one gets different ranking results, since the variance is now only that which is left after filtering out the first principal component. For this reason, only the first component rankings are presented in table 5-5. The principal components can also be used directly as weights. This is done in the construction of RINDEX3, by using the principal component multiplied by the attribute. This result is reported in the table as well. These results are discussed in the empirical section. Also, the values of the attributes were weighted by their ranks and normalized ranks ($\text{rank}_i/\text{max rank}_j$), and then these were weighted by the principal components. All of these different weighing schema were highly correlated with RINDEX3, so only RINDEX3 is reported for ease of exposition. Indices specified in these ways for each country will reflect to varying degrees the information content from each attribute relative to other countries and the country's ranking relative to other countries, as well as accounting for variation in the data. Again, the correlation (over 90 percent) between these alternative specifications of the indices made the reporting of these alternative indices with these various weighing specifications redundant.

To construct hedonic models, real gross domestic product per capita (RGDP) was used as an instrumental variable. Summers and Heston constructed this series.[16] RGDP is weighted by a country's consumption share. Many countries (for example, oil-exporting countries) have a high RGDP, but the state "owns" a large fraction of output, which thus is not available for private spending. Real gross domestic consumption (RGDC) was regressed against the various attributes,

$$(5\text{-}1) \qquad \text{RGDC} = a_o + a_i L_i + \varepsilon,$$

where L_i is the ith liberty attribute and a_i is the coefficient estimate of the effect of L_i on RGDC. The a_i's in normalized form were used as the weights in the indices; one of these results is presented in table 5-5. This index is called RINDEX4. This index is calculated by taking the ranking of the attribute and multiplying it by its weight. These results are discussed fully in the next section of this chapter. This procedure is reported in equation (5-2), but the attributes L_i were replaced by the ranks of the attribute R_i,

$$(5\text{-}2) \qquad \text{RGDC} = b_o + b_i R_i + \varepsilon,$$

where b_i is the coefficient estimate of the effect of a country's rank on its RDGC. This can be interpreted as a method of examining whether countries with little (high freedom values) liberty have high or low RGDC relative to other countries. One of these results is given in table 5-5 as well, denoted RINDEX5. It is derived by multiplying the attribute by the normalized coefficient estimate from equation (5-2). The elasticities of the attributes are also examined to see how responsive each country's relative RGDC is to its relative economic freedom measures. This specification is the same as equation (5-1) except the variables are in natural logs,

(5-3) $$\ln \text{RGDC} = c_o + c_i \ln L_i + \varepsilon.$$

One of these results is given in table 5-5. This is RINDEX6. The attribute is weighted by the normalized rank. Finally, one of the results also in the table is based on a hybrid hedonic procedure. The procedure is a hybrid one in that the same regression model as in equations (5-1) and (5-2) was used, but a stepwise procedure was employed to include only those attributes that maximize the likelihood function, or, in other words, demonstrate that they belong in the model, subsequently implying they are the major hedonic attributes with respect to RGDC. For the L_i model, these variables include economic freedom indicators 1, 2, 3, 6, 7, 8, 10, 11, 12, and 13. For the ranks (R_i) model, these factors include 1, 2, 3, 6, 8, 10, 11, 12, and 13. These are RINDEX7 and RINDEX8, respectively. These are included to capture rank and normalized rank effects. While a wide spectrum of indices was constructed for each hedonic specification, only a selected number are reported here, since the other variants were highly correlated with the ones that are reported. The indices that are reported (RINDEX2–RINDEX8) were selected to be representative of all the types of weighing that were possible. A summary was constructed by taking the average of all eight previously discussed indices, and then taking the ranking of these averages. This index is presented with all the other index rankings as a summary in table 5-5. Table 5-6 reports the Spearman correlations for all these results, which demonstrate how the indices' rankings are related to one another.

RANKINGS OF ECONOMIC LIBERTY

In constructing an overall index of economic liberty, the simplest procedure is to rank the liberty indicators (see appendix 5-3), average the ranks, and then rank the average of the fifteen separate economic liberty indicator ranks. This procedure yielded RINDEX1 in table 5-5. The rank-

TABLE 5-6
Correlation Coefficients

	RGDP	GROWTH	R1	R2	R3	R4	R5	R6	R7	R8	RR
RGDP	1.00000	.19643	−.56509	−.59409	−.52105	−.68861	−.69188	−.67619	−.65706	−.71648	−.67392
	.0000	.0294	.0001	.0001	.0001	.0001	.0001	.0001	.0001	.0001	.0001
GROWTH	.19643	1.00000	−.17859	−.18288	−.13974	−.23929	−.24789	−.23807	−.18833	−.22953	−.21677
	.0294	.0000	.0472	.0420	.1216	.0074	.0055	.0078	.0362	.0103	.0156
R1	.56509	−.17859	1.00000	.99112	.82288	.81679	.80291	.75953	.91291	.85415	.92076
	.0001	.0472	.0000	.0001	.0001	.0001	.0001	.0001	.0001	.0001	.0001
R2	.59409	−.18288	−.99112	1.00000	.81490	.82343	.81390	.77774	.91655	.87132	.92752
	.0001	.0420	.0001	.0000	.0001	.0001	.0001	.0001	.0001	.0001	.0001
R3	.52105	−.13974	.82288	.81490	1.00000	.83517	.84375	.70620	.87808	.81766	.88917
	.0001	.1216	.0001	.0001	.0000	.0001	.0001	.0001	.0001	.0001	.0001
R4	.68861	−.23929	.81679	.82343	.83517	1.00000	.99460	.90037	.95020	.97529	.96683
	.0001	.0075	.0001	.0001	.0001	.0000	.0001	.0001	.0001	.0001	.0001
R5	.69188	−.24789	.80291	.81390	.84375	.99460	1.00000	.90767	.94884	.97759	.96548
	.0001	.0055	.0001	.0001	.0001	.0001	.0000	.0001	.0001	.0001	.0001
R6	.67619	−.23807	.75953	.77774	.70620	.90037	.90767	1.00000	.85698	.93125	.90533
	.0001	.0078	.0001	.0001	.0001	.0001	.0001	.0000	.0001	.0001	.0001
R7	.65706	−.18833	.91291	.91655	.87808	.95020	.94884	.85698	1.00000	.95619	.98335
	.0001	.0362	.0001	.0001	.0001	.0001	.0001	.0001	.0000	.0001	.0001
R8	.71648	−.22953	.85415	.87132	.81766	.97529	.97759	.93125	.95619	1.00000	.97727
	.0001	.0103	.0001	.0001	.0001	.0001	.0001	.0001	.0001	.0000	.0001
RR	−.067392	−.21677	.92076	.92752	.88917	.96683	.96548	.90533	.98335	.97727	1.00000
	.0001	.0156	.0001	.0001	.0001	.0001	.0001	.0001	.0001	.0001	.0000

Notes: Numbers under correlation coefficients represent Prob $[\hat{R} > |R| / H_o: p = 0]$. $R_i = i$th index. RR = overall index.

ing of economic liberty by this simple method yields plausible results and a few anomalies. Nations such as the United States, Luxembourg, the former West Germany, Canada, and Japan rank very high; the communist bloc countries rank at the bottom; much of Europe is in the upper quartile of rankings; and much of Africa is in the lower quartile of rankings. But some anomalies are present in the rankings. Are we to believe there is more economic liberty in the Bahamas or the Dominican Republic or Ireland than there is in Hong Kong? Is Mexico (rank 48) freer than Taiwan (rank 67)? Unlikely! RINDEX1 also is highly correlated with some of the other economic liberty indices (RINDEX2 and RINDEX7), but less so with some of the others (RINDEX6) (see table 5-6).

Table 5-5 presents liberty indices based on weights obtained from principal components analysis. RINDEX2 is the rank of the index based on the first principal component. RINDEX3 is the rank of the index based on the weights obtained from the first principal component multiplied by the actual values of the fifteen attributes. Note that RINDEX2 and RINDEX3 give similar results. The two ranks of the indices are correlated ($r = .81$), but not coincident. The United States ranks first by both methods. However, there are some dramatic differences for some countries. (Note the rankings for Bahrain, Belize, Bolivia, Botswana, Chad, Congo, Cyprus, El Salvador, Guatemala, Haiti, Iceland, India, Italy, Jamaica, Jordan, Kuwait, Lebanon, Liberia, Mexico, Portugal, Qatar, Singapore, St. Lucia, Thailand, Trinidad and Tobago, and the United Arab Emirates.)

Table 5-6 presents economic liberty indices using the weights from the various hedonic models that have been discussed. RINDEX4 is the rank of the index based on the normalized coefficient estimates multiplied by the value of the liberty indicators for the full regression model (that is, all fifteen regressors). RINDEX5 is the same as RINDEX4, except that the normalized regression coefficients are multiplied by the rank of the liberty indicator. RINDEX6 is the same as RINDEX5 except that the liberty indicators (and RGDC) have been transformed into logarithms, so the coefficients are elasticities. RINDEX7 is the same as RINDEX5 except that the regressors have been restricted to only those that were statistically significant (L_1 -L_3, L_6, L_{10}, L_{11}, L_{13}). RINDEX8 is the same as RINDEX7 except that ranks rather than the values of the attributes were employed in the restricted regression. While these indices are highly correlated with one another, several of the other indices constructed but not discussed here had considerably lower correlation values. These differences in results can also be discerned by inspection of the rankings by country of these indices in table 5-5. For example, the United States ranks 1 by RINDEX7 and 15 by RINDEX6, Canada ranks 1 by RINDEX1 and 19 by RINDEX6, Spain ranks 22 by RINDEX6 and 53 by RINDEX4 or RINDEX5, and so on. A full comparison of the differences in the liberty indices by method of weighing the liberty indicators can be discerned in the table, which presents all of them in summary fashion, and by examining the rank correlation matrix in table 5-6. As can be seen also from table 5-6, the overall index (INDEX), is highly correlated with all of the rank indices, which is, of course, a consequence of its construction, and provides further evidence that it is a good summary statistic of the other indices.

To reiterate the contention that the level of liberty is important in assessing economic development, correlation coefficients for RGDP (recalling that this is the consumption share), average growth in RGDP during 1950–1985 (growth), and the nine rank indices for 1980 are presented in table 5-6. Both RGDP and the growth rate are significantly related to the nine indices, and the relationship is a negative one. These results indicate that countries that rank low with respect to their relative degree of economic freedom also have relatively low levels of economic growth and overall RGDP as a consumption share. The consistency of the results across all the rank indices suggests compelling evidence for a basic hypothesis that economic freedom is essential for economic development.

CONCLUSIONS ON ECONOMIC LIBERTY

Summary indices of economic liberty based on principal components and hedonic weighing techniques have been constructed. While overall these indices are related to one another in a statistical sense, there are sufficient differences among them to affect the rankings of the individual countries. Because the liberty indicators currently available for use are fairly coarse, the differences that these weighing techniques yield among the liberty indexes are understated. As research on liberty yields finer measures of liberty indicators, the choice of the weighing technique will become more crucial in defining an overall measure of economic liberty. As table 5-6 indicates, the simple overall ranking index created summarizes the information content of all the other indices and appears to be very robust with respect to all of them. In addition, all the rankings indicate that economic growth and RGDP are correlated with the level of economic liberty within a nation.

APPENDIX 5-1: PRINCIPAL COMPONENTS
STATISTICAL METHODS

Principal components analysis is a method whereby one can analyze how much independence there is in a group of variables. Flury has written an excellent description of this technique,[17] but a brief summary of the method is given here. Consider the case where there are k explanatory variables, some of which are collinear. The purpose of regression analysis is to explain the mean variation in the dependent variable with the variation in the independent variables. Thus, if a new set of variables can be created that contain most of the variation that was inherent in the original data set, but without being collinear, then we have something. This is the basic idea behind principal components analysis. If linear combinations of the original k explanatory variables are taken,

(5-4)
$$Z_1 = a_1X_1 + a_2X_2 + \ldots + a_kX_k,$$
$$Z_2 = b_1X_1 + b_2X_2 + \ldots + b_kX_k,$$
$$\vdots$$
$$Z_k = \ldots,$$

we want the new variable Z_1 to contain the maximum amount of variance possible. Obviously the a_i's could be chosen to make the variance infinite, but this is hardly ideal. Thus the "normalization condition" is imposed that

(5-5)
$$a_{12} + a_{22} + \ldots + a_{k2} = 1.$$

Z_1 is chosen to maximize the variance subject to the normalization constraint. Z_2 is chosen subject to the same constraint on the b_i's, and so on. Z_1 is called the first principal component of the X's, etc. We end up with the condition that

(5-6)
$$\text{Var}(Z_1) > \text{Var}(Z_2) > \ldots \text{Var}(Z_k)$$

of the k principal components. The principal components satisfy the following conditions:

1. The sum of the variances of the Z_i's equals the sum of the variances of the X_i's.

2. The Z_i's are pairwise uncorrelated, so there is no longer a collinearity problem.

Thus a regression on a subset of the Z_i's can be estimated free of collinearity. Since there are 144 countries in the sample and 15 attributes, the data matrix is an 144 x 15 matrix X, with

(5-7)
$$X = [x_{ij}] \, i = 1, \ldots, 144, j = 1, \ldots, 15.$$

This X matrix is transformed into a new matrix Z, with

(5-8)
$$Z = XA,$$

where Z is the principal components matrix of X. It is also true that

(5-9)
$$Z'Z = A'X'XA = P = \begin{bmatrix} \rho_1 & & \\ & \ddots & \\ & & \rho_k \end{bmatrix},$$

where the principal components are uncorrelated and their eigenvalues, i, represent the variances of the Z matrix. Specifically,

(5-10)
$$\rho_i / \Sigma_j = P_i$$

represents the proportionate contributions of each of the principal components to the total variation in the X matrix.

131

APPENDIX 5-2: VARIOUS LIBERTY INDICATORS
BY COUNTRY

Obs.	Country	L1	L2	L3	L4	L5	L6	L7
1	Afghanistan	2	4	4	5	5	7	9
2	Albania	4	4	5	5	5	7	8
3	Algeria	3	2	4	5	5	7	9
4	Angola	4	4	4	5	5	7	9
5	Argentina	2	3	2	2	2	3	3
6	Australia	2	1	1	1	1	1	1
7	Austria	1	2	1	1	1	1	5
8	Bahamas	1	1	1	1	2	2	1
9	Bahrain	1	1	2	1	4	5	3
10	Bangladesh	3	1	4	3	3	5	4
11	Barbados	1	3	1	1	1	2	1
12	Belgium	1	3	1	1	1	1	1
13	Beldize	3	1	1	1	2	1	1
14	Benin	2	2	4	4	5	7	9
15	Bolivia	1	2	3	2	3	3	4
16	Botswana	3	1	2	1	1	3	2
17	Brazil	2	2	3	2	3	2	3
18	Bulgaria	4	4	5	5	5	7	8
19	Burkina Faso	3	1	2	2	3	6	7
20	Burma	3	1	3	4	5	7	7
21	Burundi	3	1	3	3	5	6	5
22	Cameroon	2	3	2	3	5	7	2
23	Canada	1	1	1	1	1	1	1
24	Cape Verde	3	1	3	2	2	7	7
25	Central African Republic	2	2	2	2	4	6	4
26	Chad	2	1	3	4	5	7	2
27	Chile	2	3	2	3	3	5	1
28	China	2	2	5	5	5	6	6
29	Colombia	2	2	3	2	2	3	1
30	Congo	2	1	3	3	5	6	7
31	Costa Rica	2	1	2	1	1	1	1
32	Cuba	4	4	5	5	5	6	8
33	Cyprus	3	1	1	2	1	2	1
34	Czechoslovakia	4	4	5	5	5	6	8
35	Denmark	2	2	2	1	1	1	5
36	Dominican Republic	2	1	2	1	1	2	1

L8	L9	L10	L11	L12	L13	L14	L15	Average
3	3	4	4	4	4	4	4	4.40
3	3	4	4	4	4	4	4	4.53
3	3	1	1	4	3	2	1	3.53
3	3	4	4	4	4	4	4	4.53
2	3	1	2	1	1	2	1	2.00
1	1	1	1	2	1	1	1	1.13
1	1	1	1	1	1	1	1	1.33
1	2	1	1	1	1	1	1	1.20
3	3	2	3	4	4	4	1	2.73
1	2	2	2	4	1	2	2	2.60
1	2	1	1	1	1	1	1	1.27
1	1	1	1	1	1	1	1	1.13
1	2	1	1	1	1	1	1	1.17
3	3	1	2	4	1	4	2	3.53
2	3	1	1	2	2	1	1	2.07
1	2	1	1	2	1	1	1	1.53
1	2	1	1	1	1	2	1	1.80
3	3	4	4	4	4	4	4	4.53
3	3	1	1	3	2	4	4	3.00
3	3	4	4	4	4	4	4	4.00
3	3	1	2	4	1	4	1	3.00
3	3	4	2	4	1	4	1	3.07
1	1	1	1	1	1	2	1	1.07
3	3	1	2	4	1	4	2	3.00
2	2	2	2	4	1	4	2	2.73
3	3	3	3	4	1	4	4	3.27
2	2	2	2	4	1	4	4	2.67
3	3	3	3	4	4	4	2	3.80
1	1	3	1	2	1	3	1	1.87
3	3	2	3	4	1	4	2	3.27
1	1	1	1	1	1	1	1	1.13
3	3	1	4	4	4	3	3	4.13
1	2	3	2	1	1	1	3	1.67
3	3	2	4	4	4	4	3	4.27
1	1	1	1	1	1	1	1	1.47
1	1	1	1	1	1	1	1	1.20

APPENDIX 5-2, *cont.*

Obs.	Country	L1	L2	L3	L4	L5	L6	L7
37	Dominica	2	1	3	1	2	3	1
38	Ecuador	2	3	3	2	2	3	2
39	Egypt	2	4	3	2	4	4	5
40	El Salvador	3	4	3	4	3	4	1
41	Ethiopia	3	4	4	4	5	7	9
42	Fiji	2	1	1	1	1	2	2
43	Finland	2	1	1	1	1	2	5
44	France	2	3	2		2	2	5
45	Gabon	2	1	2	1	2	6	2
46	Gambia	2	1	1	2	2	4	2
47	West Germany	1	1	1	1	1	2	1
48	East Germany	4	3	5	5	5	6	8
49	Great Britain	3	1	1	1	1	1	5
50	Greece	2	4	2	1	1	2	5
51	Grenada	3	1	2	2	5	3	3
52	Guatemala	1	1	3	3	4	4	2
53	Guinea	4	1	4	3	5	5	7
54	Guyana	3	1	4	4	5	5	6
55	Haiti	2	1	3	3	5	6	2
56	Hong Kong	1	1	1	1	1	1	1
57	Honduras	2	2	2	1	1	3	2
58	Hungary	3	3	4	4	5	5	8
59	Iceland	3	1	1	1	1	1	1
60	India	3	1	3	3	4	3	4
61	Indonesia	2	2	3	3	4	6	4
62	Iran	3	3	3	3	3	6	4
63	Iraq	3	5	4	4	5	7	9
64	Ireland	1	1	1	1	1	1	1
65	Israel	2	5	3	2	1	2	5
66	Italy	3	2	3	1	1	1	3
67	Ivory Coast	2	1	3	1	4	5	2
68	Jamaica	3	1	3	1	2	3	3
69	Japan	2	1	3	1	1	1	1
70	Jordan	2	1	3	1	4	5	1
71	Kenya	3	1	3	1	3	5	2
72	South Korea	3	1	3	2	4	5	1
73	North Korea	4	5	5	5	5	7	8
74	Kuwait	1	1	2	2	3	4	3
75	Laos	4	1	4	5	5	7	2
76	Lebanon	1	1	2	2	2	4	1

L8	L9	L10	L11	L12	L13	L14	L15	Average
1	2	1	1	2	1	1	1	1.53
1	1	1	2	2	1	2	1	1.87
2	3	2	3	3	1	2	1	2.73
2	2	2	2	3	1	4	1	2.60
3	3	4	4	4	4	4	3	4.33
1	1	1	1	1	1	1	2	1.27
1	2	1	1	1	1	1	1	1.47
1	2	1	1	2	1	1	1	1.80
3	3	1	1	4	1	2	1	2.13
1	1	2	2	2	1	2	1	1.73
1	1	1	1	1	1	1	1	1.07
3	3	2	4	4	4	4	2	4.13
1	1	1	1	2	1	1	1	1.47
1	2	1	1	1	1	1	1	1.73
3	3	2	3	3	2	3	3	2.73
2	2	2	1	1	1	2	2	2.07
3	3	2	2	4	3	4	2	3.47
2	2	3	2	3	1	4	2	3.13
3	3	2	2	4	1	4	2	2.87
1	1	1	1	1	3	2	1	1.27
1	1	3	1	2	1	3	1	1.73
3	3	1	2	4	3	2	3	3.53
1	1	1	1	1	1	1	1	1.13
1	2	1	1	2	1	3	1	2.20
2	3	3	2	3	1	3	1	2.80
2	2	4	3	4	4	3	3	3.33
3	3	4	3	4	4	3	2	4.20
1	1	1	1	1	1	1	1	1.00
1	1	2	1	3	1	2	1	2.07
1	1	1	1	1	1	2	1	1.47
2	3	2	2	2	1	2	2	2.20
1	3	1	1	1	1	3	1	1.80
1	1	1	1	1	1	1	1	1.13
3	3	2	3	3	4	3	2	2.60
2	3	2	2	3	1	2	1	2.20
3	3	2	2	4	1	2	1	2.40
3	3	4	4	4	4	4	3	4.53
2	3	1	2	3	3	3	2	2.33
3	3	4	4	4	4	4	4	3.87
2	2	3	1	4	1	2	1	1.93

APPENDIX 5-2, *cont.*

Obs.	Country	L1	L2	L3	L4	L5	L6	L7
77	Liberia	1	1	3	3	4	5	2
78	Libya	3	1	4	3	5	6	6
79	Liechtenstein	1	1	1	1	1	1	1
80	Luxembourg	1	1	1	1	1	1	1
81	Madagascar	3	1	3	2	4	6	7
82	Malawi	3	1	2	3	5	7	2
83	Malasia	2	1	2	2	3	5	1
84	Mali	2	1	3	3	4	6	7
85	Mauritania	3	1	3	4	5	6	4
86	Mauritius	2	1	2	1	1	2	1
87	Mexico	1	1	3	2	3	4	3
88	Mongolia	4	4	5	5	5	7	8
89	Morocco	3	1	3	2	3	5	4
90	Mozambique	4	1	4	4	5	7	9
91	Nepal	3	1	2	3	3	4	2
92	Netherlands	1	4	1	1	1	1	5
93	New Zealand	3	1	1	1	1	1	1
94	Niger	2	1	1	2	5	6	2
95	Nigeria	3	1	3	2	2	5	3
96	Norway	2	4	1	1	1	1	5
97	Oman	1	1	2	2	5	6	4
98	Pakistan	3	1	3	2	5	5	4
99	Panama	1	1	3	1	3	3	3
100	Papua New Guinea	3	1	2	1	1	2	2
101	Paraguay	2	3	3	4	4	5	4
102	Peru	3	3	3	2	2	3	4
103	Philippines	3	1	3	2	3	3	4
104	Poland	4	4	3	4	4	5	6
105	Portugal	3	3	3	1	2	2	5
106	Qatar	1	1	2	2	5	5	3
107	Romania	4	3	5	5	5	7	8
108	Rwanda	3	1	1	3	3	6	7
109	Saudi Arabia	1	1	3	3	5	7	3
110	Senegal	2	1	3	1	2	4	5
111	Seychelles	3	1	3	3	5	6	6
112	Sierra Leone	2	1	2	2	4	5	2
113	Singapore	1	4	2	3	4	5	5
114	Somalia	3	1	4	5	5	7	7
115	South Africa	3	4	5	5	5	6	3

L8	L9	L10	L11	L12	L13	L14	L15	Average
3	3	2	3	2	1	4	2	2.60
3	3	2	2	4	2	3	3	3.33
1	1	1	1	1	1	1	1	1.00
1	1	1	1	1	1	1	1	1.00
3	3	2	4	4	1	4	3	.33
3	3	1	3	4	1	4	4	3.07
2	3	1	2	3	1	4	1	2.20
3	3	2	3	3	1	4	2	3.13
3	3	3	3	3	1	3	2	3.13
1	1	1	1	1	1	2	1	1.27
2	2	1	1	2	1	3	1	2.00
3	3	4	4	4	4	4	4	4.53
2	3	2	3	3	2	3	1	2.67
3	3	3	3	4	4	3	1	3.87
2	3	2	3	4	1	2	1	2.40
1	1	1	1	1	1	1	1	1.47
1	1	1	1	1	1	1	1	1.13
3	3	3	3	4	1	4	2	2.80
1	2	1	1	2	1	3	1	2.07
1	1	1	1	1	1	1	1	1.53
3	3	2	3	4	4	4	1	3.00
3	3	2	2	4	1	4	1	2.87
1	2	1	1	2	1	2	1	1.73
1	1	1	1	1	1	2	1	1.40
2	2	1	2	3	1	3	1	2.67
1		2	1	3	1	2	1	2.13
2	3	3	2	3	1	3	1	2.47
2	3	2	3	4	3	4	2	3.53
1	1	1	1	1	1	1	1	1.80
3	3	2	3	4	4	4	1	2.87
3	3	2	4	4	4	4	4	4.33
3	3	3	3	4	3	4	3	3.33
	3	2	3	4	4	4	1	3.13
2	2	1	1	2	1	1	1	1.93
3	3	2	4	4	1	4	1	3.27
3	3	2	1	3	1	1	1	2.20
3	3	1	2	3	1	2	1	2.67
3	3	4	4	4	4	4	3	4.07
2	3	4	4	4	4	4	2	3.87

APPENDIX 5-2, *cont.*

Obs.	Country	L1	L2	L3	L4	L5	L6	L7
116	USSR	4	2	5	5	7	8	3
117	Spain	3	3	2	1	2	2	1
118	Sri Lanka	3	1	3	2	2	4	3
119	St. Lucia	3	1	2	1	1	2	1
120	St. Vincent	3	1	2	1	1	2	1
121	Sudan	3	1	3	3	4	6	7
122	Suriname	3	4	3	3	4	6	1
123	Swaziland	3	1	3	2	3	6	2
124	Sweden	2	3	1	1	1	5	1
125	Switzerland	1	5	1	1	1	1	1
126	Syria	2	1	4	3	5	7	6
127	Taiwan	2	4	2	2	4	5	3
128	Tanzania	3	1	4	3	5	6	9
129	Thailand	3	3	3	1	2	4	2
130	Togo	2	1	3	2	5	6	7
131	Trinidad	3	1	3	1	1	2	3
132	Tunisia	3	2	3	3	4	5	5
133	Turkey	3	4	3	3	4	5	3
134	Uganda	4	1	4	4	5	4	4
135	United Arab Emirates	1	1	3	2	4	5	3
136	United States	1	1	1	1	1	1	1
137	Vanuatu	1	1	1	1	3	4	4
138	Venezuela	2	2	2	1	2	2	3
139	Vietnam	4	5	5	5	5	7	8
140	Yemen Arab Republic	3	1	3	3	4	5	2
141	Yugoslavia	3	3	3	3	4	5	6
142	Zaire	3	1	3	3	4	7	4
143	Zambia	3	1	3	2	4	5	7
144	Zimbabwe	3	1	3	2	4	6	5

L8	L9	L10	L11	L12	L13	L14	L15	Average
3	4	4	4	4	4	4	4	4.33
1	1	1	1	1	1	1	1	1.47
2	2	1	1	3	1	3	1	2.13
1	1	1	1	2	1	1	1	1.33
1	2	1	1	1	1	1	1	1.33
3	3	2	3	3	1	2	1	3.00
3	3	3	3	4	1	4	3	3.20
3	3	3	4	4	1	4	1	2.87
1	1	1	1	1	1	1	1	1.47
1	1	1	1	1	1	2	1	1.33
3	3	2	3	4	1	4	2	3.33
2	2	1	3	4	1	2	1	2.53
3	3	3	3	4	3	3	3	3.73
2	3	2	1	2	1	2	1	2.13
3	3	2	3	4	1	4	1	3.13
1	1	1	1	2	1	1	1	1.53
2	3	1	2	3	1	2	1	2.67
2	3	2	3	3	1	4	1	2.93
2	2	4	3	4	1	4	3	3.27
2	3	2	3	4	4	4	1	2.80
1	1	1	1	1	1	1	1	1.00
2	2	1	1	1	1	1	1	1.67
1	1	1	1	1	1	1	1	1.47
3	3	3	3	4	4	4	4	4.47
3	3	2	3	4	4	4	4	3.20
3	3	1	1	4	3	4	4	3.33
3	3	3	3	3	1	4	2	3.13
2	3	3	3	4	1	3	1	3.00
2	3	2	3	3	2	4	1	2.93

APPENDIX 5-3: RANK OF VARIOUS LIBERTY INDICATORS
BY COUNTRY

Obs.	Country	L1	L2	L3	L4	L5	L6	L7
1	Afghanistan	28	121	116	128	101	121	137
2	Albania	129	121	133	128	101	121	127
3	Algeria	72	88	116	128	101	121	137
4	Angola	129	121	116	128	101	121	137
5	Argentina	28	103	28	51	36	40	56
6	Australia	28	1	1	1	1	1	1
7	Austria	1	88	1	1	1	1	92
8	Bahamas	1	1	1	1	36	20	1
9	Bahrain	1	1	28	1	74	66	56
10	Bangladesh	72	1	116	86	56	66	76
11	Barbados	1	103	1	1	1	20	1
12	Belgium	1	103	1	1	1	1	1
13	Beldize	72	1	1	1	36	1	1
14	Benin	28	88	116	115	101	121	137
15	Bolivia	1	88	67	51	56	40	76
16	Botswana	72	1	28	1	1	40	34
17	Brazil	28	88	67	51	56	20	56
18	Bulgaria	129	121	133	128	101	121	127
19	Burkina Faso	72	1	28	51	56	94	115
20	Burma	72	1	67	115	101	121	115
21	Burundi	72	1	67	86	101	94	92
22	Cameroon	28	103	28	86	101	121	34
23	Canada	1	1	1	1	1	1	1
24	Cape Verde	72	1	67	51	36	121	115
25	Central African Republic	28	88	28	51	74	94	76
26	Chad	28	1	67	115	101	121	34
27	Chile	28	103	28	86	56	66	1
28	China	28	88	133	128	101	94	108
29	Colombia	28	88	67	51	36	40	1
30	Congo	28	1	67	86	101	94	115
31	Costa Rica	28	1	28	1	1	1	1
32	Cuba	129	121	133	128	101	94	127
33	Cyprus	72	1	1	51	1	20	1
34	Czechoslovakia	129	121	133	128	101	94	127
35	Denmark	28	88	28	1	1	1	92
36	Dominican Republic	28	1	28	1	1	20	1

L8	L9	L10	L11	L12	L13	L14	L15	Average
86	66	129	126	84	117	90	129	105.27
86	66	129	126	84	117	90	129	112.47
86	66	1	1	84	108	39	1	76.60
86	66	129	126	84	117	90	129	112.00
53	66	1	62	1	1	39	1	37.73
1	1	1	1	39	1	1	1	5.33
1	1	1	1	1	1	1	1	12.87
1	37	1	1	1	1	1	1	7.00
86	66	68	90	84	117	90	1	55.27
1	37	68	62	84	1	39	90	57.00
1	37	1	1	1	1	1	1	11.47
1	1	1	1	1	1	1	1	7.80
1	37	1	1	1	1	1	1	10.47
86	66	1	62	84	1	90	90	79.07
53	66	1	1	39	102	1	1	42.87
1	37	1	1	39	1	1	1	17.27
1	37	1	1	1	1	39	1	29.87
86	66	129	126	84	117	90	129	112.47
86	66	1	1	59	102	90	129	63.40
86	66	129	126	84	117	90	129	94.60
86	66	1	62	84	1	90	1	60.27
86	66	129	62	84	1	90	1	68.00
1	1	1	1	1	1	39	1	3.53
86	66	1	62	84	1	90	90	62.87
53	37	68	62	84	1	90	90	61.60
86	66	110	90	84	1	90	129	74.87
53	37	68	62	84	1	90	129	59.47
86	66	110	90	84	117	90	90	94.20
1	1	110	1	39	1	68	1	35.53
86	66	68	90	84	1	90	90	71.13
1	1	1	1	1	1	1	1	4.60
86	66	1	126	84	117	68	114	99.67
1	37	110	62	1	1	1	114	61.60
86	66	68	126	84	117	90	114	105.60
1	1	1	1	1	1	1	1	16.47
1	1	1	1	1	1	1	1	5.87

141

APPENDIX 5-3, *cont.*

Obs.	Country	L1	L2	L3	L4	L5	L6	L7
37	Dominica	28	1	67	1	36	40	1
38	Ecuador	28	103	67	51	36	40	34
39	Egypt	28	121	67	51	74	53	92
40	El Salvador	72	121	67	115	56	53	1
41	Ethiopia	72	121	116	115	101	121	137
42	Fiji	28	1	1	1	1	20	34
43	Finland	28	1	1	1	1	20	92
44	France	28	103	28	1	36	20	92
45	Gabon	28	1	28	1	36	94	34
46	Gambia	28	1	1	51	36	53	34
47	West Germany	1	1	1	1	1	20	1
48	East Germany	129	103	133	128	101	94	127
49	Great Britain	72	1	1	1	1	1	92
50	Greece	28	121	28	1	1	20	92
51	Grenada	72	1	28	51	101	40	56
52	Guatemala	1	1	67	86	74	53	34
53	Guinea	129	1	116	86	101	66	115
54	Guyana	72	1	116	115	101	66	108
55	Haiti	28	1	67	86	101	94	34
56	Hong Kong	1	1	1	1	1	20	1
57	Honduras	28	88	28	1	1	40	37
58	Hungary	72	103	116	115	101	66	127
59	Iceland	72	1	1	1	1	1	1
60	India	72	1	67	86	74	40	76
61	Indonesia	28	88	67	86	74	94	76
62	Iran	72	103	67	86	56	94	76
63	Iraq	72	140	116	115	101	121	137
64	Ireland	1	1	1	1	1	1	1
65	Israel	28	140	28	51	1	20	92
66	Italy	72	88	28	1	1	1	56
67	Ivory Coast	28	1	28	1	74	66	34
68	Jamaica	72	1	28	1	36	40	56
69	Japan	28	1	28	1	1	1	1
70	Jordan	28	1	28	1	74	66	1
71	Kenya	72	1	28	1	56	66	34
72	South Korea	72	1	28	51	74	66	1
73	North Korea	129	140	133	128	101	121	127
74	Kuwait	1	1	28	51	56	53	56
75	Laos	129	1	116	128	101	121	34
76	Lebanon	1	1	28	51	30	53	1

L8	L9	L10	L11	L12	L13	L14	L15	Average
1	37	1	1	39	1	1	1	17.07
1	1	1	62	39	1	39	1	33.60
53	66	68	90	59	1	39	1	57.53
53	37	68	62	59	1	90	1	57.07
86	66	129	126	84	117	90	114	106.33
1	1	1	1	1	1	1	90	12.20
1	37	1	1	1	1	1	1	12.53
1	37	1	1	39	1	1	1	26.00
86	66	1	1	84	1	39	1	33.40
1	1	68	62	39	1	39	1	27.73
1	1	1	1	1	1	1	1	2.27
86	66	68	126	84	117	90	90	102.80
1	1	1	1	39	1	1	1	14.33
1	37	1	1	1	1	1	1	22.33
86	66	68	90	59	102	68	114	66.80
53	37	68	1	1	1	39	90	40.40
86	66	68	62	84	108	90	90	84.53
53	37	110	62	59	1	90	90	72.07
86	66	68	62	84	1	90	90	63.87
1	1	1	1	1	108	39	1	11.93
1	1	110	1	39	1	68	1	29.47
86	66	1	62	84	108	39	114	84.00
1	1	1	1	1	1	1	1	5.73
1	37	1	1	39	1	68	1	37.67
53	66	110	62	59	1	68	1	62.20
53	37	129	90	84	117	68	90	102.13
86	66	129	90	84	117	68	90	102.13
1	1	1	1	1	1	1	1	1.00
1	1	68	1	59	1	39	1	35.40
1	1	1	1	1	1	39	1	19.53
53	66	68	62	39	1	39	90	43.33
1	66	1	1	1	1	68	1	24.93
1	1	1	1	1	1	1	1	4.60
86	66	68	90	59	117	68	90	56.20
53	66	68	62	59	1	39	1	40.47
86	66	68	62	84	1	39	1	46.67
86	66	129	126	84	117	90	114	112.73
53	66	1	62	59	108	68	90	50.20
86	66	129	126	84	117	90	129	97.13
53	37	110	1	84	1	39	1	33.13

APPENDIX 5-3, *cont.*

Obs.	Country	L1	L2	L3	L4	L5	L6	L7
77	Liberia	1	1	67	86	74	66	34
78	Libya	72	1	116	86	101	94	108
79	Liechtenstein	1	1	1	1	1	1	1
80	Luxembourg	1	1	1	1	1	1	1
81	Madagascar	72	1	67	51	74	94	115
82	Malawi	72	1	28	86	101	121	34
83	Malasia	28	1	28	51	56	66	1
84	Mali	28	1	67	86	74	94	115
85	Mauritania	72	1	67	115	101	94	76
86	Mauritius	28	1	28	1	1	20	1
87	Mexico	1	1	67	51	56	53	56
88	Mongolia	129	121	133	128	101	121	127
89	Morocco	72	1	67	51	56	66	76
90	Mozambique	129	1	116	115	101	121	137
91	Nepal	72	1	28	86	56	53	34
92	Netherlands	1	121	1	1	1	1	92
93	New Zealand	72	1	1	1	1	1	1
94	Niger	28	1	1	51	101	94	34
95	Nigeria	72	1	67	51	36	66	56
96	Norway	28	121	1	1	1	1	92
97	Oman	1	1	28	51	101	94	76
98	Pakistan	72	1	67	51	101	66	76
99	Panama	1	1	67	1	56	40	56
100	Papua New Guinea	72	1	28	1	1	20	34
101	Paraguay	28	103	67	115	74	66	76
102	Peru	72	103	67	51	36	40	76
103	Philippines	72	1	67	51	56	40	76
104	Poland	129	121	67	115	74	66	708
105	Portugal	72	103	67	1	36	20	92
106	Qatar	1	1	28	51	101	66	56
107	Romania	129	103	133	128	101	121	127
108	Rwanda	72	1	1	86	56	94	115
109	Saudi Arabia	1	1	67	86	101	121	56
110	Senegal	28	1	67	1	36	53	92
111	Seychelles	72	1	67	86	101	94	108
112	Sierra Leone	28	1	28	51	74	66	34
113	Singapore	1	121	28	86	74	66	92
114	Somalia	72	1	116	128	101	121	115
115	South Africa	72	121	133	128	101	94	56

L8	L9	L10	L11	L12	L13	L14	L15	Average
86	66	68	90	39	1	90	90	57.27
86	66	68	62	84	102	68	114	81.87
1	1	1	1	1	1	1	1	1.00
1	1	1	1	1	1	1	1	1.00
86	66	68	126	84	1	90	114	73.93
86	66	1	90	84	1	90	129	66.00
53	66	1	62	59	1	90	1	37.60
86	66	68	90	59	1	90	90	67.67
86	66	110	90	59	1	68	90	73.07
1	1	1	1	1	1	30	1	8.40
53	37	1	1	39	1	68	1	32.40
86	66	129	126	84	117	90	129	112.47
53	66	68	90	59	102	68	1	59.73
86	66	110	90	84	117	68	1	59.73
53	66	68	90	84	1	39	1	48.80
1	1	1	1	1	1	1	1	15.07
1	1	1	1	1	1	1	1	5.73
86	66	110	90	84	1	90	90	61.80
1	37	1	1	39	1	68	1	33.20
1	1	1	1	1	1	1	1	16.87
86	66	68	90	84	117	90	1	63.60
86	66	68	62	84	1	90	1	59.47
1	37	1	1	39	1	39	1	22.80
1	1	1	1	1	1	39	1	13.53
53	37	1	62	59	1	68	1	54.07
1	1	68	1	59	1	39	1	41.07
53	66	110	62	59	1	68	1	52.20
53	66	68	90	84	108	90	90	88.60
1	1	1	1	1	1	1	1	26.60
86	66	68	90	84	117	90	1	60.40
86	66	68	126	84	117	90	129	107.20
86	66	110	90	84	108	90	114	78.20
86	66	68	90	84	117	90	1	69.00
53	37	1	1	39	1	1	1	27.47
86	66	68	126	84	1	90	1	70.07
86	66	68	1	59	1	1	1	39.67
86	66	1	62	59	1	39	1	52.20
86	66	129	126	84	117	90	114	97.73
53	66	129	126	84	117	90	90	97.33

APPENDIX 5-3, *cont.*

Obs.	Country	L1	L2	L3	L4	L5	L6	L7
116	USSR	129	88	133	128	144	144	56
117	Spain	72	103	28	1	36	20	1
118	Sri Lanka	72	1	67	51	36	53	56
119	St. Lucia	72	1	28	1	1	20	1
120	St. Vincent	72	1	28	1	1	20	1
121	Sudan	72	1	67	86	74	94	115
122	Suriname	72	121	67	86	74	94	1
123	Swaziland	72	1	67	51	56	94	34
124	Sweden	28	103	1	1	1	66	1
125	Switzerland	1	140	1	1	1	1	1
126	Syria	28	1	116	86	101	121	108
127	Taiwan	28	121	28	51	74	66	56
128	Tanzania	72	1	116	86	101	94	137
129	Thailand	72	103	67	1	36	53	34
130	Togo	28	1	67	51	101	94	115
131	Trinidad	72	1	67	1	1	20	56
132	Tunisia	72	88	67	86	74	66	92
133	Turkey	72	121	67	86	74	66	56
134	Uganda	129	1	116	115	101	53	76
135	United Arab Emirates	1	1	67	51	74	66	56
136	United States	1	1	1	1	1	1	1
137	Vanuatu	1	1	1	1	56	53	76
138	Venezuela	28	88	28	1	36	20	56
139	Vietnam	129	140	133	128	101	121	127
140	Yemen Arab Republic	72	1	67	86	7	66	34
141	Yugoslavia	72	103	67	86	74	66	108
142	Zaire	72	1	67	86	74	121	76
143	Zambia	72	1	67	51	74	66	115
144	Zimbabwe	72	1	67	51	74	94	92

L8	L9	L10	L11	L12	L13	L14	L15	Average
86	144	129	126	84	117	90	129	115.13
1	1	1	1	1	1	1	1	17.93
53	37	1	1	59	1	68	1	37.13
1	1	1	1	39	1	1	1	11.33
1	37	1	1	1	1	1	1	11.20
86	66	68	90	59	1	39	1	61.27
86	66	110	90	84	1	90	114	77.07
86	66	110	126	84	1	90	1	62.60
1	1	1	1	1	1	1	1	13.93
1	1	1	1	1	1	39	1	12.80
86	66	68	90	84	1	90	90	75.73
53	37	1	90	84	1	39	1	48.67
86	66	110	90	84	108	68	114	88.87
53	66	68	1	39	1	39	1	42.27
86	66	68	90	84	1	90	1	62.87
1	1	1	1	39	1	1	1	17.60
53	66	1	62	59	1	39	1	55.13
53	66	68	90	59	1	90	1	64.67
53	37	129	90	84	1	90	114	79.27
53	66	68	90	84	117	90	1	59.00
1	1	1	1	1	1	1	1	1.00
53	37	1	1	1	1	1	1	19.00
1	1	1	1	1	1	1	1	17.67
86	66	110	90	84	117	90	129	110.07
86	66	68	90	84	117	90	129	75.33
86	66	1	1	84	108	90	129	76.07
86	66	110	90	59	1	90	90	72.60
53	66	110	90	84	1	68	1	61.27
53	66	68	90	59	102	90	1	65.33

147

The Choice of Law and the
Extent of Liberty

THE SOURCES OF LAW AND THE RIGHTS OF MAN

IN this chapter the concern is not with economic growth but with the effect of the legal system on freedom. There are three main legal traditions found in nations today: civil (codified, continental) law, common law, and socialist law. Other traditions of law, mainly arising from sanctioned custom or religious tenets, exist and influence civil and common law: African tribal law, Oriental law, Hindu law, and Muslim law. Among these, only Muslim law is sufficiently influential and widespread to concern us here. The tradition of civil or codified law governs non-English-speaking Europeans, the former colonies of Europe, and a number of historically independent non-European countries. For example, 94 of the countries in the sample of 167 nations used here have a civil law tradition. Civil law has the longest tradition, tracing its roots to 450 B.C., the date of the Twelve Tablets of Rome and reaching coherence in its first codification under the Byzantine emperor Justinian (A.D. 527–565) in A.D. 533. The tradition of common law governs the United Kingdom and the former colonies of England. Some fifty-four countries in the sample have been influenced by English common law. The foundations of common law were established in the years between 1154 and 1307, the reigns of Henry II through Edward I. A case casuistry of common law began with the "Year Books" in the thirteenth century. Marxist-Leninist legal tradition begins with the Russian Revolution, when whatever substantive rights the Russian peoples had ended. There are nineteen communist bloc countries in the sample. In the socialist tradition of law, the idea of justice is obscure, since personal liberty is not a concern of Marxism-Leninism. The Muslim legal tradition is based on a twenty-three-year period of legislative activity of Islam, from A.D. 609–610, the time of the Revelation, to A.D. 632, the year of the death of the Prophet. For the Muslim, law is that which God wishes it to be, as revealed to Muhammad. There are forty-one Muslim countries in the sample.

In the Institutes of Justinian (A.D. 533) it is written: "Justia est constans et perpetua voluntas jus suum cuique tribuens . . . sed et quod principi placuit, legis habet vigorem." These two short phrases reflect the recurring sharp dichotomy of views on what constitutes justice, the making of law, and the rights of man. Is justice a constant and perpetual aim granting everyone their own rights, or is it that which is pleasing to the person in power that has the force of law?

In the discussion that follows, which will be familiar to students of comparative law, those characteristic differences in the systems are identified that cause one to hypothesize that the extent of liberty differs depending on the choice of law. The general hypothesis is that the extent of individual liberty can be ranked by type of legal system. Specifically, liberty under common law is hypothesized to be greater than under civil law; liberty under Marxist-Leninist law and under Islamic law is hypothesized to be less than under civil law.

Somewhat unsatisfactorily, the choice of legal system is treated as exogenous. Partly, this is justified, because some legal systems historically were imposed on the population for "righteous" reasons—religious for Islamic law, political for the codified (for example, Napoleonic code) and Marxist-Leninist traditions—or as a result of colonization, and change is difficult. Where change is possible, at least theoretically, as in representative democracies, the evolutionary character of common law and the continuous drafting of parliamentary legislation in both common and civil law nations may yield continued political acceptance of a system of law chosen centuries before. In the former colonies of Europe and England there is evidence that precolonial legal traditions are modifying the colonial legal tradition, most importantly in Islamic countries.

The Common Law and Codified Legal Traditions

The legal systems of the West and, derivatively, their former colonies, as well as those of noncolonized countries, of course, are subdivided into two major categories: those derived from Roman law and the codification of statutes and those derived from English common law. Some scholars assert that the differences between these legal systems and the implications for human freedom are more apparent than real, since in the West both share in common Christian morals, constitutional government, and capitalist, private enterprise economic systems.[1] Others would point to the implications for freedom of the radically different sources of law in the two legal traditions.[2] This philosophical difference on the theoretical effect of the legal tradition on liberty is the subject of this section. A powerful summary by Friedrich von Hayek will introduce the reader to the main argument:

> The freedom of the British which in the eighteenth century the rest of Europe came so much to admire was thus not, as the British themselves were among the first to believe and as Montesquieu later taught the world, originally the product of the separation of powers between legislature and executive, but rather a result of the fact that the law that governed the decisions of the courts was the common law, a law existing independently of anyone's will and at the same time binding upon and developed by the independent courts; a law with which parliament only rarely interfered with and, when it did, mainly only to clear up doubtful points within a given body of law. One might even say that a sort of separation of powers had grown up in England, not because the "legislature" alone made law, but because it did *not*: because the law was determined by courts independent of the power which organized and directed government, the power namely of what was misleadingly called the "legislature."[3]

In common law countries law has evolved over the centuries from judge-made rulings on a case-by-case basis. Judicial inventiveness in creating new law out of a philosophical predisposition about how society ought to be ruled is constrained by a strict adherence to precedent, which is often ancient. Under common law, legal rules emerge from the judicial resolution of disputes between parties of equal standing. One of those parties may be the state. Under common law, individuals seek the sanctioning of private arrangements, which often arise from custom, and the resolution of disputes before an entirely neutral referee.

The legal tradition of continental Europe is codified law. In contrast with common law, which evolves continuously, codified law emerged discretely through the act of codification. All law prior to Justinian's codification was nullified and the use of any other commentaries forbidden after the code was prepared, all in the interest of preserving the "purity" of Roman law. The Code Napoleon (1804) nullified prior law in the interest of the new (bourgeois) and revolutionary order. The rights and claims of the aristocracy were abridged in favor of those of the middle class. The law of France derives its validity not from prior legal tradition, but from the act of codification. Under a regime of civil law, the government has a monopoly in the creation of law and, derivatively, in the creation of rights.

The protection of individual rights in a legal regime in which those who govern, even if they are men of good will, have the power to grant, deny, or modify rights likely is different from that in a legal system in which the government stands merely equal with the individual before an independent judiciary.

Common law arose out of the ashes of the Norman conquest of England. One hundred and fifty years of Norman tyranny followed. A truculent penal code was imposed and enforced on the Saxons to guard the privileges of the Normans. Tax collections on behalf of King John brought the English countryside to penury; it became just too much to endure. Norman rule was broken when John (1199–1216) was forced to sign the Magna Carta. Macaulay dates the commencement of the English nation with the events at Runnymede in 1215:

> Then it was that the great English people was formed, that the national character began to exhibit those peculiarities which it has ever since retained, and that our fathers became emphatically islanders; islanders not merely in a geographical position, but in their politics, their feelings, and their manners. . . . Then it was that the House of Commons, the archetype of all the representative assemblies which now meet, either in the Old or in the New World, held its first sittings. Then, it was that the common law rose to the dignity of a science, and rapidly became a not unworthy rival of the imperial jurisprudence.[4]

What features of the common law are solicitous of individual freedom? Equal protection and equal status of the litigants and strict judicial independence circumscribe the coercive power of government. Under common law the people's interest is derivative from the harmed person and, by extension, his family, peers, and society as a whole. Judicial proceedings are accusatory. Until modern times, the office of prosecutor did not exist in England. The government had to hire a lawyer to represent the people's interest, as did the defendant. Under common law, trial by jury is guaranteed in civil as well as in criminal proceedings. Trials are open and public.[5] In contrast, legal proceedings under codified systems can be inquisitional, multistage affairs, held at least partly in secret. In continental legal systems, those charged with crimes or infractions face the power of the state, not a judge, refereeing a contest between the accuser and the accused.

Independence of the judiciary implies more in common law countries than is implied by the separation of powers doctrine elsewhere. Common law is broader in scope than civil law. Civil law is confined to the range of legal subjects of the first three books of the Institutes of Justinian (that is, the law of persons, family, inheritance, torts, property, contracts, and unjust enrichment). Under common law what is lawful rests entirely with the judiciary, whose views evolve slowly and are built on the strict principle of adherence to the rule of stare decisis. Where the government chooses to intervene by statute (for example, child labor laws, city planning, and so on) a tradition of casuistry and precedent tends to result in the statutes' being construed more narrowly and limitedly than on the Continent.[6] Englishmen are less inclined to overthrow seven hundred years of legal wisdom for a modern, if popular, vision. This evolutionary character of the common law is protective of individual freedoms.

The separation of powers doctrine, of course, exists in civil law countries as well, but the independence of the judiciary is not nearly as meaningful. Judgeships in prerevolutionary France were private property. Montesquieu inherited, held for a decade, and then sold a judgeship. The thrust of codified law has been to make it as judgeproof as possible. The Code Napoleon contains 2,281 articles. Frederick the Great's distaste for judicial latitude was so great that the Prussian Landrecht of 1794 contains some sixteen thousand provisions. Completeness and coherence, which give certainty to a legal system, are an illusion in a codified system of law.[7] Statically, they are not attainable. And what is achieved erodes with human inventiveness and progress. Ultimately, someone must interpret the code and fill in the gaps. Judges shut out from participation at the front gate return through the back door. France (Italy and other nations followed the French), inundated by requests for legislative interpretation of the code, created the Tribunal of Cassation to address incorrect court interpretations. The Tribunal of Cassation, a legislative tribunal, ultimately evolved into the Supreme Court of Cassation, a judicial entity, but its roots are legislative. Moreover, the function of the court is to divine legislative intent behind the statute.[8]

Codified law is only part of the legal system in countries following the continental legal practice. Commercial law, patents, copyrights, bankruptcy, insurance, and other branches of law were omitted from the early codes. In fact, continental law is something of a hodgepodge, divided between private law (civil and commercial) and public law (administrative and constitutional), each with its separate set of courts, procedures, and hierarchies of tribunals. Disputes with the government are heard in administrative courts, which ensures that those who govern and administer judge their own conduct. In France, the review of the legality of an administrative act is the Council of State, an organ first established to advise monarchs.[9]

In civil law traditions and in England, statutes are not subject to judicial review. What guarantees individual rights in such political systems? Individuals must rely on constitutions and the good will of the legislature for the protection of their subjective rights. Yet constitutions vary in the strength of their limitation on legislative power. Moreover, there is no provision for enforcing these limitations. In contrast to the United States, where since *Marbury v. Madison*, the review of the constitutionality of legislation has been a judicial prerogative, constitutional review in civil law countries may be a nonjudicial process. In France, constitutional questions are settled by the Constitutional Council, a body composed of the former presidents of France and members chosen by the president of France, the president of the Chamber of Deputies and the president of the Senate.[10] While the authority for constitutional review rests differently in other civil law countries, the constraints on legislative power are much weaker than where constitutional questions are a judicial prerogative. Ultimately, in civil law countries liberty is at the sufferance of the legislature.

Some would argue that the rule of law is such a common cause of concern that these differences are more curious than meaningful. After all, one is as free in developed countries with a common law tradition as one is in developed countries with a civil law tradition. Perhaps. But three matters are of troublesome concern for freedom in nations without a tradition of judge-made law. First, since government is the source of all law, individual rights rest ultimately and convincingly with the state (albeit through a popular majority that elects the representative legislature). Law by legislation can weaken individual rights in several respects. First, the electoral process and the market for politicians require responsiveness to the popular will. The time horizon of the popular will and those who represent it often is short, making one less than sanguine about the durability of individual rights in an era of a shift away from private property and individual initiative to collectivism and egalitarianism. The popular will deprived a man of the right to a drink of whiskey (Volstead Act, later ratified as the Eighteenth Amendment to the U.S. Constitution). The Scopes trial raised scripture to the level of science, with a rearguard action fought to this day in parts of the South as "creation science." The Prohibition of Mixed Marriages Act made interracial marriage in South Africa illegal, and the Immorality Act made a dalliance a crime if it involved miscegenation. The habit, notorious in the United States in recent times, of spending more on public goods and social welfare than citizens are willing to pay for with taxes, leaves to posterity the burden of the debt or the debasement of the currency. Other expressions of popular will expressed as law that are infringements of individual liberty come to mind. Second, great opportunities for rent-seeking arise in the legislative process encouraged by majority voting, logrolling, and the rational political ignorance of the voter. Modern government directly controls large amounts of resources. Moreover, resources (rights) are increasingly allocated by the political process (that is, the enormous amount of regulatory activity in modern democracies). Finally, legislation imparts uncertainty about rights, since one legislature is free to alter the law of previous rulemakers. Axiomatically, uncertain prospects are of less value (utility) than certain prospects: "While legislation is almost always *certain* ... people can never be certain that the legislation in force today will be in force tomorrow. . . . As a result, people are prevented not only from freely deciding what to do, but from foreseeing the legal effects of their daily behavior."[11]

Also, the idea of individual rights seems less attractive in the West in modern times. Some view rights less as a natural endowment of man than as mere legally protected interests that must be weighed against the larger social interest. New discoveries and innovation give rise to property that may be private or collective. For example, water rights in the western United States were exclusively governed by the doctrine of appropriation (eastern water rights are riparian). The modern demands of urban development expressed politically through state legislatures has led to some socializing of western water rights. Early in its history, there were private property rights in the radio spectrum. Case law was evolving to reconcile disputes over exclusive property rights to specific radio frequencies. Government took control of the electromagnetic spectrum. Rights in the wavelength are politically allocated. Access to outer space is in the hands of the government, without debate. An entrepreneur is not free to insure (as with an airplane) a rocket and launch a vehicle for the purpose of say space manufacture or mining on the moon. The right to patent genetic changes in animals currently is being debated. Recent taxpayer revolts can be interpreted as a rebellion against the notion that the state has a greater right to the fruits of one's labor than does the worker. High taxation and the forced substitution of public for private consumption weakens individual liberty. Other examples come to mind.

Third, the West is not all of mankind. Much of the noncommunist world has adopted through colonization or on its own a common law or civil law legal system. How well do these legal systems travel? Common law, with its reliance on case law and custom and on judicial independence, likely is more protective of rights in the former British colonies than is codified law with its reliance on the legislative branch in the former European colonies. But, this remains to be shown.

Muslim Law

About one billion people are Muslims in sixty-nine countries, of which thirty-seven have a Muslim majority and twenty-three have an Islamic constitution. In common law, law is the decisions of judges. In civil law, law is the body of codified statutes. For Muslims, law is the word of God. Theologically rooted legal systems are notoriously indifferent to subjective rights. While the vast majority of Muslim countries retain common or civil law traditions from colonial days, Muslim law has lately colored these foreign traditions, in some cases beyond recognition.

An article of faith to a Muslim is that justice is an attribute of God. The *mudjtahid* is the legal expert. He is trained in the four sources of Muslim law with particular emphasis on the five hundred verses of the Koran and on solving "correctly" points that are controversial. Independent thinking is not a trait that is admired. Islamic criminal law is inflexible, even in sentencing. There is no system of appeal from either the verdict or the sentence, unless the decision is contrary to the Koran or the Sunna. Muslim civil law and commercial law are more narrowly construed and religiously flavored than Western practice.[12]

Independence of the judiciary is not a characteristic of the Muslim political system. Throughout its history, Muslim judges have served those who govern. The theory of the separation of powers is alien to Muslim tradition. Judges of the highest rank are appointed by those in power and serve at their pleasure. Judges of lesser rank are appointed by judges of higher rank and serve at their pleasure. The entire judicial structure is an instrument of government that is designed to promote conformity to the will of those who govern.

What is the standing of individual liberty and subjective rights (*hakk*) under Muslim law? Muslims do have certain inalienable rights, such as the rights of a husband over his wife and a father over his child.[13] But, the range of personal freedoms taken as a matter of course in the West are unknown to Muslims. The Koran expressly requires as a religious duty obedience to those who govern.[14] Such obligations inhibit individual freedom.

Marxist-Leninist Law

In the nations of the communist bloc, political and civil rights and the idea of justice are viewed as bourgeois precepts, the purpose of which is the suppression and exploitation of the working class. In the relevant writings of Marx, Engels, and Lenin, the concept of socialist law is as a system of rules of conduct made and enforced by the state. Politics is a recognized feature of a legal system and of legal processes. Hence, it is viewed as quite natural that the Communist Party take an active interest in the use of law as an instrument of government. In the Soviet Union, 60 percent of the defense counsels, about half of the judges, 40 percent of the assessors, and 90 percent of the procurators are members of the Communist Party. All institutions and organs of government are party controlled. Nothing in law can be written without Party approval.[15] Presumably, this contributes to the extraordinarily high criminal conviction rate in the Soviet Union.[16] In other communist bloc nations, the mutually exclusive relationship between law and individual rights is equally binding.

EMPIRICAL EVIDENCE OF THE RELATIONSHIP BETWEEN
THE SOURCE OF LAW AND THE EXTENT OF LIBERTY

The Gastil measures of political and civil liberty are employed to test the hypothesis that the choice of law determines the extent of liberty. The Gastil rankings are used in two ways. First, means and variances of POLLIB and CIVLIB are calculated by type of legal system and differences in the means tested for statistical significance. These results appear in tables 6-1 and 6-2. A summary test of the effect of choice of law on the level of political liberty and of civil liberty is presented in the form of stepwise regressions in table 6-3. Second, the scaling of the Gastil rankings is ordinal. Certainly, it is not correct to interpret them as indicating that freedom is half as great in a country with a value of POLLIB of 2.0 compared to a country with a value of 1.0. To avoid the measurement problem of the Gastil rankings used as a continuous variable, and to shed further light on the question at hand, the Gastil rankings are converted to binary variables and probabilities of the incidence of liberty are estimated. In table 6-4, a frequency distribution of the degree of political and civil liberty by type of legal system is presented. In table 6-5, OLS, Probit, and Logit models of freedom and its absence are estimated by type of legal system.

TABLE 6-1

Test of Statistical Significance of Differences in Mean Values of
Political and Civil Liberty by Type of Legal System

Category	POLLIB	CIVLIB
All nations ($n = 167$)	4.36	4.20
Standard deviation	2.04	1.85
Non–common law($n = 113$)	4.90	4.70
Common law ($n = 54$)	3.21	3.16
Difference in means	−1.69	−1.54
Student-t value	−5.44	−5.42
Non–civil law ($n = 73$)	4.10	4.01
Civil law ($n = 94$)	4.55	4.36
Difference in means	.45[a]	.35[a]
Student-t value	1.43	1.21
Non-Marxist-Leninist law ($n = 148$)	4.06	3.92
Marxist-Leninist law ($n = 19$)	6.63	6.41
Difference in means	2.57	2.48
Student-t value	5.63	6.06
Non–Muslim law ($n = 126$)	4.02	3.88
Muslim law ($n = 41$)	5.40	5.19
Difference in means	1.39	1.31
Student-t value	3.95	4.12
Non–rule of law nations ($n = 150$)	4.73	4.55
Rule of law nations ($n = 17$)	1.05	1.14
Difference in means	−3.68	−3.41
Student-t value	−8.43	−8.63

[a]Not significantly different from zero at an acceptable level.

The Gastil data are the average values of the annual indices from 1973
to 1984 of political liberty and civil rights. There were a total of 167 nations in the sample. The type of legal system by country was determined
as follows. Great Britain and her former colonies and protectorates ($n =$
54) were categorized as common law countries. While some of the former
British colonies actually stipulate common law as the legal system in their
constitutions, not all of them were so strongly influenced. All other noncommunist countries ($n = 94$) are categorized as civil law countries.

TABLE 6-2

Test of Statistical Significance of Differences in Mean Values
of Liberty Measures, Adjusted for Muslim and
Rule of Law Influences

Category	POLLIB	CIVLIB
Non-Muslim, common law ($n = 46$)	2.99	3.00
All other nations ($n = 121$)	4.87	4.66
Difference in means	−1.88	−1.66
Student-t value	−5.83	−5.62
Non-Muslim, civil law ($n = 63$)	4.05	3.85
All other nations ($n = 104$)	4.54	4.42
Difference in means	−.41[a]	−.56
Student-t value	−1.50	−1.92
Non–rule of law, common law ($n = 48$)	3.49	3.43
All other nations ($n = 119$)	4.71	4.52
Difference in means	−1.22	−1.09
Student-t value	−3.63	−3.55
Non–rule of law, civil law ($n = 83$)	5.02	4.77
All other nations ($n = 84$)	3.70	4.77
Difference in means	1.31	1.14
Student-t value	4.38	4.15
Non-Muslim, Non–rule of law, common law ($n = 40$)	3.29	3.30
All other nations ($n = 127$)	4.69	4.49
Difference in means	−1.40	−1.19
Student-t value	−3.95	−3.68
Non-Muslim, Non–rule of law, civil law ($n = 52$)	4.68	4.42
All other nations ($n = 115$)	4.21	4.11
Difference in means	.48[a]	.31[a]
Student-t value	1.41	1.00

[a]Not significantly different from zero at an acceptable level.

TABLE 6-3

Stepwise Regressions Relating the Degree of Political and Civil Liberty to the Type of Legal System

Equation:	Dependent Variable	Constant	Common	Muslim	Marxist	Lawrule	R^2
(1)	POLLIB	4.9035	−1.6943				.1471
		(27.71)	(−5.44)				
(2)	POLLIB	4.5744	−1.5321	1.1270			.1983
		(23.21)	(−5.02)	(3.39)			
(3)	POLLIB	4.0898	−1.0892	1.4084	2.3936		.3237
		(20.39)	(−3.74)	(4.56)	(5.61)		
(4)	POLLIB	4.6179	−1.1957	.9244	1.9164	−3.1488	.5312
		(25.93)	(−4.92)	(3.51)	(5.33)	(−8.55)	
(5)	CIVLIB	4.7000	−1.5370				.1462
		(29.17)	(−5.42)				
(6)	CIVLIB	4.3855	−1.3821	1.0768			.2031
		(24.52)	(−4.99)	(3.57)			
(7)	CIVLIB	3.9089	−.9465	1.3536	2.3539		.3504
		(21.85)	(−3.64)	(4.91)	(6.18)		
(8)	CIVLIB	4.3924	−1.0440	.9105	1.9170	−2.8827	.5606
		(28.00)	(−4.88)	(3.92)	(6.05)	(−8.89)	

Note: $n = 167$.

TABLE 6-4

Cumulative Frequency Distribution of the Degree of Political and Civil Liberty by Type of Legal System

Legal System	Gastil Measure of Political (Civil) Liberty					
	1.0–1.9	2.0–2.9	3.0–3.9	4.0–4.9	5.0–5.9	6.0–7.0
POLLIB						
Common law	.28	.56	.57	.78	.94	1.00
Civil law	.16	.24	.31	.48	.70	1.00
Marxist law	.00	.00	.00	.00	.00	1.00
Muslim law	.00	.07	.12	.32	.61	1.00
Rule of law	1.00	1.00	1.00	1.00	1.00	1.00
CIVLIB						
Common law	.15	.54	.65	.83	.96	1.00
Civil law	.15	.22	.35	.53	.74	1.00
Marxist law	.00	.00	.00	.00	.21	1.00
Muslim law	.00	.02	.20	.39	.61	1.00
Rule of law	1.00	1.00	1.00	1.00	1.00	1.00

TABLE 6-5

OLS and Maximum Likelihood Probit and Logit Probability Estimates of the
Incidence of Freedom and Tyranny under Common and Civil Law

Probability Model and Legal System	POLLIB		CIVLIB	
	FREEDOM	TYRANNY	FREEDOM	TYRANNY
OLS model				
Civil law	.2047	.3784	.1559	.3221
(t-value)	(4.69)	(7.64)	(3.78)	(6.45)
Common law	.2692	− .2860	.2089	− .2662
(t-value)	(4.52)	(− 4.23)	(3.72)	(− 3.90)
R^2	.4321	.3630	.4411	.2901
Probit model				
Civil law	− .9694	− .3076	− 1.1429	− .4487
(t-value)	(− 4.79)	(− 1.81)	(− 5.30)	(− 2.57)
Common law	1.0576	− 1.0931	.9212	− 1.1712
(t-value)	(3.84)	(− 3.80)	(3.23)	(− 3.66)
Log likelihood	− 54.97	− 70.53	− 50.91	− 73.57
Logit model				
Civil law	− 1.6207	− .5010	− 1.9385	− .7442
(t-value)	(− 4.41)	(− 1.81)	(− 4.73)	(− 2.58)
Common law	1.7624	− 1.8819	1.5804	− 2.1528
(t-value)	(3.70)	(− 3.55)	(3.09)	(− 3.35)
Log likelihood	− 55.22	− 70.58	− 51.14	− 73.40

Note: The variables MUSLIM, MARXIST, and LAWRULE are in each of the above equations, but are not reported to conserve space. In nearly all cases these variables were statistically significant at above the 5 percent level.

There were nineteen Marxist-Leninist countries in the sample. Of the forty-one countries classified as Muslim, thirty-two have a tradition of civil law and nine were influenced by the British legal tradition. Thus the variable MUSLIM in its own right is a combination of Muslim countries with either a common law or civil law influence. Used in conjunction with the variables COMMON and CIVIL, it adjusts for the independent effect of Islam on liberty. Additionally, it is desirable to control for the effect that a long tradition of conformity to the rule of law, independent of the choice of law, may have on liberty. Certainly, this is the case for Western Europe, where the effect on liberty of different legal systems is less apparent than elsewhere, but it is also true for the countries of North America, Australia, and New Zealand ($n = 19$). All of the independent legal system variables and the adjustment variables MUSLIM and LAWRULE are binary: equal to unity, if the characteristic is present, and zero otherwise.

Comparison of differences in the mean values of POLLIB and CIVLIB are presented in table 6-1. The average value of political liberty in the world as measured by Gastil is 4.4, with two-thirds of the world's nations in the freedom interval 2.4 to 6.4. The average value of civil liberty among the 167 nations in the sample is 4.2, with a standard deviation of 1.9. Political liberty and the protection of the individual under the law are not widely shared values outside of a relatively small fraction of nations.

The mean value of political liberty and civil liberty is lower in common law countries, and hence freedom is greater than in non–common law countries; these differences are relatively large and are statistically significant at well above the 1 percent level. On the other hand, the mean levels of political and civil liberty in civil law countries and the mean levels for non–civil law countries are not statistically different. On average, Marxist-Leninist and Muslim nations have less political and civil freedom than do non-Marxist-Leninist and non-Muslim countries, and these differences are statistically significant. The nations with a long tradition of the rule of law (LAWRULE) have the largest favorable differences in the mean values of POLLIB and CIVLIB in the comparisons made in table 6-1.

The differences in the levels of political and civil liberty in common and in civil law nations are somewhat obscured by the presence of the Islamic tradition and the tradition of the rule of law in some of these countries. In table 6-2, adjustments for the Muslim and rule of law traditions are made. In the non-Muslim, common law countries the mean value of POL-LIB (CIVLIB) is 2.99 (3.00), in comparison to a value of POLLIB (CIVLIB) of 4.05 (3.85) in the non-Muslim civil law countries. When the nations with a tradition of rule of law are omitted, the average value of POLLIB (CIVLIB) in the common law countries is 3.49 (3.43), compared to 5.02 (4.77) in the civil law nations. Finally, when the data are adjusted for the effects of both the Islamic and the rule of law traditions, the mean value of POLLIB (CIVLIB) in the common law countries is 3.29 (3.30), versus 4.68 (4.42) in the civil law nations. These favorable differences in political and civil liberty in common law relative to civil law countries are both substantial and statistically significant.

The stepwise regressions in table 6-3 conveniently summarize the differences in political liberty and in civil liberty apparent in each legal tradition. The main focus of interest is on the comparison of liberty under common law and civil law, although the adjustments for the Islamic and rule of law traditions also are of interest. In equations (4) and (8) in the table all of the adjustments have been made and the comparison of the constant terms and the coefficient on common law is the comparison of interest (that is, between civil and common law). The regressions reveal a substantial and statistically significant improvement in liberty under common law.

The incidence of political freedom and of civil liberty across legal systems can be gauged from the cumulative frequency (probability) distributions in table 6-4. The sample has been divided by type of legal system, and the fraction of nations in the six intervals of the rankings ranging from 1.0–1.9 to 6.0–7.0 has been calculated. The probability that a nation with a common law legal system will have a completely open political process is $p = .28$, while the probability in a nation with civil law is $p = .16$. If political freedom is defined as a value of POLLIB of 2.9 or less, the incidence of freedom in common law nations is 2.3 times greater than in civil law countries. At the other end of the spectrum is the lack of political freedom. The probability of the absence of political freedom (POLLIB in the interval 6.0 to 7.0) in civil law countries is $p = .30$, while in common law countries it is $p = .06$. If a closed political process is defined as one with a value of POLLIB of 5.0 or more, then the incidence of oppression is 2.3 times greater under civil law than under common law. Comparison of political freedom in Marxist-Leninist, Muslim, and rule of law nations reveals less variance in the incidence of freedom than in nations with a common or civil law heritage. Communist countries consistently deny political freedom. The rule of law nations are consistently free. Two-thirds of the Muslim countries deny or severely restrict political freedom, while very few ($p = .07$) are open politically.

In the protection of individual civil liberties, as measured by the Gastil ranking, common law countries are much more solicitous than civil law countries. If supremacy of the rights of the individual relative to the state is defined as a value of CIVLIB of 2.9 or less, the probability of having one's civil liberties protected is 2.5 times greater in common law nations than in countries with a codified legal tradition. Conversely, if the circumstance where the rights of the government take precedence over those of the individual is defined as a value of CIVLIB of 5.0 or more, than the chance of the denial of individual civil rights is 2.8 times greater in civil law than in common law nations. Other legal systems show less variance in the distribution of civil rights of the individual relative to the state. Marxist-Leninist nations deny individual civil liberties. Nations with a tradition of the rule of law relatively favor individual rights over state rights.

Islamic nations do not demonstrate a high regard for individual civil rights.

The cumulative probabilities in table 6-4 do not adjust the incidence of political and civil liberty in common and civil law countries for the Islamic and rule of law traditions. This limitation is overcome by formally estimating probability models (OLS, Probit, and Logit) of the incidence of freedom and of tyranny in common and, in civil law countries, by adjusting for the other influences.

In addition to assigning rankings of political and civil liberty by country over the period, Gastil gives an overall freedom rating: F (free), PF (partly free), and NF (not free). Guided by these categorizations and by the distribution of probabilities in table 6-4, two binary status of freedom variables for POLLIB and CIVLIB were defined. FREEDOM is equal to unity, if POLLIB (CIVLIB) is less than or equal to 2.5, and zero otherwise. TYRANNY is equal to unity, if POLLIB (CIVLIB) is equal to or greater than 5.5, and zero otherwise.

In the OLS linear probability model presented in table 6-5, after adjustment for the other independent effects, the probability of political liberty in common law countries ($p = .4739$) is 2.3 times greater than in civil law nations ($p = .2047$). Both coefficients are statistically significant at above the 1 percent level, and some 43 percent of the variance in the probability of political freedom is associated with the legal system variables. At the other end of the political spectrum, the probability of a lack of political freedom under civil law is $p = .3784$, while under common law it is $p = .0924$. Stated somewhat differently, if the choice of political environment is constrained to freedom or its absence, there is about a one in three chance that freedom will exist in a civil law country and a two in three chance that freedom is absent. In common law countries, freedom prevails eight out of ten times; its absence prevails twice in ten. Perhaps, the case for common law is even stronger. The coefficient of the probability of a lack of political freedom under civil law plus or minus its standard error is in the interval .4279 to .3289, while the coefficient on common law is in the interval $-.2184$ to $-.3540$. Since the subtraction of the two coefficients cannot rule out zero statistically, it is reasonable empirically to conclude that the probability of a denial of political freedom under common law is zero.

The probability of civil freedom is $p = .1559$ under civil law and $p = .3648$, or 2.3 times as great, under common law. Both coefficients are statistically significant above the 1 percent level. The probability of the absence of civil rights under civil law is $p = .3221$, while under common law this probability is $p = .0559$. Adding the respective standard errors to the coefficients, the range of the coefficient of the absence of civil rights under civil law is .2721 to .3421 and under common law is $-.1980$ to $-.3340$. Since zero is in the interval, after subtraction of the coefficients, the absence of the precedence of state's rights over individual rights under common law cannot be ruled out.

It is well known that linear probability models suffer certain inherent statistical weaknesses. The error term is heteroscedastic. This results in a loss of efficiency but does not result in biased or inconsistent parameter estimates. A more serious weakness is that some of the predicted probabilities can lie outside of the unit interval. Maximum likelihood estimation of Probit and Logit models overcomes these difficulties. In the Probit analysis, the model is transformed using a cumulative normal probability distribution and thus constrains the probabilities to the unit interval. The normalized values have unit variance. The Logit model is based on the cumulative logistic probability function. The dependent variable is the log of the ratio of the odds, not the actual probability.

The maximum likelihood Probit and Logit estimates of the effect of choice of law on political and civil freedom or its absence appear in table 6-5. The Probit and Logit coefficient estimates are not directly comparable to the OLS linear probability estimates; they require transformation to extract the probability estimates. The Probit estimates are Z values. Transforming the Z values to the probabilities in the standardized normal distribution yielded the following results. The probability of FREEDOM in political liberty (POLLIB) is estimated at $p = .4641$ under common law and $p = .1660$ under civil law. The probability of TYRANNY in POLLIB is $p = .0808$ under common law and $p = .3873$ under civil law. The probability of FREEDOM under civil liberty (CIVLIB) is $p = .4129$ under common law and $p = .1271$ under civil law. The corresponding values for the TYRANNY variable are $p = .0526$ and $p = .3264$. Except for the coefficient of civil law on POLLIB-TYRANNY, which is statistically significant at the 5 percent level, all of the Probit coefficients are statistically significant at above the 1 percent level. Thus the Probit estimates result is a somewhat wider predicted gap in liberty between common law and civil law than was revealed in the OLS linear probability model.

The logistic distribution has a variation of $\Pi^2/3$. The most straightforward conversion of the log probabilities is to convert them to the Z values of the Probit model.[17] The probability values of the Logit estimates for each of the liberty-legal system combinations in table 6-5 were as follows: for POLLIB-FREEDOM, common $= .4681$ and civil $= .1867$; for POLLIB-

TYRANNY, common = .0951 and civil = .3897; for CIVLIB-FREEDOM, common = .4207 and civil = .1423; and for CIVLIB-TYRANNY, common = .0559 and civil = .3409. All of the Logit coefficients were statistically significant at above the 1 percent level except one, which was significant at the 5 percent level. The wider gap in liberty between common law and civil law is apparent in the Logit estimates relative to the linear probability estimates as well. The finding of statistically greater chances of freedom and lower probabilities of tyranny under common law is invariant to the choice of the probability model.

SUMMARY AND CONCLUSIONS

In the Institutes of Justinian it is written: "Juris prudentia est divinarum atque humanarum rerum notitia, justi atque injusti scientia" (I.I.i). Indeed, the knowledge of what is right is a concept known to the gods and to civilized people, and it is the recognition of matters just and unjust. Civilization and the rule of law are synonymous.

Leoni asserts that "freedom is . . . above all, a legal concept."[18] It has been shown that the source of law crucially fixes the extent of freedom that we observe in the world today. Those nations that have chosen judge-made or common law have taken a path by which the law is to be discovered. In this tradition, judicial intervention is by the request of those concerned, is applicable mainly to the parties affected, and is decided in collaboration with the powerful legal constraints of precedent and stare decisis. The empirical evidence confirms that freedom has prospered by this arrangement. Alternatively, law is what those who govern say it is. Representative government is no guarantee that subjective rights will not be traded for a vision of society that is a twinkle in a legislator's eye. Most civil law countries are not representative democracies, and the empirical evidence presented here suggests that liberty has suffered under this legal tradition. Law by legislation, a sort of trial and error legal tinkering in the West, has resulted in a "decline of the law" to some[19] and an erosion of liberty to others.

The Constitutional Setting and
Economic Development

How much material progress has mankind made in modern times, and how much has this progress been affected by the choice of the constitutional setting designed to bring it about? The Western industrial countries and many of the former colonies chose an institutional framework that gave wide scope to individual initiative, choice, and responsibility. In general, these countries are free market, free enterprise, capitalist, democratic, and committed to the rule of law. Rising nationalism and the independence movement after World War II gave many new nations the opportunity to choose an institutional framework by which they could progress. Soviet-style state control and economic planning, with a concomitant deemphasis, if not denigration, of individual initiative, were (and remain) fashionable ideas. Prominent nationalists, such as Ghandi, Nehru, Nasser, and Nkrumah, were committed intellectually to socialist principles and central planning.[1] Many nations selected this route for economic development. Despite the recent move away from socialism in Eastern Europe, the less developed world remains committed to central government control of the economy. Certainly, sufficient time has passed to judge if these choices affected economic progress.

In this chapter the effect of the institutional framework, in terms of the choice of the economic system and the levels of political and civil liberty, on the economic growth and the economic efficiency of 115 market economies, over the period 1960 to 1980 is measured.[2] The evidence will show that nations that have chosen systems that do not encourage individual initiative have affected gravely the standard of living of their citizens.

TWO PARADIGMS OF ECONOMIC PROGRESS

The contrasting paradigms that point to the path by which men progress economically have been described. Individualism and statism compete as models of man and society today. That government direction of resources leads to material progress is the older vision. It was first articulated sys-

166

tematically by the mercantilists. In modern times, government intervention is justified by the "vicious cycle of poverty" thesis. This thesis has been
advanced by many writers, but has been elaborated substantially by Gunnar Myrdal.[3] The contrasting vision is that material progress is greatest if
individuals have the right to pursue their own affairs with little interference by the government. The conceptualization of society as a nexus of
private arrangements that are mutually beneficial is contained in the contractarian theory of the classical political theorists, the concept of law as
sanctioned private arrangements set forth by Sir Edward Coke,[4] and in the
economic theory and policy of laissez-faire set forth by Adam Smith.[5]
Modern thinkers, such as Peter T. Bauer and Basil S. Yamey, adopt these
classical liberal premises on economic development.[6]

The great concern of the twentieth century, after the reconstruction of
the war-ravaged economies and the restoration of the international economic order, has been the improvement in the standard of living of the
underdeveloped nations. The fashionable view was that the gap between
the rich and the poor nations was caused by a "vicious circle of poverty"
that required draconian measures to break. The diagnosis was as follows:
Incomes were low because productivity was low; productivity was low
because of a lack of capital formation; capital formation was low because
of a "small capacity to save"; saving was low because income was low.
Alternatively, the inducement to invest was low because income (buying
power) was small; income was small because productivity was low; productivity was low because of a low employment of capital to labor; the
low employment of capital may be due to a small inducement to invest.[7]
Thus symmetrical circularity of argument is achieved on both the supply
and the demand side.

The remedy for breaking the vicious circle of poverty is government
control of resources and economic planning. According to Myrdal, domestically the government must purposefully apply controls, interfere with
market forces, preempt many of the functions normally left to private
enterprise, guide the allocation of resources in the economy, according to
its vision of development, not via an "irrational" price system, configure
the industrial mix, raise agricultural productivity through irrigation, and
so on.[8] In its commercial relations with the world import restrictions, export subsidization and foreign exchange controls are the appropriate
commercial policy. The theories of comparative advantage and of free
trade are viewed as fallacious. There are "sound reasons why it may chose
to produce at home things which it could import more cheaply or to export things at a loss to be covered by subsidy."[9]

In *Rich Lands and Poor*, Myrdal wants to break the traditional social nexus, that in his view is a cause of economic stagnation, by "creating a psychological, ideological, social and political situation propitious to economic development," whatever that means.[10] A decade later, in *Asian Drama*, he abandons what could be interpreted as an educative approach to social change for compulsion.[11] Now, he wants a complete transformation of the values and attitudes that people hold and in the institutions that foster those values. Myrdal was not a tyrant; neither was Sir James Steuart. Yet the means of achieving the visions are not dissimilar. Steuart would allow private initiative, so long as private pursuits were in the public interest as perceived by those who govern. All that Sir James Steuart required was an "exact obedience to the laws," which were to be fashioned by the public-spirited statesman in the public interest. Transgressors would be punished.[12]

Of course, Adam Smith would have none of this. Self-interest promoted the general welfare: "It is not from the benevolence of the butcher, the brewer, or the baker, that we expect our dinner, but from their regard to their own interest. We address ourselves, not to their humanity but to their self-love, and never talk to them of our necessities, but of their advantages."[13] For the mercantilists, national wealth was the stock of precious metals at hand. There were policies to increase their sum. For Adam Smith, national wealth was the aggregation of individual wealth.[14] The conception of national wealth of Adam Smith was radically different from the mercantilist conception, and hence the appropriate institutional structure, property rights, and policies were quite different. To the mercantilist, the legal, political, and economic institutions of mercantilism were justified in the public interest of increasing the national wealth (the stock of precious metals). Restrictions on labor mobility, contract labor, wage and price regulation, the Poor Laws, industrial policy, monopoly grants from the Crown, and protectionism all were justified in the public interest. Adam Smith condemned the mercantilist institutional framework as anathema to private interests. Given Smith's theorem of the "invisible hand," mercantilist policies conflicted with the public interest as well.

Much of *The Wealth of Nations* is an examination of the institutional framework and the property rights structure and their effects on material progress. Rosenberg argues that Adam Smith recognized that self-interest, what we refer to as self-seeking with guile, can get out of hand, unless institutional restraints compel man "to use the good instrument":

Smith is in effect, searching for the appropriate definition of an institutional order which will eliminate zero-sum (or even negative-sum) games. It is the function of the institutional arrangements to cut off all avenues (and there are many) along which wealth may be pursued without contributing to the welfare of society. In modern analysis these are termed rent-seeking activities. Such a goal in practice requires a careful balancing of incentive, the provision of opportunity to enlarge one's income, against the need to minimize the opportunities for abuse.[15]

A SIMPLE MODEL OF ECONOMIC GROWTH, ECONOMIC EFFICIENCY, AND THE INSTITUTIONAL FRAMEWORK

The effects of the structure of property rights on the allocation of resources within firms now is well recognized. Firms transform inputs into marketable output. Successful firms do so with a minimum amount of inputs. Economies can be thought of as big firms. Just as the efficiency of firms is affected by the structure of property rights, so is the efficiency of economies. Firms chose a particular organizational form within a political, social, legal, and economic system that is exogenous. Economies or nations determine the rights structure or the "rules of the game" in which individual economic actors make choices. This choice of the institutional framework of the economy has consequences for the allocation of resources (efficiency) in the economy.

Economic Growth and the Rights Structure

Let an economy be described by a production function of the following form:

$$(7\text{-}1) \qquad Y = F_\theta(K, L),$$

where Y is national output, K is the capital stock, L is the labor force, θ is the property rights or institutional structure, and $F(K, L)$ is homogeneous of degree one in the inputs. This rights structure is the political, social, legal, and economic framework in which economic decisions are made. Just as differences in organizational forms of firms within a fixed rights environment affect resource allocation within firms, different rights structures affect resource allocation and hence the efficiency of economies. To the extent that differences in the institutional framework affect the efficiency of these economies, the growth rates of these economies will be affected by the choice of the rights structure.

The production function is assumed to be homogeneous of degree one.[16] The production function in intensive form is obtained by dividing equation (7-1) by L.

$$(7\text{-}2) \qquad y = f_\theta(k),$$

where $y = Y/L$ (national output per worker) and $k = K/L$ (capital-labor ratio). Differentiating with respect to time and dividing by y yields

$$(7\text{-}3) \qquad (dy/dt)/y = [\partial(f_\theta/\partial k)/f_\theta(k)](dk/dt)$$
$$= \{\partial f_\theta/\partial k)[k/f_\theta(k)]\}[(dk/dt)/k].$$

Designating g as the growth rate and e as the elasticity, we obtain

$$(7\text{-}4) \qquad g_y = e_k \cdot g_k,$$

where g_y is the growth rate of output per head, g_k is the growth rate of the capital-labor ratio, and e_k is the elasticity of output per head with respect to the capital-labor ratio. Equation (7-4) is the basis for the statistical growth model presented in equations (7-8) through (7-10) and accompanying text.

Measuring National Economic Efficiency

The effect of an increase in the growth rate of the capital-labor ratio on the growth rate of real per capita gross domestic product depends upon how efficiently resources are employed in the economy. For equal rates of capital formation, economies that transform inputs into output relatively inefficiently will grow more slowly than will efficient economies. One or more of the economies described by the production function in equation (7-2) will have values of output per head that are greater than those of other economies with similar values of the input ratio. These economies are the most technically efficient in transforming inputs into output. Such economies are said to be frontier efficient. It is hypothesized that efficiency differences between economies are the result of differences in the efficiency properties of the rights structure or the institutional framework chosen. Designate the efficient economies as y^*—the efficiency frontier. Economies can be compared to the efficiency frontier, and a measure of efficiency, EFF, can be defined as

$$(7\text{-}5) \qquad \text{EFF} = y/y^*, \quad 0 < \text{EFF} \le 1.$$

EFF is bounded between 0 and 1, and, measures the fraction of output actually achieved, y, compared to the technically efficient level, y^*.

Econometric Specification

The estimation technique for the production function depends on the nature of the assumption regarding the error term in the stochastic version of the production function. Three specifications are employed here: (1) the deterministic frontier function of Dennis Aigner and S. F. Chu; (2) the stochastic frontier function of Aigner, Knox Lovell, and Peter Schmidt, as extended by Cliff Huang; and (3) the maximum likelihood Gamma frontier function of William Greene.[17]

The deterministic frontier function is estimated by minimizing the sum of the absolute residuals. The approach, therefore, considers all deviations from the efficient, frontier function as arising from technical inefficiency. A criticism is that only part of the error may be deterministic; part may be truly stochastic. The error term may be of the form $\varepsilon = u + v$, where u is a one-sided disturbance term representing the degree of technical inefficiency and v is a symmetric, normally distributed random influence.

The EM (expected maximization) algorithm is a general approach for computing maximum likelihood estimates from incomplete data and is given by A. P. Dempster, N. M. Laird, and D. G. Rubin.[18] Huang utilizes the algorithm as a method of decomposing the estimated error, ε, into separate components, u and v. The Huang approach is an extension of Aigner, Lovell, and Schmidt.

The EM algorithm technique consists of a two-step iterative procedure. The first procedure is to estimate the sufficient statistics of the stochastic frontier function. The estimation step utilizes the predicted sufficient statistics to estimate the parameter ε by maximum likelihood. Once the estimated ε is obtained by the EM algorithm, the individual stochastic efficient frontier can then be estimated by the conditional mean. Huang can be consulted for further details.[19]

A second criticism of the deterministic frontier approach is the assumption that the error term is normally distributed. Greene has worked through the estimation of stochastic frontier functions with the assumption that the stochastic disturbance is Gamma distributed.[20] Assume that the density function follows the two parameter probability law: $f(\varepsilon) = G(\omega, p) = \omega^p \varepsilon^{p-1} e^{-\omega \varepsilon} / \rho(p)$, where $\varepsilon > 0, \omega > 0, p > 2$, and where $\rho(p)$ is the Gamma function evaluated at p. This disturbance has $\mu = p/\omega$, and $\sigma^2 = p/\omega^2$ is always positive. The parameters of the log likelihood function are estimated by using a Newton-Raphson algorithm. The Gamma function and its derivatives are approximated by utilizing a SAS subroutine known as the LIFEREG procedure. Following Greene, the starting value for the frontier function is obtained by OLS.

DATA AND VARIABLE CONSTRUCTION

The cross-country economic and institutional data employed in this study mainly come from two sources. Robert Summers and Alan Heston have constructed internationally comparable economic series for a large number of countries over time.[21] The economic data used as variables in this study are for the period 1960 to 1980. Data on some of the institutional characteristics of countries come from Raymond D. Gastil, who has annually published, since 1973, country rankings of political liberty and civil liberty, type of economic system, and other measures of freedom.[22] The institutional variables employed in this study are averages of the Gastil rankings for the period 1973 to 1980.[23]

Data on real gross domestic product per capita, population, and the percentage of real gross domestic product devoted to gross domestic investment were available annually for 115 market economies for the period 1960 to 1980. From these data the following variables were calculated (the procedures of calculation are discussed subsequently):

CAPGWTH = the compound growth rate of real per capita gross domestic product from 1960 to 1980;

L = the estimated labor force (population) annually from 1960 to 1980;

K = the estimated capital stock (buildings and machinery and equipment) annually from 1960 to 1980; and

CHGKL = the compound growth rate in the capital-labor (K/L) ratio from 1960 to 1980.

Labor Force

The use of population as a proxy for the labor force is disagreeable but conventional. Data on labor force participation rates are available for the OECD countries and Greece, Iceland, Luxembourg, and Turkey. Data for some non-OECD countries is available from UN sources. These labor force participation rates generally are not very reliable statistically. In developed countries, the labor force participation rates of young adults is relatively low because of higher schooling participation and length of schooling. Also, labor force participation is lower among older workers because alternative income sources are available (pensions, social security, etc.). Among males, population as a proxy for the labor force overstates the labor input in the developed countries relative to the less developed ones. Among females, the pattern of intercountry labor force participation differences is less clear. Much of the developed West has witnessed a secular increase in female labor force participation rates, even among married women. In less developed agricultural economies the labor force participation rate of women as family workers may be quite high. On the other hand, in some cultures there is a taboo against female employment.

Capital Stock

The construction of the series on the annual capital stock by country over the period 1960–1980 is based on the methodology suggested by Arnold C. Harberger.[24] The Summers and Heston annual data series on real gross per capita domestic product, population, and the percentage of real domestic product devoted to gross domestic investment provide the basic data for the construction of the capital stock series.

Gross investment is decomposed into three components: buildings, machinery and equipment, and inventories. The United Nations provides country data on the composition of gross domestic investment.[25] The series on the composition of gross investment hardly covers all countries in all years, but the coverage is fairly extensive. To avoid annual anomalies, the composition share data by country were averaged over the period 1965–1975, and this average was used for the country-specific composition of gross domestic investment. For those countries lacking data on the composition of capital formation, regionally averaged data were utilized. While there is intercountry dispersion in these sectoral shares of gross domestic investment, it is not so extensive as to render a regional average an unreasonable substitute for the missing data. The largest regional coefficient of variation was 23 percent.[26] Inventories are ignored in this study. Therefore, the gross investment series employed here is gross capital formation in buildings and in machinery and equipment.

Harberger assumes a depreciation rate of 2.5 percent per annum for buildings and 8.0 percent per year for machinery and equipment. These are the depreciation rates used in this study. To obtain country estimates for the capital stock in the initial year, gross investment for 1960 is multiplied by the fraction of noninventory investment and divided by the weighted depreciation rate:

(7-6) $\qquad K60 = I60(1 - c)/[0.025(a) + 0.08(b)],$

where a is the share of gross investment in buildings, b is the share in machinery and equipment, and c is the share in inventories.

Capital stock for each subsequent year is obtained by depreciating the previous year's capital stock and adding current gross investment:

(7-7) $\qquad K(t) = K(t - 1)(1 - d) + I(t)(1 - c),$

where $d = [0.025(a) + 0.08(b)]$.

There is no denying that anomalies in the investment data utilized in calculating the initial capital stock may introduce error into the capital stock series. One could reduce such possible errors by averaging the gross investment series for, say, the period 1960–1962. This has not been done. Examination of the data across countries revealed nothing extraordinary. More convincingly, as Harberger has pointed out, the longer the period used in the construction of the estimates, the less sensitive is the capital stock measure to an error in the initial capital stock data. "This is because, if the base year is twenty years back, much of the 'initial' capital stock estimated for that year will in the interim have been 'depreciated away.'"[27]

Institutional Variables

The variables employed to capture some of the effects of the institutional framework on economic development rank the level of political, civil, and economic liberty in nations of the world. Gastil has created measures of political liberty and civil liberty.[28] Political rights are ranked by Gastil from 1 (the highest degree of liberty) to 7 (the lowest), as discussed in chapter 5.

Gastil measures economic liberty in two ways. He categorizes economic systems as capitalist, mixed-capitalist, capitalist-statist, mixed-socialist, or socialist. Capitalist economies generally have a high degree of economic freedom and relatively little market intervention by government. In mixed-capitalist economies, the government is activist in income redistribution and in market intervention and regulation, although it is not particularly active in the direct allocation of resources. Capitalist-statist regimes are characterized by a much greater intervention by the government in markets and a much greater state command of resources but, in general, remain committed to private property. Mixed-socialist economies are command economies that allow some economic freedom, private property, and individual initiative. Socialist economies are command economies with very low degrees of economic freedom and with restricted private property rights. These socialist countries in the sample used in this study are more or less independent socialist regimes and are classified as market economies by Summers and Heston. Communist bloc, nonmarket economies have been excluded from this study.

Gastil also describes the level of economic liberty in nations. Economic freedom is designated by Gastil as high, medium-high, medium, low-medium, and low. Converting these rankings to the ordinal scale employed by Gastil for the political and civil liberty rankings yielded the following result: high equals 1.5; medium-high equals 3.0; medium equals 4.0; low-medium equals 5.0; and low equals 6.5. Of course, there is considerable similarity between the rankings of economic liberty (ECOLIB) and the type of economic system. The rankings of economic liberty (ECOLIB) are used as the measure of economic freedom in the institutional framework in this study.

Econometric difficulties arise in employing ordinal rankings as continuous variables. The most straightforward solution is the transformation of the continuous variable into a set of dummy variables. This is the approach adopted here. For each measure of liberty, three dummy variables were constructed, which more or less correspond to Gastil's categories of high, medium, and low levels of freedom. The variables are as follows.

POL OPEN = 1 if the Gastil ranking of POLLIB is less than 2.0, and 0 otherwise.

POL CLOSED = 1 if the Gastil ranking of POLLIB is equal to or greater than 5.0, and 0 otherwise.

INDIV RIGHTS = 1 if the Gastil ranking of CIVLIB is less than 2.0, and 0 otherwise.

STATE RIGHTS = 1 if the Gastil ranking of CIVLIB is equal to or greater than 5.0, and 0 otherwise.

FREEMKT = 1 if the ranking of ECOLIB based on Gastil is less than 2.0, and 0 otherwise.

COMMAND = 1 if the ranking of ECOLIB based on Gastil is equal to or greater than 5.0, and 0 otherwise.

The reference dummies for POLLIB, CIVLIB, and ECOLIB take the value of 1 if the Gastil ranking is greater than 2.0 and less than 5.0, and 0 otherwise.

175

EMPIRICAL EVIDENCE ON THE

RELATIONSHIP BETWEEN THE INSTITUTIONAL

FRAMEWORK AND ECONOMIC GROWTH

AND ECONOMIC EFFICIENCY

Economic Growth and the Institutional Framework

The OLS regression model utilized in this study is specified as

(7-8) $\text{CAPGWTH} = a_0 + a_1 \text{CHGKL} + \Sigma_i \, b_i \, D_i + \varepsilon,$

where CAPGWTH is the compound growth rate of real gross domestic product per capita over the period 1960–1980, CHGKL is the compound growth rate of real capital stock per capita over the same period, the D_i's are the various dummy variables for the institutional framework described in the previous section,[29] and $\varepsilon \approx iid\ N(0,\sigma^2\varepsilon)$ is the error term, which is assumed to be normally distributed.[30]

Regressions relating each of the dummy variables, which describe a characteristic of the institutional framework, to the growth rate of per capita real gross domestic product appear in table 7-1. All of the independent variables are of the expected sign and are significant at the 1 percent level (the coefficient POL OPEN is significant at the 5 percent level). The growth rates of real domestic product per capita by institutional attribute were calculated from these regressions and are presented in table 7-2. On average, politically open societies grew at a compound real per capita rate of 2.5 percent per annum, compared to a 1.4 percent growth rate for politically closed societies. On average, societies that subscribe to the rule of law grew at a 2.8 percent rate, compared to a 1.2 percent rate in societies where state rights take precedence over individual rights. On average, societies that subscribe to private property rights and a market allocation of resources grew at a 2.8 percent rate, compared to a 1.1 percent rate in nations where private property rights are circumscribed and the government intervenes in resource allocation. Thus the constitutional setting is not only a statistically significant explanation of intercountry variation in the growth rate of real per capita gross domestic product, but is a phenomenon of considerable magnitude. Growth rates in societies that circumscribe or proscribe political, civil, and economic liberty are only 40 to 56 percent (depending upon the attribute) of those in societies in which individual rights are protected.

Political, civil, and economic liberty are logically separable, although the degree to which these rights may be unbundled and remain robust is

TABLE 7-1

Regressions Relating the Separate Effects of Institutional Variables on
Economic Growth over the Period 1960–1980

Equation	Constant	CHGKL Coeffficient	Coefficient	Independent Variable	R^2
(1)	.0198	.5065			.3456
	(11.56)	(7.82)			
(2)	.0185	.5090	.0068	POL OPEN	.3571
	(9.82)	(7.93)	(1.74)		
(3)	.0255	.4992	−.0114	POL CLOSED	.4151
	(11.60)	(8.15)	(−3.80)		
(4)	.0181	.5017	.0094	INDIV RIGHTS	.3714
	(9.87)	(7.90)	(2.38)		
(5)	.0243	.5102	−.0120	STATE RIGHTS	.4181
	(12.26)	(8.36)	(−3.88)		
(6)	.0171	.5050	.0105	FREEMKT	.3893
	(9.08)	(8.07)	(3.01)		
(7)	.0233	.4765	−.0123	COMMAND	.4058
	(12.24)	(7.65)	(−3.53)		

Notes: Student-*t* values are in parentheses below the coefficients. The sample size
is 115. The dependent variable is CAPGWTH.

TABLE 7-2

Average Growth Rates of per Capita Real Gross Domestic Product by
Institutional Attribute

Institutional Attribute	Per Capita Growth Rate	Institutional Attribute	Per Capita Growth Rate	Difference in Growth
POL OPEN	2.53	POL CLOSED	1.41	1.12
INDIV RIGHTS	2.75	STATE RIGHTS	1.23	1.52
FREEMKT	2.76	COMMAND	1.10	1.66
POL OPEN		POL CLOSED		
INDIV RIGHTS	2.73	STATE RIGHTS	0.91	1.82
FREEMKT		COMMAND		

TABLE 7-3

Regressions Relating the Effects of All of the Institutional
Variables on Economic Growth, Economic Efficiency
and the Change in Economic Efficiency

Independent Variable	Dependent Variable		
	(1) CAPGWTH	(2) EFF80	(3) CHGEFF
Constant	.0261	.5124	.1153
	(8.21)	(13.83)	(4.25)
CHGKL	.4713		
	(7.64)		
POL OPEN	−.0170	−.0200	−.2196
	(−1.80)	(−.18)	(−2.67)
POL CLOSED	−.0065	−.1228	−.0628
	(−1.52)	(−2.38)	(−1.66)
INDIV RIGHTS	.0151	.1620	.1550
	(1.53)	(1.38)	(1.80)
STATE RIGHTS	−.0033	−.0080	.0071
	(−.71)	(−.15)	(.17)
FREEMKT	.0031	.1304	.0109
	(.59)	(2.06)	(.24)
COMMAND	−.0072	−.0700	−.0781
	(−1.67)	(−1.38)	(−2.11)
R^2	.4404	.4185	.0957

Notes: Student-t values are in parentheses below the coefficients. The
sample size is 115.

highly questionable. Different nations may bundle rights differently; for
example, one country may offer more economic liberty and less political
or civil liberty than does another. Undoubtedly, there are limits to this
unbundling of individual rights; that is, economic liberty may be relatively meaningless in a tyranny. If these freedoms can be unbundled, and
nations engage in such practices, then each of the variables, which measure an attribute of the institutional framework, ought to emerge statistically significant in the regression that includes all of the rights variables.
If the types of liberties used in this study cannot be unbundled, then the
matrix is singular. All of the institutional framework dummy variables
are included in equation (1) in table 7-3. The increase in the standard
errors of all of the institutional framework dummy variables indicates the
presence of some multicollinearity.[31] The statistical results suggest that

different nations do bundle rights differently but that the separability of rights is relatively weak.

The calculated compound growth rate of real domestic product per capita for the average nation that has an institutional framework with a high degree of political liberty, civil liberty, and economic liberty is 2.7 percent per annum. The calculated growth rate for the average nation with an institutional framework where political rights are proscribed, state rights take precedence over individual rights, private property is circumscribed, and the government intervenes in resource allocation is .9 percent per annum. Hence, the average growth rate in societies where these freedoms are restricted is one-third of that of free societies. These combined restrictions on liberty constitute a 67 percent tax on the wealth of the citizens of such states.

Economic Efficiency and the
Institutional Framework

Efficiency measures for each economy by each method of estimation were obtained and regressed on the institutional variables. While the size effects of the institutional variables on the measures of efficiency are somewhat different, the conclusions are invariant to the choice of the efficiency measure. To conserve space, only the results from the better estimates of the frontier production functions are reported.

In table 7-4 all of the rights variables are of the expected sign and are statistically significant at well above the 1 percent level. The average economy that is politically open (POL OPEN) or where individual rights take precedence over state rights (INDIV RIGHTS) or where private property and market allocation of resources (FREEMKT) prevail has an efficiency level of .74 to .77, depending upon the freedom measure. On the other hand, the average economy that is politically closed (POL CLOSED), where state rights prevail (STATE RIGHTS), or where private property and the market allocation of resources is circumscribed (COMMAND) has an efficiency rating of .34 to .36. Thus societies where freedom is restricted are less than half as efficient in converting resources into gross domestic product as free societies. Alternatively, more than twice the standard of living could be attained with the same resource endowment in these societies, if liberty prevailed. Combining all of the rights variables into the efficiency equation changes the results only marginally (.79 versus .31). Obviously, there is some multicollinearity present in equation (2) in table 7-4.

179

TABLE 7-4

Regressions Relating the Separate Effects of Institutional
Variables on Economic Efficiency, 1980

Equation:	Constant	Coefficient	Independent Variable	R^2
(1)	.4279	.3259	POL OPEN	.2726
	(19.41)	(6.62)		
(2)	.6237	−.2683	POL CLOSED	.2891
	(22.92)	(−6.88)		
(3)	.4266	.3473	INDIV RIGHTS	.3002
	(19.84)	(7.06)		
(4)	.5770	−.2246	STATE RIGHTS	.1867
	(21.90)	(−5.21)		
(5)	.4068	.3308	FREEMKT	.3405
	(18.63)	(7.74)		
(6)	.5452	−.2069	COMMAND	.1249
	(21.80)	(−4.16)		

Notes: Student-t values are in parentheses below the coefficients. The sample size is 115. The dependent variable is EFF80.

Economic Efficiency and Economic Growth

Obviously, growth and efficiency are linked. For equal rates of capital formation, economies that transform inputs into output relatively inefficiently will grow more slowly than will efficient economies. But the order of magnitude of this effect is unknown. The effect of the constitutional setting on economic growth and on economic efficiency has been shown. Is there evidence that the efficiency of some economies has declined and that this decline is related to choice of the institutional framework? Is there evidence that any observed decline in economic efficiency has a significant impact on the rate of economic growth? These questions are addressed in this section.

Comparative static changes in economic efficiency for each economy in the sample were calculated by estimating the frontier production function for 1960, calculating the efficiency measure for 1960, and constructing the variable CHGEFF = EFF80 − EFF60.

The computed changes in economic efficiency over the period were compared to the institutional framework variables. The results appear in table 7-5. The t-values of POL OPEN, INDIV RIGHTS, and FREEMKT indicate a lack of statistical significance, while those of POL CLOSED, STATE

TABLE 7-5

Regressions Relating the Separate Effects of Institutional
Variables on the Change in Economic Efficiency
between 1960 and 1980

Equation:	Constant	Coefficient	Independent Variable	R^2
(1)	.0587	−.0121	POL OPEN	.0011
	(3.85)	(−.35)		
(2)	.0855	−.0602	POL CLOSED	.0346
	(4.60)	(−2.26)		
(3)	.0529	.0176	INDIV RIGHTS	.0023
	(3.49)	(.51)		
(4)	.0779	−.0578	STATE RIGHTS	.0288
	(4.61)	(−2.09)		
(5)	.0468	.0363	FREEMKT	.0034
	(2.97)	(1.18)		
(6)	.0774	−.0839	COMMAND	.0550
	(5.08)	(−2.76)		

Notes: Student-*t* values are in parentheses below the coefficients. The
sample size is 115. The dependent variable is CHGEFF.

RIGHTS, and COMMAND are of the expected sign and are significant
above the 2.5 percent level. This is precisely the result one would expect.
All of the efficiency gains from freedom have been captured in free societies, and one would not expect an improvement in efficiency over time. On
the other hand, unless individual rights are proscribed in closed societies,
uncertainty about freedom or random changes in the status of the individual relative to the state or a secular decline in liberty can cause efficiency
to decline in societies where liberty is constrained.

Finally, the change in economic efficiency over the period was compared to the compound growth rate over the period. The statistical result
appears in equation (7-9). In equation (7-10) the compound growth rate
of the capital-labor ratio is included.

(7-9) $\text{CAPGWTH} = .0175 + .1342 \text{ CHGEFF}, R^2 = .8672.$
$\qquad\qquad\quad (22.98)\quad (27.30)$

(7-10) $\text{CAPGWTH} = .0165 + .1203 \text{ CHGEFF}$
$\qquad\qquad\qquad (24.21)\quad (25.23)$
$\qquad\quad + .1788 \text{ CHGKL}, R^2 = .9012.$
$\qquad\qquad (6.32)$

Although there is some circularity of argument involved in these regressions, estimation of such a relationship is legitimate on the grounds that efficiency, change in efficiency, and growth are independent relationships. The regression estimates provide some evidence of the order of magnitude of the relationship between economic efficiency and economic growth. A large portion of the variance in the growth rates of the 115 market economies over the twenty-year period is associated with changes in the efficiency with which inputs are utilized to produce output and in the growth rate of capital intensity. Previously, it was found that political (civil) illiberality and restricted private property rights reduced economic efficiency. Economies can substitute increased capital formation for the loss in economic efficiency that these illiberal conditions foster. The implicit trade-off between the growth rate of the capital-labor ratio and the efficiency loss induced by an illiberal economic and legal-political environment can be obtained from equation (7-10). Economic growth can be maintained for every 1 percentage point decline in efficiency by incrementing the growth rate of the capital-labor ratio by .7 percentage points, a very substantial increment in national resources.

SUMMARY AND CONCLUSIONS

Like water that seeks its own level, resources are predisposed to flow to their highest valued use. But a necessary condition for achieving this efficiency result is that all resources be owned exclusively by private individuals and that these resources be transferable. The political, social, legal, and economic framework of society defines what resources can be owned, who can own them, and how they can be employed. The constitutional setting sets the parameters of rights in a society. The menu of choices open to mankind is rich. What is sanctioned in law ranges from judge-made rulings, as in common law, to decisions based on the "word of God," as in Muslim law. In politics, the range is from the Vermont town hall meeting, in which everything is settled by the citizens, to totalitarian states, where even the most private of matters between people must be sanctioned by government. In economics, the range is from purely private economies, in which even the legitimacy of the public goods property of the lighthouse is disputed, to communist societies (certain religious orders), in which everything is owned in common.

A rich literature exists on the efficiency effects of different economic, political, social, and legal arrangements. While considerable testing of property rights theory, in the relatively narrow context of the U.S. institutional framework, has been undertaken at the firm or industry level, no empirical work has been done at the economywide level to assess the effects of different economic, political, and legal arrangements on economic efficiency and economic growth. The existence of comparable international economic data and measures of political and civil liberty make a test of the effect of the institutional framework on the efficiency and growth of economies possible.

For the world's 115 market economies over the period 1960 to 1980, compound growth rates of real domestic product per capita and a measure of economic efficiency were compared to measures of political, civil, and economic liberty. It was found that the choice of the institutional framework has profound consequences for the efficiency and growth of economies. Politically open societies, which bind themselves to the rule of law, to private property, and to the market allocation of resources grow at three times (2.7 to 0.9 percent annually) the rate of and are two and one-half times as efficient as societies where these freedoms are circumscribed or proscribed.

More research is required. Richer measures of the institutional framework need to be developed. More sophisticated models, which link these measures to the performance of economies, would shed more light on the topic. But if the order of magnitude of the effects of the institutional framework found here holds in subsequent research, as I believe it will, the issue of the configuration of the appropriate structure of property rights for economic development needs to be brought to the forefront in the development literature. The role of capital accumulation, innovation, human capital, and entrepreneurship widely are recognized as sources of economic growth.[32] Still more fundamental, a precondition for accumulation and innovation, is the right to capitalize.

183

The Constitutional Setting
and the Distribution
of Income

THE PROSPECTS that economic growth may have an adverse effect on income distribution is a major theme in the modern development literature.[1] Development strategies have been promoted that address problems of income distribution. These distribution-sensitive strategies greatly affected World Bank lending programs and government-to-government transfers. Many development economists called for massive government intervention in the economy, partly because they believed that it would improve equity. The view that rights regimes that give wide latitude to individual initiative and responsibility have inferior distributional outcomes compared to statist frameworks in which resources are allocated by political considerations of development and equity is very widespread in the development literature.

It was shown in the previous chapter that nations that have chosen systems that do not encourage individual initiative have much lower rates of economic growth and are less efficient in transforming resources into GDP than nations that are protective of individual rights. Here it is shown that income is more equally distributed within countries that are politically open, that have private property and market allocation of resources, and that are committed to the rule of law than in countries where these rights are abridged. Furthermore, it is shown that increased equality of rights (opportunities to compete for income streams) is associated with increased economic efficiency. This result contrasts with the conventional wisdom of a negative trade-off between efficiency and equity.[2] Previous thinking about the relationship between income inequality and economic efficiency has failed to distinguish between equality of rights or opportunities to compete for income streams and equality of economic outcomes. It appears that an increase in freedom (equality of rights to compete for income streams) yields an improvement both in efficiency and in equity, and is clearly Pareto efficient.

RIGHTS AND INCOME DISTRIBUTION

In chapter 3, the theory of "constitutional contract" was discussed. It was shown that there are many constitutional contracts in which rights are distributed unequally among the parties, but agreement between them is welfare increasing, because both parties gain from the agreement. Conceptually, "constitutional contracts" can be arrayed hierarchically from the most inequitable distribution of rights or opportunities to compete for income streams to the most equal distribution. Each "constitution" has an inherent level of economic efficiency. Efficiency is at its lowest in a society without freedom. Men who have no freedom have no incentive to work, since what they produce is for those who rule them. Moreover, those who rule must devote substantial resources to monitoring the effort of those who work. These resources are a social waste. Economic efficiency is at a maximum in a society of equal rights for all, since the gains from exchange can be exploited fully only when all have equal opportunities to compete for income (consumption) streams.

The trade-off between economic efficiency and equality of rights is negative in figure 8-1. In the figure, efficiency and equity of rights are indexed on a scale of 0 to 1.0. An efficiency level of 1.0 is the maximum. An equity level of 0 is the maximum *equality* of rights, as with the indexing of conventional measures of income inequality (for example, the Gini coefficient, Atkinson's inequality measure, etc.). An equity level of 1.0 is perfect inequality of rights. In regimes with wide inequality in the distribution of rights, wide income inequality and low economic efficiency will exist. In regimes with high degrees of equality of rights, low income inequality and high economic efficiency will exist. Thus increases in equity obtained by increases in equality of rights or opportunities are associated with increases in economic efficiency.

This theoretical insight contrasts sharply with the conventional wisdom of a negative trade-off between efficiency and income equality. For a single country at any moment of time, the rights structure is fixed. All thinking of the relationship between the income distribution and economic efficiency implicitly holds the rights structure constant and focuses on economic outcomes. However, across nations there is wide disparity in the "rules of the game." Across regimes, the variance of incomes is the sum of the variance due to differences in the distribution of rights to income streams, holding economic outcomes constant, plus the variance

185

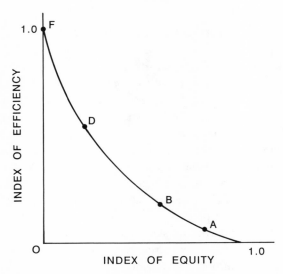

Figure 8-1. The Trade-Off between Efficiency and Equality

due to differences in economic outcomes, holding the rights structure constant, plus the covariance between the effects of the rights structure and economic outcomes. It is hypothesized that inequality of income due to differences in economic outcomes monitonically rises as inequality of rights to compete for income streams declines. Adding the theoretical variance of income inequality due to inequality of economic outcomes to the theoretical variance of income inequality due to the inequality of rights to compete for income streams yields the U-shaped income distribution function in figure 8-2. At some level of rights inequality, σ^*_R in the figure, marginal increases in rights to compete for income streams, which lower income inequality, yield marginal increases in inequality of economic outcomes. Increases in equality of rights beyond σ^*_R yield higher income inequality, because the effect of inequality of outcomes is larger than the effect of inequality of rights.

Here, only the relationship between income inequality and the rights structure is examined. Intrinsically, it is difficult to measure the effect of various individual endowments on the distribution of economic outcomes. Moreover, some individual endowments (rate of time preference, accumulation of human capital, occupational choice, etc.) are endogenously related to the distribution of individual rights. To overlook the effect of the structure of rights on income inequality is to ignore a very important source of the observed income inequality across nations.

186

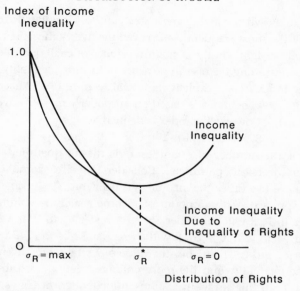

Figure 8-2. U-Shaped Income Distribution Function

DATA AND VARIABLE CONSTRUCTION

The cross-country economic data, the political and civil rights measures, and the measure of economic liberty (chapter 5) have been discussed previously. Three measures of economic liberty are employed here. ECOLIB1 is based on weights of the fifteen attributes obtained by principal components analysis. ECOLIB2 is based on weights of the fifteen attributes obtained by hedonic estimation of the regression coefficients. ECOLIB3 is based on weights of a hybrid hedonic equation (attributes entered stepwise to a noninclusion stopping rule based on the critical F-value). All of the economic liberty measures are ranks of the indices with a rank = 1 for the highest level of economic liberty.

Measuring Inequality

The income share data used to calculate the inequality measures are based on decile income data compiled by Jain[3] and revised or extended quintile data in the *World Development Report*. The income units are defined as quintile shares, where $q_i = 1, 5$ represents the ith income unit share and

$$0 < q_1 < q_2 \ldots < q_5 < 1.$$

187

Many well-known inequality measures can be formulated from this ordering. Of the most frequently employed inequality measures, all impose an implicit "weight" on the social importance of each quantile of income units in determining the overall measure of income inequality. Atkinson's inequality index makes explicit the social welfare (SW) basis for the inequality index.[4] The index is based on an underlying social welfare function. Following Cowell,[5] the index is defined as

$$SW = 1 - [1/n \sum_i (nq_i)^{1-\lambda}]^{1/1-\lambda}, i = 1, 5,$$

where n is the number of quantiles, q_i is the ith quantile, and λ is the "inequality aversion" parameter. Consider Cowell's example. Let a rich man, R, have five times the income of a poor man, P. Inequality aversion can be expressed as the amount of income society is willing to have R surrender to P. R will surrender $\$5^\lambda$ to transfer \$1 to P. If $\lambda = 0$, R will surrender \$1 to P. If $\lambda = .5$, R will surrender \$2.24 to P. If $\lambda = 2$, R will surrender \$25 to P. The higher the value of λ, the more adverse society is to income inequality and the more willing society is to transfer income from R to P. In this study, five Atkinson inequality measures were calculated with the values of λ of .5, .75, .95, 1.5, and 2. The corresponding social welfare-based inequality measures are named ATK1 through ATK5, respectively. The Atkinson inequality measures appear in appendix 8-1. As a cross-check on the sensitivity of the findings to the choice of the inequality measure, all of the specifications were reestimated with Theil's entropy coefficient measure of inequality (not reported here).[6] The findings were similar for either measure of inequality.

EVIDENCE: THE EFFECT OF RIGHTS ON INCOME INEQUALITY

Income Inequality within Nations

Evidence of the effect of the rights structure on income quintiles within countries appears in table 8-1. The Gastil measures of political and civil liberty are specified in three ways: (1) as the original, continuous variables; (2) as rank variables; and (3) as dummy variables. POLLIB and CIVLIB are the Gastil measures. A difficulty with the scaling of such variables is that it can introduce spurious correlation. To ensure against a potentially false empirical conclusion, a Spearman rank correlation analysis was performed. As an alternative confirmation, the Gastil measures were converted to dummy variables. Values of the Gastil measures less than 2.0 represent regimes that are relatively free (POL OPEN, INDIV RIGHTS), while values above 4.0 represent regimes that are relatively re-

TABLE 8-1
Regressions Relating the Separate Effects of Rights Measures on Quintile Income Share

Measure	Q1	Q2	Q3	Q4	Q5
Political liberty					
Constant	.0574	.1137	.1670	.2374	.4245
	(10.95)	(20.55)	(28.51)	(37.15)	(22.49)
POLLIB	−.0007	−.0048	−.0075	−.0084	.0214
	(.59)	(3.64)	(5.46)	(5.57)	(4.81)
R^2	.0050	.1507	.2942	.3030	.2425
Spearman R	−.0746	−.4285	−.5775	−.5876	.5255
Constant	.0539	.0900	.1305	.1979	.5277
	(17.57)	(27.91)	(36.70)	(49.09)	(46.19)
POL OPEN	.0031	.0230	.0325	.0320	−.0906
	(.53)	(3.71)	(4.76)	(4.13)	(4.13)
R^2	.0042	.1562	.2391	.1889	.1888
Constant	.0581	.1067	.1549	.2228	.4575
	(15.37)	(26.48)	(35.28)	(45.38)	(32.82)
POL CLOSED	−.0063	−.0199	−.0295	−.0307	.0864
	(1.22)	(3.59)	(4.89)	(4.54)	(4.51)
R^2	.0070	.1468	.2493	.2216	.2186
Civil Liberty					
Constant	.0600	.1179	.1722	.2396	.4103
	(10.58)	(20.09)	(27.91)	(33.88)	(20.42)
CIVLIB	−.0015	−.0063	−.0095	−.0095	.0268
	(1.04)	(4.16)	(6.01)	(5.25)	(5.20)
R^2	.0012	.1911	.3370	.2780	.2743
Spearman R	−.1235	−.4479	−.5865	−.5517	.5360
Constant	.0522	.0883	.1291	.1978	.5326
	(17.50)	(30.01)	(39.57)	(50.21)	(50.65)
INDIV RIGHTS	.0010	.0309	.0394	.0342	−.1145
	(1.69)	(5.33)	(6.12)	(4.40)	(5.52)
R^2	.0264	.2841	.3461	.2102	.2993
Constant	.0573	.1056	.1540	.2224	.4607
	(15.79)	(27.21)	(37.02)	(48.20)	(34.65)
STATE RIGHTS	−.0053	−.0193	−.0303	−.0324	.0873
	(1.01)	(3.47)	(5.08)	(4.90)	(4.58)
R^2	.0004	.1376	.2654	.2502	.2243

TABLE 8-1, *cont.*

Measure	Q1	Q2	Q3	Q4	Q5
Economic liberty					
Constant	.0532	.1080	.1604	.2274	.4510
	(10.75)	(19.83)	(27.24)	(34.29)	(23.40)
ECOLIB1	.2731E-04	−.2103E-03	−.3771E-03	−.3716E-03	.9322E-04
	(.36)	(2.55)	(4.23)	(3.70)	(3.21)
R^2	.0019	.0738	.1964	.1551	.1185
Constant	.0534	.1078	.1592	.2268	.4527
	(10.90)	(20.01)	(26.99)	(34.43)	(23.75)
ECOLIB2	.2187E-04	−.1872E-03	−.3202E-03	−.3250E-03	.8117E-03
	(.33)	(2.55)	(3.99)	(3.63)	(3.13)
R^2	.0016	.0741	.1779	.1470	.1130
Constant	.0534	.1086	.1606	.2284	.4488
	(11.17)	(20.84)	(28.68)	(36.41)	(24.54)
ECOLIB3	.2146E-04	−.2064E-03	−.3560E-03	−.3643E-03	.9062E-03
	(.32)	(2.84)	(4.56)	(4.16)	(3.55)
R^2	.0015	.0928	.2226	.1913	.1440

Note: $n = 70$.

stricted (POL CLOSED, STATE RIGHTS). The economic liberty measures (ECOLIB1, etc.) are the ranks of the economic liberty indexes.

The evidence strongly suggests that free societies have higher shares of income going to the second through the fourth quintiles (twentieth to eightieth percentiles) and lower shares being received by the fifth quintile (eightieth to one hundredth percentiles). Conversely, societies in which political, civil, and economic rights are restricted have lower shares among the income recipients in the twentieth to eightieth percentiles and higher income shares among those in the eightieth to one hundredth percentiles. The relative share of the poorest in society (Q1) is invariant to the choice of the institutional framework. Thus the poor are no better off in terms of relative income, which is only one aspect of quality of life, in free or tyrannical societies. However, overall, as measured by the relationship between the various rights variables and the quintile income shares, free societies have more income equity than do societies in which rights are restricted. The conclusion is strengthened by the fact that the statistical significance of all of the coefficients in the table exceeds the 1 percent level, except for those relating to the first income quintile.

TABLE 8-2

Income Shares and Income Inequality by Institutional Attribute

Measure	Q1[a]	Q2	Q3	Q4	Q5
Political liberty					
Most free	.057	.107	.160	.229	.446
Least free	.053	.080	.115	.179	.574
Difference	.004	.027	.045	.050	− .128
Civil liberty					
Most free	.059	.112	.163	.230	.437
Least free	.050	.074	.106	.173	.598
Difference	.009	.038	.057	.057	− .161
Economic liberty[b]					
Most free	.055	.108	.160	.228	.450
Least free	.056	.080	.111	.177	.576
Difference	− .001	.028	.049	.051	− .126

[a] Since the coefficients (shown in table 8-1) for the Q1 quintile are mainly statistically insignificant, the comparisons for Q1 should be interpreted with caution.

[b] ECOLIB3 is the measure of economic liberty.

In addition to the statistical significance, the order of magnitude of the effect of freedom on equity is quite large. The statistical results from table 8-1 were used to calculate the income shares for the most free and the least free societies across quintiles; these shares are presented in table 8-2. For quintiles Q2 and Q3 on average across liberty measures, income shares are nearly 50 percent higher in the most free compared to the least free societies. The share of income going to the fourth quintile is about 30 percent higher in the most free nations compared to the least free. On the other hand, the share going to the richest members of society is 25 percent lower in the most free societies.

Evidence of the effect of the rights structure on overall measures of income inequality appears in table 8-3. The evidence strongly suggests that free societies have more income equality due to a more equal distribution of rights (opportunities) than do societies where individual rights are restricted. The statistical results from table 8-3 were utilized to calculate the Atkinson social welfare measures of income inequality for the most and the least free societies; these measures are presented in table 8-4. Averaging the results across the five Atkinson measures and the three liberty measures, income inequality is somewhat more than 50 percent higher in

TABLE 8-3
Regressions Relating the Separate Effects of Rights
on Atkinson Measures of Income Inequality

Measure	ATK1	ATK2	ATK3	ATK4	ATK5
Political liberty					
Constant	.1011	.1509	.1898	.2876	.3625
	(7.03)	(7.44)	(7.86)	(9.24)	(10.67)
POLLIB	.0118	.0158	.0181	.0205	.0196
	(3.47)	(3.31)	(3.17)	(2.80)	(2.45)
R^2	.1379	.1261	.1162	.0899	.0676
Constant	.1579	.2274	.2773	.3870	.4575
	(18.45)	(18.88)	(19.35)	(21.02)	(22.84)
POL OPEN	−.0500	−.0674	−.0773	−.0879	−.0842
	(3.04)	(2.92)	(2.81)	(2.49)	(2.19)
R^2	.1070	.0981	.0910	.0700	.0522
Constant	.1176	.1728	.2144	.3141	.3862
	(11.28)	(11.77)	(12.27)	(13.98)	(15.79)
POL CLOSED	.0506	.0688	.0793	.0926	.0915
	(3.53)	(3.40)	(3.30)	(3.00)	(2.72)
R^2	.1423	.1331	.1252	.1037	.0848
Civil liberty					
Constant	.0904	.1359	.1720	.2656	.3395
	(5.91)	(6.31)	(6.70)	(8.00)	(9.36)
CIVLIB	.0156	.0211	.0243	.0281	.0274
	(3.97)	(3.82)	(3.69)	(3.31)	(2.95)
R^2	.1765	.1649	.1549	.1259	.1004
Constant	.1620	.2334	.2846	.3971	.4690
	(20.28)	(20.76)	(21.28)	(23.06)	(24.95)
INDIV RIGHTS	−.0687	−.0945	−.1102	−.1323	−.1338
	(4.36)	(4.26)	(4.18)	(3.90)	(3.61)
R^2	.2072	.1992	.1926	.1705	.1483
Constant	.1196	.1757	.2179	.3189	.3916
	(12.00)	(12.50)	(13.02)	(14.79)	(16.66)
STATE RIGHTS	.0508	.0688	.0789	.0909	.0886
	(3.55)	(3.41)	(3.29)	(2.94)	(2.63)
R^2	.1442	.1335	.1244	.0997	.0787

TABLE 8-3, *cont.*

Measure	ATK1	ATK2	ATK3	ATK4	ATK5
Economic liberty					
Constant	.1176	.1734	.2158	.3190	.3952
	(8.28)	(8.69)	(9.10)	(10.51)	(12.00)
ECOLIB1	.4766E-03	.6371E-03	.7223E-03	.7865E-03	.7040E-03
	(2.22)	(2.11)	(2.01)	(1.71)	(1.41)
R^2	.0536	.0475	.0422	.0271	.0142
Constant	.1199	.1767	.2197	.3233	.3989
	(8.47)	(8.90)	(9.32)	(10.72)	(12.21)
ECOLIB2	.3928E-03	.5221E-03	.5896E-03	.6403E-03	.5740E-03
	(2.04)	(1.93)	(1.84)	(1.56)	(1.29)
R^2	.0440	.0382	.0333	.0204	.0100
Constant	.1170	.1728	.2152	.3185	.3944
	(8.57)	(9.00)	(9.43)	(10.88)	(12.42)
ECOLIB3	.4547E-03	.6051E-03	.6837E-03	.7444E-03	.6709E-03
	(2.39)	(2.26)	(2.15)	(1.82)	(1.51)
R^2	.0637	.0561	.0497	.0326	.0184

Note: $n = 70$.

TABLE 8-4

Atkinson Measures of Income Inequality by Institutional Attribute

Measure	ATK1	ATK2	ATK3	ATK4	ATK5
Political liberty					
Most free	.1129	.1667	.2079	.3081	.3821
Least free	.1837	.2615	.3165	.4311	.4997
Difference	.0708	.0948	.1086	.1230	.1176
Civil liberty					
Most free	.1060	.1570	.1963	.2937	.3669
Least free	.1996	.2836	.3421	.4623	.5313
Difference	.0936	.1266	.1458	.1686	.1644
Economic liberty[a]					
Most free	.1175	.1734	.2159	.3192	.3951
Least free	.1807	.2575	.3110	.4227	.4883
Difference	.0632	.0841	.0951	.1035	.0932

[a] ECOLIB3 is the measure of economic liberty.

societies where individual rights are restricted. The lack of rights of individuals to compete for income streams has a large and bad effect on the income distribution.

Equity of Rights and Economic Efficiency

Transfers of high income to low income types can only be made with a "leaky bucket"—the efficiency-reduced shrinkage of the income pie. At a particular time for a particular regime in which the rights structure is fixed, redistribution is about altering economic outcomes. In this sense of the analysis of efficiency and equity, there is no quarrel with the Okun hypothesis. However, rights structures differ across nations and within nations differ across time. A move from an inequitable distribution of individual rights to a more equitable distribution increases the opportunities to compete for income streams of those previously excluded from competition. This increase in rights expands the gains from exchange in the postconstitutional stage. Thus efficiency and equity may be higher in free societies than in societies where individual rights are restricted.

It has been shown that free societies are more efficient and have higher growth rates of real per capita GDP than do closed societies. Income inequality is lower in free nations. Evidence of a "trade-off" between equity of rights and efficiency is presented in table 8-5. The efficiency measure employed has been described previously and is the best among the deterministic and stochastic specifications of the efficiency frontiers. The conclusions are invariant to the choice of the specification. The relationship between efficiency and quintile income share is very revealing. The share of income going to the poorest members of society appears not to affect efficiency. Redistribution to the middle class, broadly measured as the twentieth to eightieth percentiles, increases efficiency. It is among these income classes that an expansion of individual rights is likely to yield the largest gains from exchange. The larger the share of income going to the richest members of society, the lower the level of efficiency.

Further evidence on the trade-off relationship is presented in table 8-6. The rights variable utilized in the analysis is ECOLIB2. The estimated relationship between EFF80 and ECOLIB2 is

$$\text{EFF80} = \quad .7992 - .4479\text{E-}02\ \text{ECOLIB2}, R^2 = .4350.$$
$$\quad\quad (19.56) \quad\ (7.24)$$

This equation is utilized to obtain the predicted values of efficiency in table 8-6. Three of the five Atkinson measures were selected. The predicted values are obtained from the regression equations in table 8-3.

TABLE 8-5
Regressions Relating Efficiency and
Quintile Income Share

Constant	Coefficient	Variable	R^2
.6143	− 1.2034	Q1	.0025
(7.89)	(.91)		
.3578	1.9815	Q2	.0291
(3.18)	(1.75)		
.1640	2.7606	Q3	.0999
(1.23)	(2.94)		
− .0879	3.0803	Q4	.1574
(.51)	(3.73)		
.9265	− .7513	Q5	.0675
(5.91)	(2.45)		

Note: $n = 70$.

TABLE 8-6
The Relationship between Economic Efficiency and
Atkinson Measures of Income Inequality

Rank of Economic Liberty	Efficiency	ATK1	ATK3	ATK5
1	.79	.1181	.2166	.3198
10	.75	.1224	.2231	.3269
20	.71	.1272	.2303	.3348
30	.66	.1319	.2375	.3426
40	.62	.1367	.2447	.3505
50	.58	.1415	.2519	.3584
60	.53	.1462	.2592	.3662
70	.49	.1510	.2664	.3741
80	.44	.1558	.2736	.3820
90	.40	.1606	.2808	.3898
100	.35	.1653	.2881	.3977
110	.31	.1701	.2953	.4056
120	.26	.1749	.3025	.4134
130	.22	.1796	.3097	.4213
140	.17	.1844	.3170	.4292

Within countries, those with more unequal income distributions, as measured by the Atkinson measures of inequality, have lower levels of efficiency. The effect of increases in income inequality on efficiency is quite elastic. Each 1 percent increase in ATK1 is associated with a 3.2 percent reduction in efficiency. The elasticities of ATK3 and ATK5 with respect to efficiency are -3.7 and -4.8, respectively.

It appears that an increase in individual rights is relatively Pareto efficient. Both an increase in equity and an increase in efficiency occur from the movement from a more restricted to a less restricted rights regime.

SUMMARY AND CONCLUSIONS

The premise that economic development and equity are incompatible is not supported by the evidence of a strong relationship between equality of rights and the income distribution. The premise that equity requires the denial of individual rights and the affirmation of government control of resources is not true. What has been overlooked in the literature on growth and equity is the effect of the rights structure on both economic efficiency and the income distribution. The evidence is that free societies have much larger shares of income going to the middle 60 percent of the distribution than is observed in societies where men are not free to choose. In politically open societies compared to politically closed regimes the share of income of the middle three quintiles is as follows: for Q2, 10.7 versus 8.0; for Q3, 16.0 versus 11.5; and for Q4, 22.9 versus 17.9. In the aggregate, the shares of the middle quintiles are 49.6 versus 37.4. In nations that obey the rule of law compared to regimes in which the rights of the state relative to the individual are paramount the comparisons are as follows: for Q2, 11.2 versus 7.4; for Q3, 16.3 versus 10.6; and for Q4, 23.0 versus 17.3. Summing the three quintiles yields a comparison of 50.5 versus 35.3. In countries that have private property, market allocation of resources, and minimum intervention by government compared to command economies, the shares of income of the middle quintiles are as follows: for Q2, 10.8 versus 8.0; for Q3, 16.0 versus 11.1; and for Q4, 22.8 versus 17.7. Aggregated, the shares of the middle class in regimes with high levels of economic liberty are 49.6, versus 36.8 for regimes with restricted private economic rights.

Equally revealing as a matter of equity is the status of the poor and the rich in free and statist nations. The income share of the highest income group is much larger in nations that repress individual rights than in those where rights are protected. Averaged across the rights measures, the share of income going to the highest income quintile is 58.3 percent among the least free nations and is 44.4 percent among the most free, a staggering difference of nearly 14.0 percentage points. Among the poorest members of society choice of the rights regime does not have much of an impact on their share of income. While the share averaged across rights measures is larger in the most free nations (5.7 versus 5.3), the difference is not statistically significant.

Economic progress and equity are not incompatible. Nations can move to a less restrictive rights regime and increase economic efficiency, economic growth, and equity. Collectivism is a lubricious path to economic progress and equity.

APPENDIX 8-1: ATKINSON MEASURES OF INCOME INEQUALITY

FOR SEVENTY NATIONS

Country	ATK1	ATK2	ATK3	ATK4	ATK5
Benin	.1182	.1691	.2055	.2864	.3392
Chad	.0835	.1222	.1513	.2222	.2751
Egypt	.1178	.1720	.2125	.3094	.3794
Gabon	.3023	.4224	.5006	.6461	.7207
Ivory Coast	.1394	.1960	.2348	.3156	.3642
Kenya	.2264	.3271	.3988	.5520	.6423
Madagascar	.1958	.2797	.3386	.4645	.5418
Malawi	.1065	.1502	.1806	.2454	.2855
Morocco	.2184	.3011	.3543	.4524	.5018
Niger	.0819	.1205	.1498	.2221	.2770
Nigeria	.1914	.2676	.3185	.4189	.4741
Senegal	.2364	.3347	.4020	.5389	.6179
Sierra Leone	.1431	.2060	.2513	.3534	.4213
South Africa	.2528	.3725	.4589	.6361	.7276
Sudan	.1460	.2161	.2694	.3990	.4908
Tanzania	.1290	.1868	.2290	.3269	.3947
Tunisia	.2288	.3191	.3786	.4928	.5538
Zambia	.2129	.3034	.3665	.4992	.5792
Bangladesh	.1100	.1607	.1987	.2901	.3567
Burma	.0948	.1344	.1622	.2232	.2625
Hong Kong	.1170	.1722	.2140	.3163	.3919
India	.1211	.1747	.2138	.3028	.3631

APPENDIX 8-1, *cont.*

Country	ATK1	ATK2	ATK3	ATK4	ATK5
Iraq	.2827	.3996	.4781	.6309	.7123
Israel	.0860	.1295	.1671	.2551	.3289
Japan	.0586	.0870	.1092	.1666	.2133
Korea	.1077	.1591	.1984	.2958	.3693
Malayasia	.1869	.2712	.3324	.4690	.5562
Nepal	.1880	.2666	.3211	.4357	.5053
Pakistan	.1011	.1483	.1842	.2716	.3368
Philippines	.1541	.2215	.2698	.3773	.4478
Sri Lanka	.0868	.1273	.1578	.2327	.2890
Thailand	.1311	.1906	.2345	.3369	.4078
Belgium	.0579	.0872	.1105	.1731	.2263
Denmark	.0884	.1345	.1718	.2724	.3554
Finland	.0783	.1185	.1507	.2370	.3084
France	.1121	.1659	.2073	.3105	.3887
Germany	.0703	.1043	.1306	.1979	.2515
Greece	.1077	.1534	.1859	.2576	.3045
Ireland	.0736	.1097	.1380	.2116	.2712
Italy	.0997	.1475	.1842	.2758	.3457
Netherlands	.0551	.0826	.1044	.1624	.2115
Norway	.0790	.1198	.1527	.2416	.3163
Portugal	.1297	.1898	.2346	.3414	.4173
Spain	.0780	.1164	.1464	.2244	.2873
Sweden	.0773	.1141	.1424	.2138	.2703
Switzerland	.0715	.1080	.1373	.2162	.2830
Turkey	.1866	.2702	.3308	.4663	.5533
United Kingdom	.0806	.1203	.1513	.2309	.2941
Barbados	.1584	.2336	.2904	.4264	.5211
Canada	.0931	.1411	.1796	.2823	.3657
Costa Rica	.1777	.2597	.3205	.4611	.5549
El Salvador	.1209	.1777	.2204	.3235	.3978
Jamaica	.2413	.3491	.4257	.5875	.6800
Mexico	.2060	.2993	.3669	.5159	.6078
Panama	.2516	.3650	.4456	.6133	.7057
Trinidad and Tobago	.1480	.2179	.2706	.3959	.4832
United States	.0927	.1405	.1789	.2814	.3649
Argentina	.1433	.2104	.2607	.3808	.4654
Bolivia	.2071	.2948	.3559	.4856	.5652
Brazil	.2780	.3957	.4757	.6330	.7180
Chile	.1506	.2202	.2719	.3929	.4759

APPENDIX 8-1, *cont.*

Country	ATK1	ATK2	ATK3	ATK4	ATK5
Colombia	.2848	.4023	.4807	.6305	.7077
Ecuador	.1034	.1527	.1903	.2828	.3515
Peru	.2515	.3665	.4489	.6210	.7150
Suriname	.0702	.1016	.1246	.1792	.2183
Venezuela	.1880	.2768	.3428	.4938	.5903
Australia	.1209	.1779	.2210	.3255	.4012
Fiji	.1644	.2407	.2971	.4273	.5136
Indonesia	.1349	.1957	.2402	.3409	.4072
New Zealand	.1199	.1668	.2094	.3169	.3989

The Economic Effect of the
Size of the State

IN THE eighteenth century and through most of the nineteenth century, the economic resources at the command of government were limited. Government enforced rights, protected property, and provided public goods. Perhaps, beginning with the social welfare programs of Bismarck as a general model, government became much more active in its income distribution function toward the end of the nineteenth century. The resources available for redistribution rose by an order of magnitude with the innovation of progressive income taxation. Now, modern governments provide direct income redistribution and supply a wide array of collective goods and services. The fiscal regime has expanded as government has taken responsibility for stimulating aggregate demand during cyclical downturns, for planning economic development through the political allocation of resources, and for altering the income distribution through fiscal and social policy. Domestically, citizens make behavioral adjustments as political incentives replace those of the market. Coalitions of special interests withdraw resources from the productive sector to obtain economic rents, available to those who expend sufficient political capital to capture the coercive power of the state. This transfer of resources from productive to directly unproductive activities reduces economic growth.

THE SIZE OF THE STATE, ECONOMIC GROWTH,
AND THE EFFICIENT UTILIZATION OF NATIONAL RESOURCES

The size of the state conventionally is measured as government expenditures as a fraction of national output. So measured, government has grown enormously in modern times.[1] During this century, among developed nations, central government spending has risen from under a tenth to more than a third of a share of GNP. The rise of government control over national resources is ubiquitous.[2] Is this substitution of public choice for private choice beneficial or harmful to society on the basis of some objective criterion? Obviously, an array of criteria must be specified and their interrelationships modeled before an definitive, overall judgment can be made. The objective here is more limited. Evidence is offered on the effect of the size of the fiscal sector, net of resource growth, on economic growth, and on the efficiency of resource allocation for 115 market economies for the period 1960 to 1980. The overall conclusion is that for these criteria at least, the growth of the public sector has been harmful.

INCREASES IN THE SIZE OF GOVERNMENT:
BENEFICIAL OR HARMFUL?

Several caricatures of the state are found in the literature. In the English-speaking public finance tradition the democratic state is characterized as benevolent. The agents (politicians and bureaucrats) benignly serve the polity in performing the Musgravian fiscal functions.[3] From a public choice perspective, the bureaucratic state in majoritarian, representative democracies is fiscally expansionist, redistributive, and self-serving, with public resources being allocated in a political market.[4] In the Italian public finance tradition the state is characterized as malevolent.[5] Unshackled of constitutional rules, revenue-maximizing Leviathan drives the polity to penury.[6]

While malevolence for its own sake cannot be ruled out, political self-seeking with guile naturally is linked with rent-seeking.[7] In majoritarian, representative democracies, logrolling politicians redistribute public income by concentrating net benefits (benefits minus taxes) among the majority coalitions electing them. This tends to lead to a growth of the public sector[8] and toward a redistribution of public resources toward the middle class.[9] In nonrepresentative governments, the public sector is a source of rents to the ruling class and a source of much mischief. Gordon Tullock's important theoretical insight on rent-seeking identifies monopoly- and tariff-induced rents as a prize up for grabs.[10] In a constitutional setting of laissez-faire, free trade, and market allocation of resources, competition erodes rents. Government command of resources through its fiscal function and government rules, regulations, licensing, etc., gives rise to economic rents that are allocated in a political market. Because the prize of special treatment, enforced by the coercive power of government, has value, resources (political capital) are expended to capture it. A rational rent-seeker expends resources equal to the expected value of the prize. As

201

such, competitive rent-seeking games, by exhausting the value of the prize, are a social waste of productive resources. James Buchanan argues that the level of rent-seeking and the resources devoted to this socially unproductive pursuit are directly related to the relative size of the public sector in the economy.[11] Therefore, the increased size of government is harmful. Resources are reallocated from productive activities into directly unproductive, rent-seeking pursuits. A consequence of the rent-induced distortions in resource allocation is a decline in economic growth and in efficiency.

Traditional arguments also plausibly link the size of the government sector with a reduction in national economic performance. Value added in the government sector is lower than in the private sector. Resources are not allocated to highest valued use but on a political (bureaucratic) criterion. High taxes, tax progressivity, and the substitution in consumption of politically priced public goods for market-priced private goods reduces the incentives of economic actors.

The secular rise in the size of government and the near-universal appeal of the relatively large public sector suggests that large segments of these societies find this result desirable. Arguments that the increased size of the public sector is beneficial and may promote growth and efficiency would be of the following sorts. (1) The larger the government sector, the greater the macroeconomic stability, since government expenditures exhibit less variance than do private sector expenditures. *Ceteris paribus*, economies with low variance in GNP grow at a higher rate than do those with a high variance in GNP. (2) The larger the size of the government, the greater is the scope for income redistribution. Too much income inequality may create incentives for the poor to seek another social order. Redistributions may reduce work incentives, but may be an inexpensive (efficient) means of preserving the social order. Satisfying the demand for income redistribution promotes political and social stability, which are preconditions for growth and efficiency. Thus the income distribution partly may reflect the opportunity cost of rebellion. (3) Traditional public goods-externalities (market failure) arguments and the effect of reduced transaction costs are associated with the government-supplied infrastructure. A variant of this hypothesis has been suggested by Robert Barro.[12] (4) Among the less developed countries there is a widespread belief that the private sector is incapable of modern transformation of the economy.

Empirical testing of the hypothesis of a rent-seeking Leviathan is difficult. The relatively little empirical evidence that exists is conflicting.[13] Ideally, the vector of government policies (tariffs, quantitative restrictions, licenses, export marketing boards, foreign exchange controls, etc.) that give rise to rent-seeking and that yield negative net social benefits would be identified and their effects estimated. Data limitations preclude wide testing of this proposition.

Alternatively, but, less adequately, the effect of the size of the public sector on economic growth and efficiency can be tested. Utilizing IMF, World Bank, and UN sources, D. Landau found that the size of government was negatively correlated with the compound growth rate of per capita gross domestic product for a sample of sixty-five less developed countries over the period 1960 to 1980.[14] A weakness of the Landau study is that a multiplicity of regressors (frequently more than twenty) appear in the equations without concern for a theoretical specification of relationships and interrelationships among the variables. Using an earlier version of the data set employed here, Landau found for a sample of 104 developed and less developed countries over the period 1961–1976 a negative relationship between size of government and the growth rate of per capita GDP.[15] Marlow found a negative relationship between the size of the public sector and the compound growth rate of real gross domestic product for the industrialized countries over the period 1960–1970.[16] In sharp contrast, Ram (1986) using the Summers and Heston data for the period 1960–1980 concluded that the size of the public sector had a positive effect on growth.[17] Ram's dependent variable is the country-specific trend (per capita growth) regression coefficient; the independent variables measuring the growth rate of government expenditure and population are also trend regression coefficients. This procedure violates the normality assumption of the underlying distribution of the estimators. In the Ram specification, the growth rate of the government sector and the growth rate multiplied by the size of the government sector are entered as separate regressors, when in fact they are not independent. Econometric difficulties of this sort weaken his findings.

A major limitation of these empirical studies on the effect of the size of the public sector on the economy is that a growth model has not been specified, nor has the effect of state allocation of resources on economic efficiency been studied. The growth rate of inputs, such as the capital stock and the labor force, affect the growth rate of output. Failure to adjust for input growth may render inaccurate the estimates of the effect of the size of the public sector on economic growth.

DATA AND VARIABLE CONSTRUCTION

The cross-country economic data employed in this study come from Robert Summers and Alan Heston, previously discussed. Data on real gross domestic product per capita, population, and the percentages of real gross domestic product devoted to gross domestic investment and to government expenditures (public consumption) were available annually for 115 market economies for the period 1960 to 1980. From these data, the following variables were calculated (the procedures of calculation have been discussed in chapter 7):

CAPGWTH = the compound growth rate of real per capita gross domestic product from 1960 to 1980;

L = the estimated labor force (population) annually from 1960 to 1980;

K = the estimated capital stock (buildings and machinery and equipment) annually from 1960 to 1980;

KLGWTH = the compound growth rate in the capital-labor (K/L) ratio from 1960 to 1980;

GOVT60 = government expenditures as a percentage of gross domestic product, 1960;

GOVT80 = government expenditures as a percentage of gross domestic product, 1980; and

CHGGOVT. = GOVT80-GOVT60.

Size of Government

The variable chosen to capture the effect of the size of the public sector on economic growth and economic efficiency is government expenditure as a share of gross domestic product. Sam Peltzman points out that the role of government is far more pervasive in economic life than is implied by this variable (for example, statutes and administrative rules, regulation, etc., reallocate resources as much as do fiscal activities), but data limitations dictate the choice.[18] Notwithstanding this caveat, the size of the government sector so measured represents a substitution of public choice for private choice in the allocation of resources, and this substitution is hypothesized to adversely affect economic growth and efficiency. The three government expenditure variables measure the initial, terminal, and comparative static absolute percentage point change in government share over the period of study.

EMPIRICAL EVIDENCE ON THE RELATIONSHIP BETWEEN
GOVERNMENT EXPENDITURE, ECONOMIC GROWTH,
AND ECONOMIC EFFICIENCY

The Size of the State and Economic Growth

The relationship between economic growth, as measured by the compound growth rate of real gross domestic product over the period 1960–1980, and the share of government in the national economy (GOVT60) and the interperiod change in the share of government (CHGGOVT) was estimated by linear OLS. The error term is assumed to be normally distributed. The regression results appear in table 9-1. In equation (1) in the table only the government share variables appear as regressors. In equation (2) the compound growth rate of the capital-labor ratio over the period is included as a regressor. As the size of the public sector grows, government plays a more direct role in the allocation of physical capital.[19] While public investment may be less productive than private investment, such investment (positively) affects growth. Hence, because of the absence of the compound growth rate in the capital-labor ratio, the negative effect of government share on growth may be overstated.

TABLE 9-1
Regressions Relating the Effects of Government Expenditures on
Economic Growth, 1960–1980

	All Economies Equation:		Less Developed Economies Equation:	
	(1)	(2)	(3)	(4)
Variable	CAPGWTH	CAPGWTH	CAPGWTH	CAPGWTH
Constant	.0467	.0372	.0466	.0361
	(7.04)	(6.70)	(5.14)	(4.73)
KLGWTH		.4752		.4571
		(7.61)		(6.58)
GOVT60	− .1123	− .0889	− .1129	− .0842
	(3.16)	(3.05)	(2.47)	(2.22)
CHGGOVT	− .1140	− .0871	− .1159	− .0856
	(3.66)	(3.41)	(3.05)	(2.70)
R^2	.1007	.1617	.0758	.3713
(n)	(115)	(115)	(93)	(93)

Note: Student-t values are in parentheses below the coefficients.

205

Both GOVT60 and CHGGOVT are of the correct sign and are statistically significant in a one-tailed test at better than the 1 percent level. With all of the independent variables in equation (2) in the table set equal to zero, the compound growth rate is 3.7 percent. Each 1 percentage point increase in the compound growth rate of the capital-labor ratio (mean CHGKL = 1.04, st. dev. = 2.45) adds about a half of a percentage point to the growth rate of real per capita income. Each 1 percentage point increase in government expenditures as a fraction of GDP in 1960 (GOVT60) or in the interperiod change in the fraction reduces the growth rate by roughly one-tenth of a percentage point. The average value of GOVT60 is 16.2 percent (st. dev. = 6.6), the average value of CHGGOVT is 3.08 percent (st. dev. = 7.56), and the average real per capita growth rate is 2.51 (st. dev. = 2.09).

The negative effect of government expenditure on economic growth can be seen more clearly in table 9-2, in which average predicted growth rates based on equation 2 in table 9-1 for a range of values of GOVT60 and CHGGOVT across these 115 market economies are presented. At one standard deviation below the mean the least interventionist states have values of GOVT60 = 9.55 and CHGGOVT = -4.48. Such hypothetical economies would have real per capita income growth rates of 3.8 per annum. The most interventionist states (at one standard deviation above the mean) have values of GOVT60 = 22.78 and CHGGOVT = 10.64. Such hypothetical economies would have real per capita growth rates of 1.3 per annum. Obviously, the negative impact of the size of government on growth is of an important order of magnitude.

An objection to the analysis is that the sample of economies contains developed and developing countries, where the objectives of government expenditures may differ. Among developed countries a larger fraction of government expenditure is directly redistributive, while in developing countries a larger fraction may be for "productive," development purposes. The equations were reestimated for the sample of less developed countries (n = 93). The results appear in table 9-1. Naturally, there are changes in the size of the coefficients and standard errors, but these changes are trivial. The signs of the coefficients remain unchanged and the results remain statistically significant.

The Size of the State and Economic Efficiency

Efficiency measures were calculated for each economy by utilizing the various production function specifications discussed previously. The technical efficiency measures obtained are for 1980, and the best of these were

TABLE 9-2

Predicted Average Growth Rates for Various
Levels of GOVT60 and CHGGOVT

CHGGOVT	GOVT60				
	0	10	20	30	40
0	4.2	3.3	2.4	1.5	.6
5	3.8	2.9	2.0	1.1	.2
10	3.3	2.5	1.6	.7	− .2
15	2.9	2.0	1.1	.2	− .6
20	2.5	1.6	.7	− .2	− 1.1

Note: Based on equation (2) in Table 10-1, with
KLGWTH set equal to its mean value.

TABLE 9-3

Regressions Relating the Effect of Size of the Government Sector on
Economic Efficiency

Variable	All Economies Equation:		Less Developed Economies Equation:	
	(1) EFF80	(2) Logit EFF80	(3) EFF80	(4) Logit EFF80
Constant	.8426	− 2.1152	.6766	− 1.6082
	(12.83)	(4.56)	(8.41)	(2.61)
GOVT80	− 1.8477	10.6936	− 1.2183	8.9630
	(5.65)	(4.67)	(3.25)	(3.12)
R^2	.2136	.1542	.0939	.0866
(n)	(115)	(115)	(93)	(93)

Note: Student-t values are in parentheses below the coefficients.

regressed against the share of government expenditures in GDP for 1980
(GOVT80). The conclusions are not sensitive to the choice of the efficiency
specification. The result appears in table 9-3. If GOVT80 is set at zero, the
technical efficiency of the average economy among the 115 countries is
EFF80 = .84. Thus, on average, such an hypothetical economy produces
84 percent of its potential or frontier real GDP per capita with its observed
capital-labor ratio. For each 1 percentage point increase in the size of the
public sector there is a loss of technical efficiency of about 1.8 percentage
points. The coefficient relating GOVT80 to EFF80 is very highly statistically significant. At one standard deviation above and below the mean,
the difference between the most interventionist and the least intervention-

ist state is 12.5 percentage points. This difference yields a 23 percentage point difference in technical efficiency. Alternatively, the least interventionist state hypothetically produces 62 percent more output per worker with the same input ratio as the most interventionist state.

Restricting the sample of countries to the less developed countries does not change the conclusion that government expenditures and economic efficiency are inversely related and that this trade-off is statistically significant. On the whole, the less developed countries are less technically efficient in transforming inputs into output; that is, the intercept in equation (3) in table 9-3 is .1660 less than that of equation (1). While there may be other reasons for this difference, most of the difference in terms of the model is due to the fact that the less developed countries are more interventionist than the developed economies. There is a 7.1 percentage point difference in the size of the government sector in 1980 between these two groups of countries. The higher mean GOVT80 for the less developed countries and the lower variance yield the somewhat smaller coefficient relating GOVT80 to EFF80 in equation (3) in the table.

It is clear from these results that increments in the relative amount of resources allocated by the government sector reduce the efficiency of the economy in transforming inputs into output. Symmetry of argument requires that the greater the share of private sector allocation in the economy, the greater the efficiency with which inputs are transformed into output. To test this proposition, the efficiency measure was regressed against the share of gross investment out of GDP in 1980 (I80). Since some government investment in state-owned enterprises may be included in the gross investment data, the coefficient of I80 on efficiency may be biased downward to some unknown degree. The results appear as equations (1) and (3) in table 9-4. The coefficient of I80 on EFF80 is positive and very highly significant. Moreover, the size of these coefficients are of the same order of magnitude as the absolute value of the coefficients of GOVT80 on EFF80 in equations (1) and (3) in table 9-3. Thus, although one should bear in mind the potential bias in the coefficient, each unit of resource converted from private sector allocation to public sector allocation is associated with a unit proportional loss of efficiency for the economy.

It is well known that bounded variables, such as EFF80, may have distributions that are truncated, which limits the power of the tests on the hypothesis. The appropriate solution econometrically is to transform the dependent variable into the Logit of the variable.[20] The dependent variable then is interpreted as the logarithm of the ratio of the odds of the event, and the coefficient, the signs of which change naturally, is inter-

TABLE 9-4

Regressions Relating the Effects of Gross Investment Share on
Economic Efficiency in 1980 and the Change in Economic
Efficiency, 1960–1980

Variable	All Economies Equation:		Less Developed Economies Equation:	
	(1) EFF80	(2) CHGEFF	(3) EFF80	(4) CHGEFF
Constant	.1407	−.1315	.1542	−.1621
	(2.74)	(3.88)	(3.05)	(4.35)
I60		.9481		1.2197
		(5.72)		(6.07)
I80	1.7438		1.4379	
	(7.40)		(5.85)	
CHGI		.8215		.8892
		(5.10)		(5.15)
R^2	.3204	.2333	.2655	.2912
(n)	(115)	(115)	(93)	(93)

Note: Student-t values are in parentheses below the coefficients.

preted as the effect of the independent variable on changing the log of the relative odds. The empirical results appear in table 9-3 as equations (2) and (4). OLS estimation of the logistic specification is a maximum likelihood estimate of the parameters. The results of equations (2) and (4) in the table confirm that the negative relationship between the size of the government sector and economic efficiency remains robust. The standard errors are marginally larger in the Logit specification, but the coefficients remain significant at above the 1 percent level. Apparently, the distribution of EFF80 is approximately normal, which offers some further assurance about the strength of the findings reported here.

The Size of the State and the Comparative Change in Efficiency

The negative effect of the share of government expenditure out of GDP on economic growth and on economic efficiency has been shown. A possible source of a decline in the rate of economic growth is a decline in economic efficiency resulting from the observed growth in the size of the government sector. It is an important natural extension of the empirical argu-

209

ment to test for the effect of these observed changes in the size of the government sector on interperiod economic efficiency.

Comparative static changes in economic efficiency for each economy in the sample were calculated by estimating the frontier production functions for 1960, calculating the efficiency measure for 1960, and constructing the variable CHGEFF = EFF80 − EFF60. CHGEFF was regressed against GOVT60 and CHGGOVT. The results appear in table 9-5. Both coefficients are negative and are statistically significant at the 1 percent level. For the least interventionist hypothetical state (that is, at one standard deviation below the mean for GOVT60 and CHGGOVT), economic efficiency between 1960 and 1980 improved (predicted CHGEFF = .1433). For the most interventionist hypothetical state (that is, at one standard deviation above the mean), interperiod economic efficiency declined (predicted CHGEFF = − .0267).

If the increase in the size of the government sector between 1960 and 1980 resulted in a reduction in efficiency, symmetry of argument requires that an increase in private sector allocation of resources result in an increase in interperiod efficiency. To test this proposition, CHGEFF was regressed against the share of gross domestic investment out of GDP in 1960 (I60) and the absolute interperiod change in the share of gross investment (CHGI = I80 − I60). The results appear as equations (2) and (4) in table 9-4. The coefficients are positive and highly significant. Economies with relatively high levels of gross domestic investment as a share of GDP in 1960 and with increases in that share during the period of study increased their efficiency in transforming inputs into output. Economies with relatively high levels of government expenditure as a fraction of GDP in 1960 and with increases in the size of the government sector during the period experienced a decline in the efficiency in transforming inputs into output.

SUMMARY AND CONCLUSIONS ON THE SIZE OF THE STATE

The motives of government in projecting a more than minimal presence in the economy may be conceived of as benevolent or malevolent. Whatever the characterization of the motivation, increases in the size of the government share of the economy adversely affect economic growth and the allocation of resources. Nations with relatively large government shares in 1960 on the whole grew more slowly than nations with relatively small state sectors. Interperiod increases in the size of government were associated with lower growth rates over the period. The size of the gov-

TABLE 9-5

Regressions Relating the Effects of Size of the Government
Sector and Changes in Size to Changes in Economic
Efficiency, 1960–1980

Variable	All Economies Equation (1) CHGEFF	Less Developed Economies Equation (2) CHGEFF
Constant	.1769	.2256
	(3.74)	(3.57)
GOVT60	− .6324	− .8383
	(2.49)	(2.63)
CHGGOVT	− .5986	− .7692
	(2.70)	(2.90)
R^2	.0533	.0721
(n)	(115)	(93)

Note: Student-t values are in parentheses below the coefficients.

ernment share coefficients in the regressions were of sufficiently large magnitude to conclude that the rise in the size of the government has had a substantial depressing effect on economic growth. These results are consistent with those reported by Landau and Marlow.[21] Landau did not adjust economic growth for the growth in factor endowment. Consequently, his results overstate the adverse effect of government size.

Government allocation of resources is thought to be less efficient than private allocation. For the first time in the literature, this hypothesis was tested directly by comparing efficiency measures with the measures of the size of the government sector. It was found that the size of the government share in the economy was negatively correlated with economic efficiency and with the interperiod change in economic efficiency. Nations with relatively large public sectors produced a lower standard of living with the same input ratio than did nations with relatively small government sectors.

What Is to Be Done?

Reform of the Institutional Framework

and Economic Policy for Progress

FREEDOM IS PARETO-EFFICIENT

THE NEOCLASSICAL paradigm correctly identifies many of the sources of economic growth. There is strong empirical evidence that capital formation, human capital accumulation, and technical progress contribute positively to economic growth. But the predictions of the neoclassical model have not been borne out. Largely, Western capital does not flow to the less developed countries in pursuit of higher returns. Domestic capital formation in many countries is low. Human capital formation also is low. Frequently, those with high levels of education emigrate to free societies or employ their talents in rent-seeking activities at home. In many nations, relatively little of the entrepreneurial and human capital talent is employed in the commerce that is a key to the economic transformation of society.

The failure of the neoclassical paradigm to produce predictions consistent with our observations of the real world is due to the fact that it treats capital accumulation and technical progress as exogenous to the institutional setting. Capital formation and inventiveness are determined endogenously in a narrow sense by the nature of the property rights facing individual economic actors and more broadly by the constitutional setting or rule space.

Thus the first implication of this research is that the model of man and society promulgated by the classical liberals is as valid for the transformation of the Third World (and, the socialist world) as it was for the West. John Locke and Adam Smith, the intellectual giants of a sociopolitical and economic philosophy of free men and free markets, have much to say to the human condition of the late twentieth century. All societies have persons of talent, ability, and ambition who are capable of transforming their lives, their families, and, in the aggregate, their nations from a rude state to one of a high level of economic and human development. There are many talented and ambitious people in the less developed world. Consider the contributions of Indians, Chinese, Russians, Eastern bloc residents, Latins, Africans, and others in the pure sciences, mathematics, engineering, literature, art, sports, and a wide array of human endeavor. That there has been a lack of economic progress speaks not of the people but of their institutions and ideology: a failure to structure a rule space that leaves men free to go about the business of self-betterment, with a minimum of government interference.

The necessary conditions for these universal human characteristics to be unleashed is a constitutional setting that fosters and protects private property and the rule of law and allows for competition among political agents who aspire to govern. Private property, freedom of contract, and free market exchange free the Scotsman in everyone. Collective ownership and the political allocation of resources waste a nation's natural endowment.

Nor is extensive government intervention justified on the grounds of equity. Again, the failure of neoclassical economics to recognize the effect on income distribution of the variance in rights to compete for income streams has led to a preoccupation with variance in economic outcomes as the exclusive explanation of observed differences in income distributions. While the variance in economic outcome due to exogenous (for example, genes, luck, inheritance) and endogenous (parsimony, human capital, motivation, ambition, etc.) factors is an important source of income inequality, the variance in the right to compete for income streams is a much more important source of the observed transnational income inequality. It has been shown that liberty is Pareto efficient in the sense that a free people obtain not only higher economic growth rates and economic efficiency but a more equitable income distribution than those of mankind that live in an illiberal rule space.

In a society of equal rights for all, the distribution of resources is efficient, but may result in an income distribution that is socially unacceptable. An unresolved dilemma of modern times is the crafting of a system of rules and order that balances considerations of efficiency and equity. Common law, as a system of spontaneous legal rules and order, fosters economic efficiency. Equity is a matter of individual altruism, not governmental compulsion. Legislation is a political system of rules and order. Statutes are crafted in a political market, where political agents must respond to the coalitions of special interests that elect and retain them in office. In representative government, with universal suffrage and majority rule, there is opportunity for politicians to concentrate net benefits to the groups that elect them and diffuse the costs to others. Universal suffrage and majority rule grants ethical justification to legislative redistribution of rights and of income. The inherent danger in representative government is that this process of concentrating net benefits to special interests and diffusing costs can lead to a rise in the size of the public sector and a political allocation of resources sufficiently large to undermine economic progress. Theorists of the public choice and constitutional economics tradition have pointed to constitutional restrictions on the size of the fiscal state and to supermajority voting rules in the legislature as means of retarding the growth of rent-seeking.

The second implication of this research is to get the policies right. Free trade, a small public sector, and conservative fiscal and monetary policy are growth promoting. Restricted trade, licensed monopoly, regulation, a large public sector, budget deficits, and inflation promote rent-seeking. The gap between the West and the Third World with respect to these policies probably is not as wide as it is with respect to the rights accorded their respective citizens. Yet it remains true that the Third World is more protectionist and interventionist, and economic growth has suffered for it.

PROSPECTS FOR FREEDOM

The close of the decade of the 1980s witnessed the spontaneous uprisings of the peoples of Eastern Europe, who have overthrown the monopoly of the Communist Party. Communism was an externally imposed regime on these peoples. These countries are moving toward a system of political competition and are cautiously seeking to incorporate Western economic and legal institutions into their systems. Also, witnessed were the expressions of separatism among the Baltic nations that had been absorbed into the Soviet Union. Other Soviet republics and ethnic groups are asserting demands for autonomy. Absent the reimposition of a Stalinist-type rule, there is a prospect of the dissolution of the Soviet Union. But the situation in the Soviet Union and in Eastern Europe is too chaotic to make credible predictions about the ultimate political, legal, and economic structure of these nations.

But national independence and freedom are not the same. The Third World became independent, but for the most part is not free. A domestic ruling elite took power from a foreign ruling elite. While I cannot prove the proposition empirically, on the whole and particularly for the former British colonies, I think the peoples of the Third World enjoy less freedom under their own ruling elites than they did under colonization. The current events in the Third World offer only slim prospects for freedom. The Latin countries have been moving toward civilian government, but the military remains a force in the background that may reassert its power. There has been some movement toward multiparty political competition in Africa; yet that continent largely is unfree. Some Asian countries have institutionalized a high level of economic freedom (Hong Kong, Singapore, Korea, and Taiwan), but not a great deal of political freedom. The prospects for greater personal freedom seem relatively bright in Korea and Taiwan, but less so elsewhere in Asia.

The self-acknowledged failure of socialism to bring economic progress to its citizens has weakened the intellectual justification for the continued suppression of rights in the Third World. But legitimacy is a mere convenience in a dictatorship. Power is what counts. No one knows what it would take to topple these dictatorships. Perhaps, it is only a little courage, as with the peoples of Eastern Europe. But if they are overthrown, another dictatorship or ruling elite is as likely an outcome as is liberty for all and representative government. After all, Haiti moved from one dictatorship to another, Iran from a despotic monarchy to a despotic theocracy, and the Philippines from one ruling clique to another.

The prospects for freedom throughout the world in part will depend on what Eastern Europe does now that it is largely free of Communist Party rule. These peoples seem united in their opposition to the coercive features of the socialist model of man and society. It is not clear that they are prepared to move fully to a model of man as independent and responsible. Poland has chosen a policy of rapid transition to a market economy. The short-run costs of adjustment are high and politically dangerous. There is little difference in austerity under socialism (shoddy but cheap goods in short supply) and in the transition to capitalism (available goods but at high prices). These high short- and intermediate-run costs of adjustment will test the will and patience of Polish citizens and offer opportunities for the resurgence of the idea of government intervention. In May 1990, in free elections, the Romanians overwhelmingly returned communists to power (the presidential candidate got 85 percent of the vote and two-thirds of the elected legislators were former communists). And the bureaucrats of the new Eastern European order are the same ones employed by the masters of the old order.

Failure was socialized in Eastern Europe. Integration with Western Europe through the Common Market is a powerful attraction for Eastern Europe. Full integration will require the structuring of a constitutional setting in Eastern Europe along the lines of the West. And the West European welfare state has insured against failure perhaps to a sufficient degree to make those who are timid after five decades of socialism willing to try freedom.

PROSPECTS FOR TRADE LIBERALIZATION

In an effort to determine the appropriate design of a trade liberalization policy, the World Bank conducted an extensive study of the timing and sequencing of trade liberalization episodes in nineteen developing countries.[1] The study is the most recent investigation of the comparative experience of countries that attempt to move away from a protected and distorted trade regime to a more neutral one.[2] One of the distressing aspects of the study is the paucity of developing countries that even have attempted trade liberalization. There is not one African country in the study. The countries studied are from Latin America (six countries), Asia and the Pacific (seven countries), and the Mediterranean (six countries). Moreover, the liberalizations studied were not once and for all, episodic events. Rather, they were multiple events (twelve of the nineteen countries had two liberalization episodes). There were thirty-six liberalization episodes in the nineteen countries. Distressingly, a third of these attempts utterly failed, and nine reversed from a more liberal to a more restrictive (partial failure) trade regime.[3]

Most attempts at liberalization arise not from an intellectual conviction of the net benefits from freer trade but from distress, when the country is reeling under economic catastrophe: an acute balance-of-payments crisis, low or negative economic growth, disemployment, and inflation. Most of the countries in the study only flirted with liberalization. Where a freer trade regime was sustained, most often it was fairly radical and swiftly imposed. And it was part of a general scheme to shift the economy to freer markets; that is, trade liberalization was part of an overall policy goal of improved resource allocation, increased economic growth, increased growth of exports, and reduced inflation. Hence, where trade liberalization was sustained, it was accompanied by more restricted macroeconomic (reduced budget deficits) and monetary policies and adherence to a stable real exchange rate. The liberalizers tended to be resource-poor, small or medium-sized economies, with a relatively high per capita income and with a modicum of political stability. The degrees of freedom (market size, own home production) of such economies are few; hence, trade liberalization is more compelling prima facia. The nonliberalizers were relatively large economies and rich in resources.

Some of the fears concerning the economic consequences (costs) of trade liberalization are not supported by the evidence of the nineteen-country experience. Theoretically, when protection is removed from an activity, output contracts and inputs are disemployed. In the long run, resources are absorbed into the expanding (for example, export) sectors of the economy. But in the short run, unemployment is considered to be a consequence of liberalization. The empirical evidence from the studies did not support a finding of significant unemployment arising from the trade liberalization episodes. Additionally, trade liberalization alters relative product prices. Rapid price changes redistribute income. Although income redistribution effects are difficult to verify, because of a paucity of data, the available evidence did not indicate significant effects. Further, because protected trade regimes have a strong export bias, trade liberalization increases imports relative to exports, and a balance-of-payments crisis is a feared consequence of trade reform. The evidence from the studies is that trade liberalization induces rapid export growth (the export growth rate of the liberalizers was twice that of the nonliberalizers) and the deficit in the current account, in general, was not a serious consequence of trade reform.

Thus there is little evidence of extreme short- and intermediate-term economic distress arising from the experience with trade liberalization among these countries. And there is evidence of static and dynamic gains from freer trade. Then, if the net benefits from freer trade are so transparent, why do we see such stubborn resistance to freer trade among so many nations of the world? I believe we are drawn to a public choice hypothesis that protection yields economic rents and that the special interest ruling elites that control the economic affairs of these trade-distorted regimes have a vested interest in maintaining the illiberal economic regime. In a political environment in which Leviathan is unconstrained, economic policy in general and commercial policy in particular will be an instrument

217

of rent-seeking by the ruling elite. Thus the prospects for trade liberalization inextricably are linked with the prospects for freedom. Only if men are free to chose will trade policy possibly reflect the self-interest of the masses and not that of a ruling elite.

PROSPECTS FOR A SHRINKAGE OF THE SIZE OF GOVERNMENT

The constitutional setting and the size of the state are not linked, particularly. While the public sector is a little larger in the less developed world than in the West, the difference in the size of the public sector, measured as government expenditures out of GDP, is not that great. But government control of the economy is more pervasive in the Third World, and the scope and purpose of intervention differs from that in the West. In the universal suffrage, representative democracies, majority coalitions "lease" the coercive power of government to redistribute income to themselves. This public choice hypothesis seems to be the most tractable explanation of the rise of the size of the public sector in the West. In the Third World, where citizens are not free, the public command of resources by the ruling elite is the mechanism of extracting rents from citizens. All that differs among Leviathans constrained by popular sovereignty and those unconstrained is the size of the brokerage fee. Thus a move to greater freedom in the less developed world, particularly economic liberty, likely will not shrink the size of the public sector. But it will alter the pattern of public expenditure and reduce the size of the brokerage fee of those who rule. In itself, such a transformation is beneficial. If the analysis of the evolution of the constitutional setting, described earlier, is a reasonably accurate description of the way political markets work, the introduction of a rule space of liberty will lead to the introduction of Pareto- and Hicks-Kaldor-efficient rules. These changes in the institutional setting unleash the force of the private pursuit of wealth and reduce the level of rents (brokers' fees) available to those who govern.

The United States and Great Britain have structured a rule space that gives the widest latitude to individuals. During the twentieth century, both countries have frittered away individual liberty in the public interest and in humanitarian policies of subsidizing failure. The welfare state remains robust in both countries. But a new perspective on the public interest seems to have been born in the mid-1970s. The United States chose a policy of regulation for observed or suspected market failure. The British regulate, also, but they chose government ownership of many economic activities that had a "public" character. During the Carter administration and the first term of the Reagan presidency, substantial deregulation of economic activity occurred. This public policy process largely has ended, perhaps because all of the politically cheap regulatory reforms were exhausted (those special interests, that is, unions, shareholders, etc., that could not muster credible political opposition to deregulation). In Great Britain, under the Thatcher government, considerable progress toward privatization took place. Without much credible political opposition, the Thatcher government was able to structure sufficiently attractive net benefits to coalitions of special interests that made it possible for the government to liquidate its public assets or services in a variety of activities. The privatization movement has slowed as it has run into those activities in which it is expensive both politically and economically to buy off the credible special interest opposition. The lesson of a century of regulation and state ownership is that such policies do not do what they were envisioned to do and impose an efficiency drag on the economy. A deregulation and privatization program of an order of magnitude larger than has been experienced would have been a salutary lesson to the Third World. Deregulation in the United States and privatization in Great Britain, in theory, are capable of shrinking the scope and power of modern government. Alas, they seem to have run their course. Moreover, neither public policy seems to have traveled well: The other OECD countries have remained largely immune to this form of liberalization.

☆ *Notes* ☆

CHAPTER 1

1. Robert L. Heilbroner, *The Future as History* (New York: Harper, 1960).

2. Id., "The Triumph of Capitalism," *New Yorker* 64 (January 23, 1989): 98–109.

3. In 1990, the Communist Party in the Soviet Union, through the Soviet legislature, approved a law that provides for "citizens' property" in small-scale businesses, with limitations on the amount of labor that can be hired. In companion legislation, the private ownership of land is forbidden but a small amount of land may be leased to citizens. Through statute, the powers of the presidency have been expanded, and in theory are separate from holding the leadership of the Communist Party. Interest has been expressed in reforming Soviet socialist law by making it less an instrument of the Communist Party.

4. There are numerous meanings to the terms "freedom" and "liberty," depending on one's position on the sociopolitical spectrum. My sense of these terms is within the Anglo-American political tradition, and within that, the classical liberal tradition. Freedom or liberty in the words of Hayek is "independence of the arbitrary will of another." Among some neoclassical economists (for example, George Stigler) freedom means maximization of the choice set. Freedom is increased with an increase in our wealth. The neoclassical definition is too narrow, and the direction of causation is wrong. Freedom stands as a moral principle whether it is correlated with wealth or not. As this book will show, freedom leads to wealth, not vice versa. That a constitutional setting of liberty promotes economic progress is fortuitous. Had this not been the case, my own priorities would cause me to choose to live in a society of free men over a society of wealthy slaves. F. A. Hayek, *The Constitution of Liberty* (Chicago: University of Chicago Press, 1960), 12; George J. Stigler, "Wealth and Possibly Liberty," *Journal of Legal Studies* 7 (June 1978): 213–17.

5. The cost to West Germans of absorbing East Germany is not certain. A recent estimate puts the cost during the decade of the 1990s at one trillion dollars. Ferdinand Protzman, "As Marriage Nears, Germans in the Wealthy West Fear a Cost in Billions," *New York Times*, September 24, 1990, A6.

6. In the March 1990 legislative elections in Hungary, not one Communist was elected. The leftist parties were routed in the election. The two leading parties are center-rightist politically, and the issue is the pace of the transition to a free market economy.

7. In a survey of 2,485 Soviet citizens interviewed in their homes in November and December of 1989 by the National Center for Public Opinion Research, in Moscow, of the respondents answering whether the state should or should not be mainly responsible for people's success and well-being, 51 percent of the Rus-

sians, 43 percent of the Balts, 77 percent of the Georgians, and 40 percent of the Central Asians answered in favor of statism over individualism. *New York Times*, March 29, 1990, A6. The demand for freedom and individual responsibility likely is higher in Eastern Europe, but I have not seen any survey evidence. Perhaps, one should not take such polls too seriously. If the question were asked of residents of New York or Seattle, the responses might be similar.

8. If empirical evidence is required to see the point consider Hong Kong, Taiwan, and the People's Republic of China. Hong Kong is a rock devoid of resource endowments. Economic liberty and a work ethic (the Protestant work ethic that has died in the West is alive in Oriental form in the countries constituting the Asian tigers) have produced a per capita income that is several times that of mainland China. On a personal level, I lived in Taiwan in 1963. I got around Taipei on buses or in pedicabs. Private cars and taxis were rare. In 1986–1987, I was in Taiwan and mainland China. Taipei is horridly congested with private cars; Peking is horridly congested with bicycles. There are plenty of taxis for the tourists in Peking, but it is hard to get one. Brilliant communist policy has led to simultaneous excess supply and demand in the taxi market, a rather unique achievement. When taxis were first introduced as part of the development of the tourist (foreign exchange) industry, drivers kept a fixed share of the fare, just as in the West. They were ambitious and worked long hours, and soon were making more money than the premier. Can't have that! To reduce their income, their earnings were fixed. Taxi drivers earn the maximum in a short time. Not willing to drive for free, they sleep the rest of the day away—so queues of irate customers line up waiting for a cab, and the parking lot is full of them, with the drivers asleep. Nothing separates the economic outcomes of these nations other than the choice of the model of man and society.

9. Gunnar Myrdal, "The Equality Issue in World Development," *American Economic Review* 79, no. 6 (December 1989): 13.

10. Robert M. Solow, "A Contribution to the Theory of Economic Growth," *Quarterly Journal of Economics* 70 (1956): 65–94.

11. Kenneth J. Arrow, "The Economic Implications of Learning by Doing," *Review of Economic Studies* 29 (June 1962): 155–73; id., "Economic Welfare and the Allocation of Resources for Invention," in *The Rate and Direction of Inventive Activity* (Princeton: Princeton University Press, 1962).

12. Armen A. Alchian and Harold Demsetz, "Production, Information Costs, and Economic Organization," *American Economic Review* 62 (December 1972): 777–95.

CHAPTER 2

1. John Maynard Keynes, *The General Theory of Employment, Interest, and Money* (New York: Harcourt, Brace, 1936).

2. Roy F. Harrod, *Towards a Dynamic Economics* (London: Macmillian, 1948);

Evsey D. Domar, *Essays in the Theory of Economic Growth* (New York: Oxford University Press, 1957).

3. Robert M. Solow, "A Contribution to the Theory of Economic Growth," *Quarterly Journal of Economics* 70 (1956): 65–94. See also David Cass, "Optimum Growth in an Aggregative Model of Capital Accumulation," *Review of Economic Studies* 32 (1965): 233–40; and T. C. Koopmans, "On the Concept of Optimum Economic Growth," in *The Econometric Approach to Development Planning* (Amsterdam: North Holland, 1965).

4. Mathematically, the country's output function is written as $Y = F(K, L)$, where Y is national output, K is capital stock, and L is labor. The production function is subject to the laws of production (diminishing marginal productivity). Thus, the first derivatives (marginal products of the inputs) are positive, and the second derivatives are negative (diminishing marginal products of the inputs).

Subsequently, Solow allows for factor-neutral technological change in the model. The effect of neutral technical change is to increase the marginal product of each of the factors of production but to leave the ratio of the marginal products unchanged.

5. Since the production function is assumed to be homogeneous of degree one in the inputs it may be rewritten in intensive form as $y = f(k)$, where $y = Y/L$, output per worker, and $k = K/L$, capital per worker.

The production function is subject to the standard neoclassical restrictions; that is, the production function is assumed to be constant returns to scale, continuous, concave, twice differentiable, to satisfy the Inada conditions, and absent of corner solutions (both factors are essential to production at all levels of output). Solow later relaxes the restriction on the shape of the production function by exploring the effect on the stability condition of introducing fixed-proportions technology (Leontieff production function), the Cobb-Douglas function, and the constant elasticity of substitution (CES) function. Imposing homogeneity of degree one on the production function rules out resources in fixed supply (for example, land), which would induce diminishing returns in the manner described by Ricardo.

6. Thus, $S/Y = sY_{(t)}$. Under the asumption of the identity of savings and investment $I = sY = sF(K, L) = sf(k)$. Solow later relaxes this assumption by considering a variable savings ratio that depends on the real return to capital.

7. Thus the growth of the labor force is given as: $L = L_0 e^{nt}$. Solow later permits population growth to be dependent on per capita income.

8. Robert Summers and Alan Heston, "Improved International Comparisons of Real Product and Its Composition: 1950–1980," *Review of Income and Wealth* 30 (June 1984): 207–62; and "A New Set of International Comparisons of Real Product and Price Levels: Estimates for 130 Countries, *Review of Income and Wealth* 34 (March 1988): 1–25.

9. Intercountry comparisons of per capita income have suffered for several reasons: the intractable index number problem; differences in national accounting conventions and in the coverage and reliability of the accounts data; and problems

in exchange rate conversion of income in different national currencies to the U.S. dollar, the conventional, common standard. The Summers-Heston technique tackles some of these problems and provides the only avaible set of international product and product composition data. For criticisms of this technique, see Douglas W. Caves, Lauritus R. Christensen, and W. Erwin Diewert, "Multilateral Comparisons of Output, Input, and Productivity Using Superlative Index Numbers," *Economic Journal* 92 (March 1982): 73–86.

10. Robert G. King and S. Rebelo, "Transitional Dynamics and Economic Growth in Neoclassical Economies" (unpublished manuscript, University of Rochester, July 1989).

11. Robert J. Barro and Xavier Sala i Martin, "Economic Growth and Convergence across the United States" (unpublished manuscript, Harvard University, September 1989).

12. Robert E. Lucas, Jr., "Why Doesn't Capital Flow from Rich to Poor Countries?" *American Economic Review, Papers and Proceedings* 80, no. 2 (May 1990): 92–96. See also, id., "On the Mechanics of Economic Development," *Journal of Monetary Economics* 22 (January 1988): 3–22.

13. Anne O. Krueger, "Factor Endowments and per Capita Income Differences Among Countries," *Economic Journal* 78 (September 1968): 641–59.

14. Property rights were incorporated into the production function of the firm by Michael C. Jensen and William H. Meckling, "Rights and Production Functions: An Application to Labor-Managed Firms and Codetermination," *Journal of Business* 52 (October 1979): 469–506.

15. S. C. Tsiang, "Success or Failure in Economic Takeoff," *Journal of Political Economy*, 1991, in press.

16. Gary S. Becker and Robert J. Barro, "A Reformulation of the Economic Theory of Fertility," *Quarterly Journal of Economics* 103 (February 1988): 1–25

17. Gary S. Becker and Kevin M. Murphy, "Economic Growth, Human Capital and Population Growth," *Journal of Political Economy*, 1991, in press.

18. $\text{RGDP85} = -1282.8 + 272.6 \quad \text{Invest share, } R^2 = .33$
                    $(1.86) \quad (7.71)$
        $\text{Growth} = .1392 + .1180 \quad \text{Invest share, } R^2 = .16$
                    $(.30) \quad (4.91)$

19. Gary S. Becker and Nigel Tomes, "Human Capital and the Rise and Fall of Families," *Journal of Labor Economics* 4, no. 3, pt. 2 (July 1986): S1–S39; Gary S. Becker and Robert J. Barro, "A Reformulation of the Economic Theory of Fertility," *Quarterly Journal of Economics* 103 (February 1988): 1–25; and Gary S. Becker, Kevin M. Murphy, and Robert Tamura, "Human Capital, Fertility, and Economic Growth," *Journal of Political Economy* 98, no. 5, pt. 2 (October 1990): S12–S37.

20. Simon Kuznets, "Economic Growth and Income Inequality," *American Economic Review* 65 (1955): 1–28.

21. Robert M. Solow, "Technical Change and the Aggregate Production Function," *Review of Economics and Statistics* 39 (1957): 312–20.

22. Kenneth J. Arrow, "The Economic Implications of Learning by Doing," *Review of Economic Studies* 29 (June 1962): 155–73; and id., "Economic Welfare and the Allocation of Resources for Invention," in *The Rate and Direction of Inventive Activity* (Princeton: NBER and Princeton University Press, 1962).

23. Hirofumi Uzawa, "Optimum Technical Change in an Aggregative Model of Economic Growth," *International Economic Review* 6 (January 1965): 18–31; Robert G. King and Sergio Rebelo, "Business Cycles with Endogenous Growth" (unpublished manuscript, University of Rochester, March 1986); and Becker, Murphy, and Tamura, "Human Capital."

24. See Paul M. Romer, "Endogenous Technological Change," *Journal of Political Economy* 98, no. 5, pt. 2 (October 1990): S71–S102. See also the series of papers by Grossman and Helpman cited in Gene M. Grossman and Elhanan Helpman, "Trade, Innovation, and Growth," *American Economic Review Papers and Proceedings* 80 (2) (May 1990): 86–91.

25. Adam Smith, *An Inquiry into the Nature and Causes of the Wealth of Nations* (New York: Modern Library, 1937); David Ricardo, *The Principles of Political Economy and Taxation* (New York: E. P. Dutton, 1957); John Stuart Mill, *Principles of Political Economy*, 2 vols. (New York: Co-operative Publication Society, 1900); and, Gottfried Haberler, *International Trade and Economic Development* (Cairo: National Bank of Egypt, 1959).

26. Friedrich List, *The National System of Political Economy*, trans. Sampson S. Lloyd (London: Longmans, Green, 1904); Mihail Manoilesco, *The Theory of Protection and International Trade* (London: P. S. King and Son, 1931); Raul Prebisch, *The Economic Development of Latin America and Its Principal Problems* (Lake Success, N. Y.: United Nations, 1950); id., "Commercial Policy in the Underdeveloped Countries," *American Economic Review* 49 (May 1959): 251–73; and Hans W. Singer, "The Distribution of Gains between Investing and Borrowing Countries," *American Economic Review* 40 (May 1950): 473–85.

27. Gottfried Haberler, "Some Problems in the Pure Theory of International Trade," *Economic Journal* 60 (June 1950): 223–40.

28. Cf. Paul A. Samuelson, "The Gains from International Trade," *Canadian Journal of Economics and Political Science* 5 (May 1939): 195–205.

29. Under a regime of high tariffs or quota restrictions, those goods subject to the regime are imported in relatively small quantities, and those subject to low tariffs or quotas are imported in relatively high quantities. Hence such a weighted measure would be biased downward.

30. Robert J. Barro, "Government Spending in a Simple Model of Endogenous Growth," *Journal of Political Economy* 98, no. 5, pt. 2 (October 1990): S103–S125.

31. Roger Kormendi and Philip G. Meguire, "Macroeconomic Determinants of Growth: Cross-country Evidence," *Journal of Monetary Economics* 16, no. 2 (September 1985): 139–63; K. Grier and Gordon Tullock (1987); D. Landau, "Government Expenditure and Economic Growth: A Cross-country Study," *Southern Economic Journal* 49 (January 1983): 783–92.

CHAPTER 3

1. James M. Buchanan and Gordon Tullock, *The Calculus of Consent: Logical Foundations of Constitutional Democracy* (Ann Arbor: University of Michigan Press, 1962).

2. James M. Buchanan, *The Limits of Liberty: Between Anarchy and Leviathan* (Chicago: University of Chicago Press, 1975).

3. Thus, altruism, anonymous gift transfer without any expected return, is ruled out as a driving force in structuring an institutional framework. Undoubtedly, altruism occurs within family life and may occur among unrelated individuals. However, altruism is sufficiently rare behavior to be ruled out as a driving motive of human behavior.

4. Absent externalities, which are a characteristic of a constitutional setting that has some inefficiency (not all property is owned by someone and/or there are socially inefficient restrictions on the use or exchange of property), private and social wealth maximization are synonymous.

5. For example, the introduction of commodity-based money as a substitute for barter exchange facilitates the gains from exchange and reduces transaction costs. Similarly, the rise of a stock or an insurance market diversifies risk. Such rules or institutions are Pareto efficient.

6. Examples might include fiat money and bankruptcy laws.

7. Gordon Tullock was the first to show that the competition for special favor (licensed monopoly, tariff protection, etc.) was socially wasteful. If the value of the monopoly prize is $1 million and there are ten competitors for the prize, each with an equal chance of winning, the rational expenditure in securing the prize of each contestant is $100,000. There is only one winner, of course, but the game of seeking the prize has exactly exhausted the value of the prize. Such an activity is a zero-sum game. Anne Krueger was the first to term this type of activity "rent-seeking." See Gordon Tullock, "The Welfare Costs of Tariffs, Monopolies and Theft," *Western Economic Journal* 5 (June 1967): 224–32; and Anne O. Krueger, "The Political Economy of the Rent-seeking Society," *American Economic Review* 64 (June 1974): 291–303.

8. Examples might include licensed monopoly, trade unions, price controls, and trade protection.

9. The division of functions of the state into the protection of individual rights, provision of public goods, and a fiscal mechanism that redistributes income is conventional but ambiguous. Income can be redistributed via rights assignment and public goods. If a license is required to perform an activity (for example, carry passengers or cargo, hold foreign exchange, etc.), those having the license get the right to the income stream. If schools are financed out of common taxation, those without children pay for something from which they do not benefit, directly.

10. F. W. Maitland, *The Constitutional History of England* (Cambridge: Cambridge University Press, 1968).

11. Paul A. Samuelson, "The Pure Theory of Public Expenditure," *Review of Economics and Statistics* 36 (November 1954): 387–89.

12. Buchanan showed that many goods have an element of publicness about them (for example, a golf course) and may be privately provided through voluntary organizations or clubs. James M. Buchanan, "An Economic Theory of Clubs," *Economica* 32 (February 1965): 1–14.

13. Buchanan, *The Limits of Liberty*, 36–41.

14. Buchanan and Tullock, *The Calculus of Consent*, 192–95.

15. John Rawls, *A Theory of Justice* (Cambridge: Harvard University Press, 1971).

16. Buchanan and Tullock, *The Calculus of Consent*, 194.

17. A figure similar to figure 3-5 can be drawn. Utility of each person would be from the present discounted value of the lifetime stream of income. Point G would represent the utility associated with the income stream without income redistribution. Point H would represent the income stream with a Pareto-efficient agreement on income redistribution. Points H^* and H^{**} reflect potential outcomes when income is redistributed by an unconstrained simple majority.

18. Article 1 of the Virginia Bill of Rights recognizes the possession of property as an inherent, individual right. Article 6 stipulates that all men have the right not to be taxed or deprived of property without their own consent. These articles did not carry over to the Bill of Rights Amendments to the U.S. Constitution.

19. The corollary to the efficiency of the marketplace of ideas is the efficiency of the market in the allocation of all economic resources. If it is irrational and inefficient for the state to regulate the marketplace for ideas, why is it rational for the government to regulate product and factor markets? The logic escaped Holmes, but not Aaron Director. Aaron Director, "The Parity of the Economic Market Place," *Journal of Law and Economics* 7 (1964): 1–10.

20. A.V. Dicey has defined the attributes of the "rule of law" as follows: (1) No man is punishable by the state except for a breach of law as defined by the ordinary courts and not through the exercise of arbitrary or discretionary power of those who govern; (2) all men, including those who rule, equally are before the law and subject to its jurisdiction through ordinary tribunals; and (3) the general principles of law and the constitution are the result, not the source, of individual law. A. V. Dicey, *Introduction to the Study of the Law of the Constitution* (Indianapolis: Liberty Classics, 1982) 110–15; 8th ed., London: Macmillan, 1915).

21. Friedrich A. Hayek, *Law, Legislation and Liberty*, Vol. 1, *Rules and Order*, (Chicago: University of Chicago Press, 1973), 74.

22. F. W. Maitland and F. C. Montagu, *A Sketch of English Legal History*, ed. J. F. Colby (New York: Putnam's, 1915), 213; Arthur R. Hogue, *Origins of the Common Law* (Indianapolis: Liberty Press, 1985), 190–203.

23. Roscoe Pound, *An Introduction to the Philosophy of Law* (New Haven: Yale University Press, 1922); and id., *Social Control through Law* (New Haven: Yale University Press, 1942).

24. Nock claims that much of English civil behavior arises not from law but from a self-imposed, customary constraint of "doing the right thing" (women and children first in the lifeboat, refusing to satisfy one's thirst when there is not enough water to go around, standing in queue waiting one's turn, etc.). He claims that there are some two million laws in America and that having a legal instead of a customary order does not work very well: "In this respect, living in America is like serving in the army; ninety percent of the conduct is prescribed by law and the remaining ten percent by the *esprit de corps*, with the consequence that opportunity for free choice in conduct is practically abolished." Albert Jay Nock, *On Doing the Right Thing* (New York: Harper, 1928), 171.

25. Iredell Jenkins, *Social Order and the Limits of Law* (Princeton: Princeton University Press, 1980), 341–42.

26. Bruno Leoni, *Freedom and the Law* (Princeton: D. Van Nostrand, 1961), 10.

27. F. W. Maitland, *The Constitutional History of England*; and D. A. Binchy, *Celtic and Anglo-Saxon Kingship* (Oxford: Oxford University Press, 1970).

28. W. C. Mitchell, *Lecture Notes on Types of Economic Theory*, 2 vols. (New York: August M. Kelley, 1949), 1:30.

29. R. H. Coase, "The Federal Communications Commission," *Journal of Law and Economics* 2 (October 1959): 1–40.

30. Richard A. Posner, *Economic Analysis of Law* (Boston: Little, Brown, 1973), 41–44.

31. See also George L. Priest, "The Common Law Process and the Selection of Efficient Rules," *Journal of Legal Studies* 6 (1977): 65–82; and Paul H. Rubin, "Why Is the Common Law Efficient?" *Journal of Legal Studies* 6 (1977): 51–63.

32. Posner, *Economic Analysis of Law*, 98, 100.

33. Legislative unanimity on a statute is no guarantee of constituent unanimity. If legislators vote on the basis of the majority position of their constituents, constituent views are normally distributed, and each constituency has the same distribution of views, statutes pass unanimously with simple constituent majority. Thus constituent opposition may be as strong in this case as where the constituents of the majority of constituencies support the statute unanimously and the constituents of the minority of constituencies are unanimously opposed.

34. Robert F. Martin, *National Income in the United States, 1799–1938* (New York: Arno Press, 1976), 6.

35. See Sam Peltzman, "The Growth of Government," *Journal of Law and Economics* 23, no. 2 (October 1980): 209–88.

36. Knut Wicksell, "Ein neues Prinzip der gerechten Besteuerung," in *Finanz-theoretische Untersuchungen* (Jena, Germany: Gustav Fisher, 1896), trans. J. M. Buchanan, "A New Principle of Just Taxation," in R. A. Musgrave and A. T. Peacock, eds., *Classics in the Theory of Public Finance* (London: MacMillan, 1958), 72–118.

37. Ibid., 95.

38. In the case of schooling, medical care, and some other services the objection

is that the poor might not value the service sufficiently to pay the fee, and to the extent that these services provide a means of upward socioeconomic mobility, this may promote a permanent underclass. Friedman's voucher plan which can be distributed progressively, solves this problem nicely. A problem with the current allocation of central and state government aid to education to equalize district school expenditures is that it is based on attendance. Thus, for school administrations to maximize their budgets they must maximize attendance or minimize school dropout rates and truancy. This is achieved by making the school environment as pleasant and nonacademically demanding as possible. The incentive structure in the public finance of public schooling is inconsistent with either the goal of quality education or the goal of providing opportunities for the children of the poor to acquire the educational skills necessary to function productively in the economy.

39. George J. Stigler, "Director's Law of Public Income Redistribution," *Journal of Law and Economics* 13 (April 1970): 1–10.

40. Gordon Tullock, *Economics of Income Redistribution* (Boston: Kluwer-Nijhoff, 1983); and id., *The Economics of Wealth and Poverty* (New York: New York University Press, 1986).

41. Anthony Downs, *An Economic Theory of Democracy* (New York: Harper and Row, 1957); Buchanan and Tullock, *The Calculus of Consent*; and Mancur Olsen, *The Logic of Collective Action* (Cambridge: Harvard University Press, 1965).

42. Gerald W. Scully and Daniel J. Slottje, "The Paradox of Politics and Policy in Redistributing Income," *Public Choice* 60 (January 1989): 55–70.

CHAPTER 4

1. James M. Buchanan and Gordon Tullock, *The Calculus of Consent* (Ann Arbor: University of Michigan Press, 1962).

2. James M. Buchanan, *The Limits of Liberty: Between Anarchy and Leviathan* (Chicago: University of Chicago Press, 1975).

3. Geoffrey Brennan and James M. Buchanan, *The Power to Tax: Analytical Foundations of a Fiscal Constitution* (Cambridge: Cambridge University Press, 1980).

4. Gary S. Becker, "A Theory of Competition among Pressure Groups for Political Influence," *Quarterly Journal of Economics* 98 (August 1983): 371–400.

5. Donald Wittman, "Why Democracies Produce Efficient Results," *Journal of Political Economy* 97 (December 1989): 1395–1424.

6. William M. Landes and Richard A. Posner, "Legal Precedent: A Theoretical and Empirical Analysis," *Journal of Law and Economics* 19 (August 1976): 283

7. Ibid.

8. See Robert Staaf and Bruce Yandle, "The Calculus, Coase, and the Common Law" (unpublished photocopy, Center for Policy Studies, Clemson University, April 1989).

9. Ruben A. Kessel and Armen A. Alchian, "Effects of Inflations," *Journal of Political Economy* 70, no. 6 (December 1962): 521–37.

10. Armen A. Alchian and Ruben A. Kessel, "Redistribution of Wealth through Inflation," *Science* 130, no. 3375 (September 4, 1959): 535–39.

11. Real full income is a measure of individual utility and can be added across individuals without loss in generality, if relative prices of different commodities are the same for all persons. See Becker, "A Theory of Competition," for an application of real full income and a discussion of its derivation.

12. The production function is subject to the standard neoclassical restrictions that guarantee concavity and an interior solution.

13. That is, $dk/dt = sy - nk$, where s is the average propensity to save and n is the population growth rate.

14. Thus, capital is $k^i = k^{Fi} + k^{Vi}$, where F designates specific capital and V designates variable capital.

15. From equation (4-1) for any k this implies that $f_k^i = f_k^j = MPk(\theta)$ for all i's and j's.

16. That is, for any rule change, $d\theta$, there are $n^p(\theta)$ proponents for which $dw^i/d\theta > 0$, and $n^o(\theta)$ opponents for which $dw^i/d\theta < 0$. Then, $dw^p/d\theta = \Sigma_i dw^i/d\theta$, $i = 1, n^p$, and $dw^o/d\theta = -\Sigma_j dw^j/d\theta, j = 1, n^o$ is the total benefit of a rule change for the group of proponents and the total cost of a rule change for the group of opponents, respectively.

17. The individual is assumed to be a "rule taker"—too small to have political influence. The group therefore is the unit of account in paying for rule changes.

18. That is, $dw^p/d\theta > dw^o/d\theta$.

19. Write the political payment functions of the proponents and the opponents, measured in units of real full income, as

$$\overset{+ \quad -}{P^p(M^p, n^p)} \text{ and } \overset{+ \quad -}{P^o(M^o, n^o)},$$

respectively. Signs reflect direct ($+$) and indirect ($-$) partial influences. Either group's offer to pay for a rule change, P^i ($i = p, o$), is a function of the group's monetary resources, M, and voting resources, n.

20. George J. Stigler, "The Theory of Economic Regulation," *Bell Journal of Economics and Management Science* 2 (Spring 1971): 12, makes this point concerning the employment of party workers.

21. Therefore, write the member contribution functions for each group as

$$\overset{+ \quad -}{M^p = M^p(dw^p, n^p, X^p)} \text{ and } \overset{+ \quad -}{M^o = M^o(dw^o, n^o, X^o)},$$

where the vectors, X, reflect other influences on the groups' ability to raise money.

22. Mancur Olsen, *The Logic of Collective Action* (Cambridge: Harvard University Press, 1965).

23. Buchanan and Tullock, *The Calculus of Consent*.

24. Note that $f^i = 0$ for $k^{Fi} = 0$.

25. It is possible to make rule changes that have only marginal consequences,

$f_\theta = 0$ and $MPk_\theta \neq 0$. This might be characteristic of rule changes that "grandfather" existing uses of inputs. Rule changes that have only inframarginal consequences, $f \neq 0$ and $MPK_\theta = 0$, are not likely. This would require new sanctions on the use of sunk assets that perhaps because these assets have no substitutes, do not influence the use of other resources.

26. Technically, $MPk^L \geq MPK^* \equiv f_k(k^*, \theta^*)$, where k^* and θ^* are the steady-state, equilibrium values of k and θ, respectively.

27. This confirms the results in Wittman, "Why Democracies Produce Efficient Results."

28. Olson, *Logic of Collective Action*.

29. Anthony Downs, *An Economic Theory of Democracy* (New York: Harper and Row, 1957); Gordon Tullock, "Some Problems of Majority Voting," *Journal of Political Economy* 67 (December 1959): 571–79.

30. That is, $dw^p/dw^o = dn^p/dn^o$.

31. Becker, "A Theory of Competition," 377.

32. For the theory of clubs see James M. Buchanan, "An Economic Theory of Clubs," *Economica* (February 1965): 1–14.

33. Ronald H. Coase, "The Nature of the Firm," *Economica* 4 (1937): 386–405.

34. Gerald W. Scully, "The Choice of Law and the Extent of Liberty," *Journal of Institutional and Theoretical Economics* 143, no. 4 (December 1987): 602.

35. It is not that common law does not change. However, even in modern times, the durability of the legal capital of common law is longer than that of statutory law. Landes and Posner, "Legal Precedent," 283, calculate an average durability of precedent in common law by the Supreme Court of forty years. On the other hand, precedents of statutes on economic regulation have an average life of eighteen years.

36. See Staff and Yandle, "The Calculus," 19–23.

37. Whittman, "Why Democracies Produce Efficient Results."

38. With full compensation, both groups clearly will favor the rule change. In this context "opponent" is meant in the sense of "opposed to the change without full compensation."

39. The sufficient condition is $dP^p/d\theta > dP^o/d\theta + (g_k L^L)MPk$.

40. When, $dP^p/d\theta < dw^o/d\theta + (h_k L)MPk$.

41. That is, when $dw^p/d\theta - dP^o/d\theta > 0$.

CHAPTER 5

1. A. Banks and R. Textor, *A Cross-polity Survey* (Cambridge: MIT Press, 1963); Robert Dahl, *Polyarchy: Participation and Opposition* (New Haven: Yale University Press, 1971); R. P. Claude, ed. *Comparative Human Rights* (Baltimore: Johns Hopkins University Press, 1976).

2. Raymond D. Gastil, *Freedom in the World* (Westport, Conn.: Greenwood Press, 1987).

3. Ibid., 9.

4. Ibid., 10.

5. Charles Humana, *World Human Rights Guide* (New York: Pica Press, 1982); id., *World Human Rights Guide* (London: Hodder and Stoughton, 1986).

6. Michael A. Walker, ed., *Symposium on Rating Economic Freedom* (Vancouver: Fraser Institute, forthcoming).

7. Alvin Rabushka, "Preliminary Definition of Economic Freedom," in Walker, *Symposium*.

8. See Z. Spindler and L. Still, "Economic Freedom Ratings," in Walker, *Symposium*, for a discussion of the weighing of the four subindices of economic freedom in the Gastil-Wright ratings.

9. Ibid.

10. Gastil, *Freedom in the World*.

11. Humana, *World Human Rights Guide*.

12. E. Maasoumi and G. Nickelsburg, "Multivariate Measures of Well Being and an Analysis of Inequality," *Journal of Business and Economic Statistics* 6 (1988): 327–34.

13. Zvi Griliches, *Price Indexes and Quality Changes: Studies in New Methods of Measurement* (Cambridge: Harvard University Press, 1971).

14. R. Frank, *Choosing the Right Pond: Human Behavior and the Quest for Status* (Oxford: Oxford University Press, 1985).

15. A brief and more technical discussion of principal components analysis appears in appendix 5-1.

16. Robert Summers and Alan Heston, "A New Set of International Comparisons of Real Product and Price Levels: Estimates for 130 Countries," *Review of Income and Wealth* 34 (March 1988): 1–25.

17. B. Flury, *Common Principal Components and Related Multivariate Methods* (New York: Wiley, 1988).

CHAPTER 6

1. Rene David, *Traite elementaire de droit civil compare* (Paris: Librairie generale de droit et de jurisprudence, 1950), 224.

2. Friedrich A. Hayek, *Law, Legislation and Liberty*, 3 vols. (Chicago: University of Chicago Press, 1973); Bruno Leoni, *Freedom and the Law* (Princeton: D. Van Nostrand, 1961).

3. Hayek, *Law, Legislation and Liberty* 1:85.

4. Thomas Babington Macaulay, *History of England*, Butler's edition (Philadelphia, Butler, n.d.), 5.

5. T.F.T Plucknett, *A Concise History of the Common Law*, 5th ed. (London: Butterworth, 1956).

6. See John H. Merryman and David S. Clark, *Comparative Law: Western and Latin American Legal Systems* (Indianapolis: Bobbs Merrill, 1978); Owen H. Phil-

lips, *A First Book of English Law*, 6th ed. (London: Sweet and Maxwell, 1970), 177–206; and Plucknett, *Concise History*, 342–50.

7. John H. Merryman, *The Civil Law Tradition* (Stanford: Stanford University Press, 1985), 39–47.

8. A. T. von Mehren, *The Civil Law System* (Englewood Cliffs, N.J.: Prentice Hall, 1957), 138–249.

9. Ibid., 250–336.

10. Merryman and Clark, *Comparative Law*, 759.

11. Leoni, *Freedom and the Law*, 8.

12. N. P. Aghnides, *Mohammedan Theories of Finance* (Lahore: Premier Book House, 1961).

13. Gerald W. Scully, "Mullahs, Muslims, and Marital Sorting," *Journal of Political Economy* 87 (1979): 1139–43.

14. M. Asad, *The Principles of State and Government in Islam* (Berkeley: University of California Press, 1961), 69–94.

15. William E. Butler, *Soviet Law* (London: Butterworths, 1983), 160–61.

16. Ibid., 317.

17. G. S. Maddala, *Limited-Dependent and Qualitative Variables in Econometrics* (Cambridge: Cambridge University Press, 1983), 23.

18. Leoni, *Freedom and the Law*, 2.

19. G. Ripert, *Le declin du droit* (Paris: Librairie generale de droit et de jurisprudence, 1949).

CHAPTER 7

1. The socialist model remains popular in the less developed world. Nelson Mandela, imprisoned for twenty-seven years (released in 1990) for his agitation for full suffrage for blacks in South Africa, is a Marxist. The African National Congress is allied with the Communist Party of South Africa. Under black majority rule and political control of the African National Congress, the constitutional setting of South Africa may well be altered from capitalist to socialist.

2. By choice of the institutional framework, I mean the observed outcome, not the political process of choice. In some cases, the choice was with the "consent" or acquiescence of the governed; in others it was the will of the "ruling class." Even the meaning of the terms "individual initiative, choice and responsibility" has been modified with the rise of the "welfare state" and the projection of the government into economic affairs the outcome of which it finds undesirable. In the case of nations that were former colonies, the institutional framework partly was inherited from (imposed by) the colonizer. But the institutional framework in these nations has been modified, often by a "ruling class" and often beyond recognition. Here, the extent of economic, political, and civil liberty is treated as a given. The objective is to determine to what extent these choices of the structure of rights, however made, affect economic progress.

3. Gunnar Myrdal, *Economic Theory and Under-developed Regions* (London: Duckworth, 1957) published in the United States as *Rich Lands and Poor* (New York: Harper, 1957); id., *Asian Drama: An Inquiry into the Poverty of Nations* (London: Penguin, 1968).

4. Edward Coke, *First Institute: A Commentary on Littleton* (London: E. and H. Brooke, 1794).

5. Adam Smith, *An Inquiry into the Nature and Causes of the Wealth of Nations* (New York: Modern Library, 1937).

6. Peter T. Bauer and Basil S. Yamey, *The Economics of Underdeveloped Countries* (Chicago: University of Chicago Press, 1957); Peter T. Bauer, *Dissent on Development* (Cambridge: Harvard University Press, 1972. See also W. Arthur Lewis, *The Theory of Economic Growth* (London: G. Allen and Unwin, 1955).

7. Ragnar Nurkse, *Problems in Capital Formation in Underdeveloped Countries* (New York: Oxford University Press, 1953): 5.

8. Myrdal, *Rich Lands and Poor*, 81–94.

9. Ibid., 98.

10. Ibid., 83–84.

11. Myrdal, *Asian Drama*, 67, 115–16, passim.

12. James Steuart, *An Inquiry into the Principles of Political Economy: Being an Essay on the Science of Domestic Policy in Free Nations* (London: A. Millar and T. Cadell, 1767), 162–65.

13. Smith, *Inquiry*, 14.

14. Ibid., 423.

15. Nathan Rosenberg, "Some Institutional Aspects of the Wealth of Nations," *Journal of Political Economy* 68 (December 1960): 560.

16. The assumption of homogeneity of degree one of the production function is testable. Equation (7-1) in growth form was estimated by OLS for the entire sample of 115 market economies utilized in this study. The coefficient of $e^K \cdot g^K$ on g^Y was .5415 ($t = 8.05$). The coefficient of $e^L \cdot g^L$ on g^Y was .6067 ($t = 4.90$). An F-test on the unrestricted model versus the restriction on unity for the sum of the coefficients yielded $F(1,112) = 1.39$, which is significant at the .2405 level. Hence, the assumption of homogeneity of degree one is reasonable.

17. Dennis J. Aigner and S. F. Chu, "Estimating the Industry Production Function," *American Economic Review* 58 (September 1968): 826–39; Dennis J. Aigner, C. A. Knox Lovell, and Peter Schmidt, "Formulation and Estimation of Stochastic Production Models," *Journal of Econometrics* (January 1977): 21–37; Cliff J. Huang, "Estimation of Stochastic Frontier Production Function and Technical Efficiency via the EM Algorithm," *Southern Economic Journal* 50 (1984): 847–56; William H. Greene, "Maximum Likelihood Estimation of Econometric Frontier Functions," *Journal of Econometrics* 13 (1980): 27–56; id., "The Estimation of a Flexible Frontier Production Model," *Journal of Econometrics* 13 (1980): 101–15.

18. A. P. Dempster, N. M. Laird, and D. G. Rubin, "Maximum Likelihood from Incomplete Data via the EM Algorithm," *Journal of the Royal Statistical Society*, ser. B, 39 (1977): 1–38.

19. Huang, "Estimation of Stochastic Frontier," 848–50.

20. Greene, "Maximum Likelihood Estimation"; id., "Estimation of a Flexible Frontier."

21. Robert Summers and Alan Heston, "Improved International Comparisons of Real Product and Its Composition: 1950–1980," *Review of Income and Wealth* 30 (June 1984): 207–62.

22. Raymond D. Gastil, *Freedom in the World* (Westport, Conn.: Greenwood, 1982).

23. Use of institutional data over the period 1973–1980 as a predictor of economic growth and efficiency over the period 1960–1980 is suspect. Small changes in freedom occur frequently, but gross changes in liberty are relatively rare events. Dictatorships rarely become representative democracies or vice versa. The categorization of societies as "free" or "not free" prior to 1973 on the basis of their status of observed freedom in 1973 and thereafter may be quite appropriate.

A partial and inferential test of this proposition is to show that the status of political freedom in 1973 is a reasonably good predictor of political freedom in 1984, more than a decade later. The Gastil rankings of political liberty for 1973 were regressed on the rankings for 1984. The simple correlation coefficient was $r = .68$. With 115 observations, the relationship is statistically significant at well above the 1 percent level.

Perhaps a more meaningful test is to determine the incidence of gross misclassification in using 1973 observations of freedom to predict 1984 observations. Three of the 115 countries (Bangladesh, Chile, and Suriname) that were classified as politically free in 1973 were actually not free in 1984. Five countries (Greece, Honduras, Argentina, Ecuador, and Peru) that were classified as not free in 1973 were free in 1984. The frequency of error in classification between free and not free over this twelve-year period is 7 percent. It is likely that this classification error is on the same order of magnitude for the period 1960–1972. The empirical results—see text accompanying equations (7-8) through (7-10)—employ the institutional variables as dummy variables, where "free" and "not free" are the essential categories. Therefore, any incidence of misclassification of the status of political, civil, or economic freedom over the period 1960–1980 resulting from use of freedom data for 1973–1980 is likely to be tolerably small.

Further evidence of the reasonableness of using the Gastil data for the whole period of study is the comparison of Gastil's rankings with rankings by Arthur S. Banks, *Cross-Polity Time-Series Data* (Cambridge: MIT Press, 1971), for the period 1960–1965. Banks reports several measures of the legislative process, including a ranking of the effectiveness of the legislature. The Banks rankings characterize the legislative process as effective (3) partly effective (2) largely ineffective (1), or no legislature (0). These categories are compared with Gastil's categories of free, partly free and not free for 1973. The simple correlation between the Gastil measure for 1973 and the Banks measure for the early 1960s for the eighty-two available observations was $R = .72$, which is significant at above the 1 percent level.

As a final check, types of government by country were compared for the early

1960s and the early 1970s by using the annual *Statesman's Yearbook*. The general pattern described above was confirmed with these comparisons.

24. Arnold C. Harberger, "Perspectives on Capital and Technology in Less-Developed Countries," In *Contemporary Economic Analysis*, ed. Michael J. Artis and A. R. Nobay (London: Croom-Helm, 1978).

25. United Nations, *Yearbook of National Accounts Statistics*, various years.

26. For buildings the regional coefficients of variation were as follows: Africa, 20 percent; Asia, 20 percent; Europe, 9 percent; the Americas, 22 percent. For machinery and equipment, the regional coefficients of variation were as follows: Africa, 21 percent; Asia, 17 percent; Europe, 17 percent; the Americas, 23 percent.

27. Harberger, "Perspectives," 19.

28. Gastil mainly uses newspaper reports, journals, Amnesty International and other rights reports, the U.S. Department of State and its reports to Congress on the human rights of nations receiving American assistance, and other public sources for the data to construct these rankings. He compares his measures with other measures.

29. The specification asserts that the direction of causation is from the institutional framework or property rights regime to the growth rate. Some believe that the causation is reversed: that liberty is a sort of "luxury" good for high-growth regimes; low growth environments cannot "afford" liberty. If one views the state as benign, this view of the direction of causation is at least plausible. If one views the state as predatory, as with the public choice theorists, the belief that state control is for the purpose of growth requires a great leap of faith.

No empirical evidence on causation or exogeneity can be offered here. Granger causality tests, which require the use of lagged values of the dependent and independent variables, cannot be employed, because of the few degrees of freedom. The institutional variables are available annually from 1973 to 1980. Therefore, whether liberty promotes growth, or whether growth promotes liberty, or whether the two are intertwined empirically is an open question.

30. Heteroskedasticity is a possibility in cross-section studies. Given the wide range of sizes of economies in this study, the violation of constant variance across countries ranked by size is a possibility. Three procedures were employed to test for heteroskedasticity: (1) the residuals were ranked by 1980 population (a measure of the size of the economy); (2) the residuals were squared and regressed against 1980 population; and (3) the Goldfeld-Quandt test was employed, with 1980 population as the exogenous ordering variable. Examination of the residuals plotted against 1980 population indicated normality. The t-statistic of the squared residuals on 1980 population was well below the 5 percent acceptance level. For the Goldfeld-Quandt test, the data was ranked by 1980 population size and the sample was divided into thirds. Two regressions were estimated: one for countries with small populations; one for countries with large populations. An F-test on the ratio of the residual sum of the squares was well below the 5 percent significance level. The assumption of normality is validated.

31. The standard errors of the regression coefficients of the rights variables in equation (1) in table 7-3 in comparison to the standard errors in equations (2)–(7) in table 7-1 rose by a factor of 1.2 to 2.5.

32. Edward F. Denison, *The Sources of Economic Growth in the United States and the Alternatives before Us* (New York: Committee for Economic Development, 1962); Jacob Schmookler, *Invention and Economic Growth* (Cambridge: Harvard University Press, 1966); T. W. Schultz, "Investment in Human Capital," *American Economic Review* 51 (March 1961): 1–17; Joseph A. Schumpeter, *The Theory of Economic Development* (Cambridge: Harvard University Press, 1934); R. M. Solow, "Technical Progress and the Aggregate Production Function, *Review of Economics and Statistics* 39 (August 1957): 312–20.

CHAPTER 8

1. Irma Adelman and Cynthia Taft Morris, *Society, Politics and Economic Development* (Baltimore: Johns Hopkins University Press, 1967); Adelman and Morris, *Economic Growth and Social Equity in Developing Countries* (Stanford: Stanford University Press, 1973); Hollis B. Chenery et al., *Redistribution with Growth* (New York: Oxford University Press, 1974).

2. Arthur M. Okun, *Equality and Efficiency: The Big Tradeoff* (Washington, D.C.: Brookings, 1975).

3. S. Jain, *Size Distribution of Income* (Washington, D.C.: World Bank, 1975).

4. A. T. Atkinson, "On the Measurement of Inequality," *Journal of Economic Theory* 2 (1970): 244–63.

5. F. Cowell, *Measuring Inequality* (Oxford: Phillip Allan, 1977).

6. Henri Theil, *Economics and Information Theory* (Amsterdam: North-Holland, 1967).

CHAPTER 9

1. Peltzman presents data on the share of government out of GNP for the period 1860–1974 for the United States, United Kingdom, Germany, and Sweden. Sam Peltzman, "The Growth of Government," *Journal of Law and Economics* 23 (October 1980): 209–87.

2. Marlow presents data on the share of government expenditures out of GDP for nineteen OECD countries. The average increase in the share (G/GDP) over the period 1960 to 1980 was 25 percent. Michael L. Marlow, "Private Sector Shrinkage and the Growth of Industrialized Economies," *Public Choice* 49 (1986): 143–54.

3. Richard A. Musgrave, *The Theory of Public Finance* (New York: McGraw Hill, 1959).

4. Anthony Downs, *An Economic Theory of Democracy* (New York: Harper and Row, 1957); James M. Buchanan and Gordon Tullock, *The Calculus of Consent* (Ann Arbor: University of Michigan Press, 1962); Gordon Tullock, *The Politics of*

Bureaucracy (Washington, D.C.: Public Affairs Press, 1965); Mancur Olsen, *The Logic of Collective Action* (Cambridge: Harvard University Press, 1965); William A. Niskanen, Jr., *Bureaucracy and Representative Government* (Chicago: Aldens and Atherton, 1971).

5. James M. Buchanan, "La Scienza Della Finanze': The Italian Tradition in Fiscal Theory," in *Fiscal Theory and Political Economy, ed. id.* (Chapel Hill: University of North Carolina Press, 1960); 24–74; id., *The Limits of Liberty: Between Anarchy and Leviathan* (Chicago: University of Chicago Press, 1975); Geoffrey Brennan and James M. Buchanan, *The Power to Tax: Analytical Foundations of a Fiscal Constitution* (Cambridge: Cambridge University Press, 1980).

6. Brennan and Buchanan, *The Power to Tax*, 40.

7. Robert D. Tollison, "Rent Seeking: A Survey," *Kyklos* 35 (1982): 575–602.

8. Buchanan and Tullock, *The Calculus of Consent*.

9. George J. Stigler, "Director's Law of Public Income Redistribution," *Journal of Law and Economics* 13 (April 1970): 1–10; Gordon Tullock, *Economics of Income Redistribution* (Boston: Kluwer-Nijhoff, 1983); id., *The Economics of Wealth and Poverty* (New York: New York University Press, 1986).

10. Gordon Tullock, "The Welfare Costs of Tariffs, Monopolies and Theft," *Western Economic Journal* 5 (June 1967): 224–32. See also Anne O. Krueger, "The Political Economy of the Rent-seeking Society," *American Economic Review* 64 (June 1974): 291–303.

11. James M. Buchanan, "Rent Seeking and Profit Seeking," in *Toward a Theory of the Rent-Seeking Society*, ed. James M. Buchanan et al. (College Station: Texas A and M Press, 1980); 3–15, at 9.

12. See the discussion in chapter 2, the section on Government Expenditures, 1950–1985.

13. Oates has examined the hypothesis that decentralization of the fiscal function induces intergovernmental competition for resources, which constrains the taxing power of the state. For data consisting of state and local government units in the United States and for a sample of forty-three countries, Oates could not confirm the decentralization hypothesis. Employing a different measure of decentralization Nelson finds support for the hypothesis. Wallace Oates, "Searching for Leviathan," *American Economic Review* 75 (September 1985): 748–57; Michael A. Nelson, "Searching for Leviathan: Comment and Extension," *American Economic Review* 75 (September 1975): 198–204.

14. Daniel Landau, "Government and Economic Growth in the Less Developed Countries" (mimeo, n.d).

15. Id., "Government Expenditure and Economic Growth: A Cross-Country Study," *Southern Economic Journal* 49 (January 1983): 783–92.

16. Marlow, "Private Sector Shrinkage."

17. Rati Ram, "Government Size and Economic Growth: A New Framework and Some Evidence from Cross-section and Time Series Data," *American Economic Review* 76 (March 1986): 191–203.

18. Peltzman, "Growth of Government," 209.

19. The simple correlation between the share of national investment going to state-owned enterprises averaged over the period 1970 to 1980 and GOVT80 (GOVT70) was $R = .41$ (.37), which is statistically significant at above the 1 percent level for the sample size ($n = 69$). The data on the share of national investment going to state-owned enterprises are from R. P. Short, "The Role of Public Enterprises: An International Statistical Comparison," in *Public Enterprise in Mixed Economies: Some International Aspects*, ed. R. Floyd, C. Gray, and R. P. Short (Washington, D.C.: International Monetary Fund, 1984), 99, 110–94.

20. The Logit transformation is $1/1 + e^{-X\beta + \alpha}$. Hence, $\log(1 - p/p) = -X\beta + \alpha$. Compared with the linear specification, the Logit transformation changes the signs of the coefficients.

21. Landau, "Government Expenditure"; Marlow, "Private Sector Shrinkage."

CHAPTER 10

1. These countries and the author(s) of the study were as follows: Argentina (D. Cavallo and J. Cottani); Brazil (D. Coes); Chile (S. de la Cuadra and D. Hachette); Colombia (J. Garcia Gracia); Greece (G. Kottis); Indonesia (M. Pitt); Israel (N. Halevi and J. Baruh); Korea (K. S. Kim); New Zealand (A.C. Rayner and R. Lattimore); Pakistan (S. Guisinger and G. W. Scully); Peru (J. Nogues); Philippines (G. Sheperd and F. Alburo); Portugal (J. de Macedo, C. Corado, and M. Porto); Singapore (B. Y. Aw); Spain (G. de la Dehesa, J. Ruiz, and A. Torres); Sri Lanka (A. G. Cuthbertson and P. Athukorala); Turkey (T. Baysan and C. Blitzer); Uruguay (E. Favaro and P. Spiller); and Yugoslavia (O. Havrylyshyn). The country studies are published in a series by Basil Blackwell, 1990.

2. An investigation of six countries was conducted by the OECD and summarized in a volume of comparative study by I. M. D. Little, T. Scitovsky, and M. Scott. OECD, *Industry and Trade in Some Developing Countries*, 6 vols. (1970). The National Bureau of Economic Research (NBER) studied ten countries, and the results were synthesized in volumes by J. Bhagwati and A. Krueger. NBER, *Foreign Trade Regimes and Economic Development*, 11 vols. (1974–1978); id., *Trade and Employment in Developing Countries*, 3 vols. (1981–1983). See also Bela Balassa and Associates, *Developing Strategies in Semi-Industrial Economies* (Baltimore: Johns Hopkins University Press, 1982).

3. Michael Michaely, Demetrios Papageorgiou, and Armeane Choksi, *Liberalizing Foreign Trade: Lessons of Experience in the Developing World* (Oxford: Basil Blackwell, 1990).

☆ *Index* ☆

capital stock, 173–74

development economics, 6–9; concern with income distribution, 12; domestic price distortions, 8; import-substitution policy, 7; market failure, 7; vicious circle of poverty, 167

economic efficiency measure, 170; econometric specification of, 171–72

inequality measures, 187–88; country comparisons, 197–99; trade-off with economic efficiency, 194–96

international economic comparisons, 16–55; capital formation, 28–32; commercial policy, 42–43; correlations of variables with per capita income and economic growth, 28, 32–33, 36, 41, 43–44, 46; economic growth rates, 16–23; human capital, 34–36, 47–50; inflation, 45–46; per capita income, 16–23; population growth, 36–37, 52–55; real interest rates, 32–34; size of government, 43–44; technological change, 40–42

liberty, 106–20; criticism of measures, 116–17; current measures of, 106–12, 114–20; defined, 221n.4; early measures of, 235–36n.23; and effect on growth and efficiency, 169–72, 176–82, 194–96; and effect on income distribution, 188–96; rankings of, 127–30, 140–47; rule of law, 227n.20; statistical weighing techniques, 120–21, 125–27, 130–31; and type of legal system, 149–56; weighing attributes of, 120–27

neoclassical growth model, 9, 14–16, 23–26; capital formation in, 15, 28–32; convergence of growth rates in, 15–16, 23–24; growth of labor force in, 15, 24; incorpo-

rating constitutional setting in, 81–82, 84–85, 168–70; public policy implications of, 26–28; savings rate in, 15, 25–26

paradigms of human progress, 4–6, 166–69; classical liberalism, 5, 13; public interest, 5; socialism, 3–4, 7–8, 99–100

reform of institutional framework, 212–19; prospects for freedom, 214–16; prospects for reduced size of government, 218–19; prospects for trade liberalization, 216–18

rule change in constitutional settings, 82–105; constitutional amendment, 82; effect of technical change on production of, 88–89, 101; effect on wealth, 86; endurance of rules, 98–101; inputs into production of, 86–88, 90, 92–94, 102–5; legislation, 83; political income from, 88–89; precedent, 82–83; production of, 84–85, 102–4; rent-seeking and revolution caused by inefficient rule change, 101–5; supply of rules, 88

rules of constitutional settings, 56–79; constitutional protection of, 66–68; custom in, 69–70; distribution of rights in, 58, 60; efficiency of legal system, 72–74; efficient and inefficient rules, 56–57, 89, 96–98; enforcement of rights in, 62–63; and gains from exchange, 63–66; income redistribution, 57–58; public goods, 57, 76; rent-seeking, 57; restrictions on fiscal state and income redistribution in, 74–79; type of legal system, 57, 68–73; and voting rule, 63–64, 76–77, 101

size of government, 200–204; beneficial effects of, 202; and effect on economic growth and efficiency, 205–10; measuring, 204; rent-seeking and growth of, 201–2; trend in, 200

241